MURDER
AMONG
FRIENDS

ALSO BY CANDACE FLEMING

YOUNG ADULT

*The Family Romanov: Murder, Rebellion, and the Fall
of Imperial Russia*

Fatal Throne: The Wives of Henry VIII Tell All

The Lincolns: A Scrapbook Look at Abraham and Mary

The Rise and Fall of Charles Lindbergh

MIDDLE GRADE

Amelia Lost: The Life and Disappearance of Amelia Earhart

Ben Franklin's in My Bathroom!

Eleanor Roosevelt's in My Garage!

The Fabled Fifth Graders of Aesop Elementary School

The Fabled Fourth Graders of Aesop Elementary School

*The Great and Only Barnum: The Tremendous, Stupendous Life
of Showman P. T. Barnum*

Strongheart: Wonder Dog of the Silver Screen

YOUNGER READERS

Clever Jack Takes the Cake

Imogene's Last Stand

Oh, No!

MURDER AMONG FRIENDS

How Leopold and Loeb Tried to Commit the Perfect Crime

CANDACE FLEMING

a·s·b
anne schwartz books

Text copyright © 2022 by Candace Fleming
Front cover photograph copyright © 2022 by Bettmann/Getty Images
Back cover photograph courtesy of the *Chicago Daily News* Collection, Chicago History Museum

All rights reserved. Published in the United States by Anne Schwartz Books, an imprint of
Random House Children's Books, a division of Penguin Random House LLC, New York.

Anne Schwartz Books and the colophon are trademarks of Penguin Random House LLC.

For image credits, please see page 345.

Visit us on the Web! GetUnderlined.com

Educators and librarians, for a variety of teaching tools, visit us at
RHTeachersLibrarians.com

Library of Congress Cataloging-in-Publication Data is available upon request.
ISBN 978-0-593-17742-6 (trade) — ISBN 978-0-593-17743-3 (lib. bdg.) —
ISBN 978-0-593-17744-0 (ebook)

The text of this book is set in 10.4-point Cheltenham ITC Pro Book.
Interior design by Cathy Bobak

Printed in the United States of America
10 9 8 7 6 5 4 3 2 1
First Edition

CONTENTS

PART ONE: WHERE IS BOBBY?

Chapter One: Wednesday, May 21, 1924 3

Chapter Two: The Longest Night 8

PART TWO: BOYS WILL BE BOYS

Chapter Three: Nathan and Richard 15

Chapter Four: The Superman and the Master Criminal 32

Chapter Five: Apart and Together 44

Chapter Six: Planning the Perfect Crime 56

PART THREE: TRACKING THE KILLERS

Chapter Seven: Thursday, May 22, 1924 71

Chapter Eight: Search for the Killers 84

Chapter Nine: A Murderer's Theories; A Coroner's Inquest 95

Chapter Ten: Saturday, May 24–Sunday, May 25, 1924 105

Chapter Eleven: Interrogation 113

Chapter Twelve: Another Day in Custody 127

PART FOUR: CONFESSIONS

Chapter Thirteen: "I Will Tell You the *Real* Truth" 137

Chapter Fourteen: Murderers' Field Trip 149

Chapter Fifteen: "Impaling a Beetle on a Pin" 158

Chapter Sixteen: Darrow for the Defense 171

Chapter Seventeen: Searching for Insanity 183

PART FIVE: COURTROOM BATTLE

Chapter Eighteen: Surprise Strategy. 205

Chapter Nineteen: A Hot Day in Court 212

Chapter Twenty: Battles in and out of Court. 219

Chapter Twenty-One: New-School Psychiatry Takes the Stand . . 230

Chapter Twenty-Two: "The Ageing Lion" vs. "Fighting Bob" . . . 248

Chapter Twenty-Three: Waiting 263

Chapter Twenty-Four: "Nothing but the Night" 267

Chapter Twenty-Five: "Life in Prison Is Just What You Make". . 279

Afterword 290

Acknowledgments 293

Bibliography 295

Notes 307

Image Credits 345

Index 347

PART ONE

WHERE
IS BOBBY?

CHAPTER ONE

WEDNESDAY, MAY 21, 1924

Nineteen-year-old Nathan Leopold would kill a child today. He didn't expect to get much pleasure from it. Still, it *would* be an interesting intellectual experiment, like an entomologist sticking a pin through a beetle. Besides, his friend Richard wanted this murder . . . badly. And Nathan would do anything for Richard Loeb.

Nathan lit a cigarette and looked over at Richard. The eighteen-year-old appeared calm as he drove the rental car. But Nathan could see a muscle in Richard's right cheek twitching. He knew that sign. Richard was ready, eager even, to kill somebody.

On the floor of the backseat, wrapped in a blanket, lay their gear—rope, chisel, adhesive tape, gags, hydrochloric acid, and hip boots. They had everything they needed. Everything but a victim.

Nathan looked at his watch.

Two-thirty.

School was letting out.

The pair drove into their Chicago neighborhood of Kenwood, a little pocket of fashionable homes on the city's South Side.

A street away from the Harvard School for Boys, Richard pulled to the curb. He turned off the ignition. They sat there. Who should they grab? They hadn't settled on a specific victim. Any boy would do.

Leaving Nathan in the car, Richard walked to the school. Kids poured out onto the playground. He noticed nine-year-old Johnny Levinson, who was in the same fourth-grade class as Richard's little brother, Tommy. Just days earlier, the boy had played at the Loeb house.

There couldn't be a better victim. Stick thin and small for his age, Johnny would be easy to nab.

Richard turned on his charm. "What are you doing after school?" he asked Johnny in his friendliest voice.

"I'm going to play baseball," replied Johnny.

Where? Richard wanted to know. Who with?

It was just a pickup game with some friends, Johnny told him. He was headed over to the vacant lot at 49th Street and Drexel.

Richard wondered how to lure the boy to the car. Should he offer him a ride?

But before he got the chance, Johnny ran off.

Frustrated, Richard walked around to the front of the school. He saw Tommy standing on the steps. Maybe he should grab him.

Just then Nathan whistled for Richard to return to the car. When he did, Nathan said, "There are some children playing on Ingleside Avenue." Maybe they could catch one of them.

Richard had a better idea. Why not go over to the vacant lot on 49th Street and watch Johnny's baseball game? They could snatch the boy afterward as he was walking home.

Nathan agreed. They drove toward the lot. Yes, the boys were there. But from the moving vehicle, Richard and Nathan couldn't recognize anybody. They parked again, a block from the lot, and walked down an alley to a spot where they could see the game. Still, they couldn't make out faces. Could they get closer? Not without being seen. And they couldn't let that happen. When Johnny vanished, the police would put two and two together. No, they'd have to watch the boy from a distance. To do that, they needed Nathan's field glasses.

It was only four blocks to the Leopolds' house. After dropping Nathan off, Richard drove to a nearby drugstore. He bought two packages of gum before heading to the phone booth in the back to look up Johnny's address in the telephone book. Chewing away, Richard flipped through the pages until he found it. He nodded. He now knew the route Johnny would take to walk home.

Minutes later, he picked Nathan up. They returned to the alley near the vacant lot. Passing the field glasses back and forth, they watched the children play. Nathan pointed out a few other possible victims. What about the shortstop, or the kid on third base? Richard nixed those ideas. He had his heart set on killing Johnny.

At four-thirty, Johnny and some others suddenly walked away from the game. Richard grew worried. Was Johnny coming back? He and Nathan waited, but there was no further sign of the boy.

They drove around and around the neighborhood.

Who knew it would be so hard to nab a child?

Nathan looked at his watch again. It was getting late, almost dinnertime. They'd been searching for a victim for more than two hours. He suggested they try again tomorrow.

Richard refused. They'd been planning this for so long. They couldn't quit. Not yet. One more time around the neighborhood, he insisted.

This time, Nathan drove. They passed by the vacant lot again. They went by the Levinson house, too.

No luck.

That was when they saw him, walking on the opposite side of the street all by himself. He wore a tan jacket, knickers, wool golf stockings with checkered tops, a necktie, and a tan cap.

"I know him," said Richard.

It was his second cousin, fourteen-year-old Bobby Franks. Bobby lived across the street from Richard. Just yesterday they'd played tennis together on the Loebs' court.

The car passed the boy. Richard signaled for Nathan to turn around and drive up behind him. As Nathan did, Richard climbed in back, behind the front passenger seat.

The car pulled up alongside Bobby.

"Hey, Bob," Richard called. He leaned forward and opened the passenger door. "Do you want a ride home?"

Bobby shook his head. His house was only two blocks away.

"Come on in," urged Richard. "I want to talk to you about the tennis racket you had yesterday. I want to get one for my brother."

Bobby moved closer to the car. He was so close Richard could have grabbed him and dragged him in. Instead, Richard kept talking, kept smiling.

Bobby hesitated a moment longer. Then he slid into the front passenger seat. He looked over at Nathan.

"You know Leopold, don't you?" said Richard.

Bobby didn't. He turned around to the backseat, eager to talk tennis with his older cousin.

"You don't mind [us] taking you around the block?" Richard asked.

"Certainly not," said Bobby.

Nathan pulled away from the curb as Richard groped around on the floor for the chisel.

CHAPTER TWO

THE LONGEST NIGHT

"Baby."

That was what Flora Franks called her youngest child, Bobby.

"Don't you realize my age?" Bobby would grumble. He'd turned fourteen that year, although he didn't look it. Small-boned and just eighty pounds, with dark wavy hair, he liked sports and school and joking around with his friends. His big, soulful eyes belied his mischievous streak.

But Flora found his naughtiness part of his charm. Bobby *could* be a rascal. But he also possessed a sensitive and generous nature. The school essay he'd written weeks earlier proved that. The topic had been capital punishment, and in it Bobby opined that executing murderers was senseless and immoral. "Most criminals have diseased minds," he'd argued. It was not just or fair for the state to kill these people. Flora had been proud of his stance. At a time when most people believed executing convicted murderers was the most effective way of deterring crime, Bobby had disagreed. Boldly and articulately, he'd expressed an unpopular position. And afterward, he'd told his family he wanted to become a lawyer to help people.

Was it any wonder that of Flora's three children, he was her favorite? She freely admitted it. And every night, she tiptoed into his room to kiss his cheek while he slept.

So when Bobby didn't come home by six-thirty on that drizzling, gray evening, Flora grew frantic. Where was Baby?

Her husband, Jacob, tried to calm her. The boy had probably just gone to a friend's house and lost track of time. Had he said anything about being late?

Bobby had come home at lunchtime, she recalled. He'd reminded her that he was umpiring the freshman baseball game after school that day. But he should have been home long before this.

"Maybe he's playing tennis across the street [at the Loebs' house] and forgot the time," suggested their fifteen-year-old son, Jack.

Jacob went to look.

The court was empty.

Walking down Ellis Avenue, he peered into backyards and alleys. He, too, was growing worried.

He returned home to find Flora phoning Bobby's friends. Was he there? When was the last time they'd seen him? Had they seen him leave?

Some of the boys remembered spotting Bobby at the baseball game. One of them had even seen him headed toward home. Yes, he'd been alone.

It was seven o'clock now. The maid came into the living room and asked if she should serve dinner.

Eat? How could they eat? Flora paced around the room, stopping again and again to pull back the curtains and look out the tall arched windows. Her eyes strained for Bobby's familiar figure walking along the sidewalk.

With every passing minute, Jacob grew more alarmed. Still, he tried to stay calm. He suggested they sit down at the table. Bobby, he told them, would surely be back by dessert.

It was a tense meal. Jack fidgeted nervously in his chair. Seventeen-year-old Josephine pushed food around her plate. And Flora just stared at her untouched dinner. At the sound of every passing car, Jacob jumped. Might one of them be bringing his son home?

By the time the maid cleared the uneaten meal, Jacob's mind had become a jumble of fear. He had to do something. Was it too soon to contact the police? Should they telephone Bobby's friends again? Finally, he called his friend Samuel Ettelson, a prominent lawyer and former state senator. Jacob figured Sam would know what to do.

Ettelson—who lived next door to the Leopolds—arrived in minutes. Could Bobby have gotten locked in the school? he asked.

Possibly, conceded Jacob.

Grabbing their coats, the two men hurried out the door. It took just five minutes to cover the three and a half blocks to school. The men walked around the building, eventually finding an open basement window. They clambered inside and called out Bobby's name.

No answer.

They hunted through every room, opening supply closets and peeking under desks. Over and over, Bobby's name echoed down the empty corridors.

They found no sign of him.

"There must be some explanation," said Jacob.

Meanwhile, as the men searched, the telephone in the Frankses' living room rang.

Flora snatched it up.

A man's voice on the other end asked for Mr. Franks.

"Mr. Franks isn't here," she said.

"Your son has been kidnapped," the voice said. "He is all right. There will be further news in the morning."

"Who is this?" Flora managed to say.

"Johnson," replied the voice.

"What do you want? What do you want?" Flora screamed.

But the man on the other end hung up.

Flora fainted.

Minutes later, Jacob and Sam found her crumpled on the Persian rug. A whiff of smelling salts brought her around. Then the story came tumbling out, followed by hysterical sobbing.

Tenderly, Jacob helped her upstairs to bed. It was, he assured her, the best place for her. There was nothing she could do for Bobby right now. She needed to save her strength for when it was needed. He left her weeping into her pillows.

Back downstairs, he and Sam weighed their options. Should they notify the police? Doing so was sure to alert the press. After all, Jacob Franks was the millionaire president of the Rockford Watch Company, as well as a member of the city's library board. His son's kidnapping would make headlines. Would the publicity force the kidnappers to do something desperate? Jacob was dead set against any action that might put his son in danger.

After some discussion, the men decided not to report the crime. Instead, they sat next to the telephone, waiting and hoping for another call from the kidnappers.

PART TWO

BOYS WILL BE BOYS

CHAPTER THREE

NATHAN AND RICHARD

Nathan Leopold loved birds. They were magical in that manner of all things just a little beyond his understanding. To him, they were creatures of wing and air, and it frustrated him that he could never get to know them as completely as he wanted. With the legs of his trousers tucked into waterproof boots and his field glasses hanging around his neck, Nathan would creep almost daily through the wild bits of unused land around Chicago. When a few notes of unexpected birdsong caught his ear, he'd crouch and raise the field glasses to his eyes.

There—a flash of red! It was a scarlet tanager on the branch of an oak tree.

For long minutes, Nathan would focus on the bird, his lips curving into an admiring smile. Then, slowly, he would raise the rifle he always carried when bird-watching, take careful aim, and squeeze the trigger.

The creature of wing and air now belonged to Nathan. He would add it to his collection.

Nathan's bird collection was immense. By 1924, he possessed

close to three thousand specimens. Stuffed birds crammed the second-floor study adjoining his bedroom. They stared out from glass-fronted cabinets and lined shelves and mantels. Nathan had killed each one. Most had been sent off to a taxidermist to be mounted in lifelike positions. But he'd held back a few. These he'd gutted himself, pulling out their tiny organs until only their feathered skins remained intact. After tagging each with its scientific name, he tucked the birds away into specially made drawers. None of this bothered Nathan. Killing small creatures had become second nature to him.

Nathan was just five years old when he discovered his passion for birds. That year, 1909, had been an especially unhappy one. He was sent to the Douglas Public School, a school near the Leopolds' Michigan Avenue mansion. His parents, pleased with the school's proximity, apparently gave little thought to academics. The place, Nathan later recalled, was full of "tough boys" who came from poor families.

Nathan knew he was different from them. He was shy and far more studious than most children his age. While he consistently got excellent grades, he detested sports and had no athletic ability. At recess, as the other boys tumbled and ran in the schoolyard, Nathan sat on the sidelines with a book. Magnifying these differences was his parents' wealth. He was the only student at Douglas who lived on posh Michigan Avenue, and his governess would take him to and from school, setting him even further apart. His classmates teased him relentlessly. They called him names he didn't understand but recognized as dirty. They stole his pocket change. They knocked him to the ground and forced him to eat grass.

Nathan didn't say a word to his parents about this bullying. His father, Nathan Leopold Sr., had made a fortune manufacturing aluminum cans and paper and was one of the wealthiest men in Chicago. Aloof and uninvolved, Nathan Sr. was too absorbed in his business dealings to take much notice of his youngest son's problems.

Nathan's mother, Florence, was no help, either. A semi-invalid since Nathan's birth on November 19, 1904, she spent most of her time in her darkened bedroom. Doctors had diagnosed her illness as kidney disease and believed it had been caused by her pregnancy. Nathan, who adored his mother, blamed himself for her illness. If he had never been born, he told himself, she would be well. How could he bother her with his bullying problems when he'd already made her sick?

He did have two brothers—Foreman (called Mike) and Samuel. But the siblings weren't close. Mike, who was ten years older, wasn't around much. And Samuel, five years older, made it clear he didn't have time for his baby brother.

That left Nathan's governess, Paula Van den Bosch. A Roman Catholic, she regaled him with gory stories of the saints. Because he was Jewish, Nathan knew very little about the Christian faith. The saints' cruel and sadistic deaths fascinated the small boy. He thrilled at the idea of Saint Lawrence being grilled alive. And his eyes lit up as he imagined a group of children hacking away at their teacher, Saint Cassian, with iron pencils. But it was the Crucifixion that especially enchanted him. "The idea of nailing anybody to anything appealed to me greatly," he later admitted. He filled notebook after notebook with drawings of headless bodies and crucifixion scenes. "Nathan," Paula said years later, "was a mean child."

She also found his mania for killing and collecting birds peculiar . . . and dangerous. She remembered a day when six-year-old Nathan had shot at a blue jay in his backyard. The shot went wild, shattered the next-door neighbors' window, and just missed hitting one of their servants.

Paula had raced outside and scolded him. His carelessness could have killed somebody.

"I should give a damn," Nathan had snapped back.

That a six-year-old would be allowed to carry a gun (or curse) seemed idiotic to lots of people. But inside the family, Babe, as he was affectionately called, was considered extraordinary and precocious. According to his baby book, he'd spoken his first words at four months: *"Nein, nein, Mama!"* ("No, no, Mama!" The English-speaking Leopolds, whose family had emigrated from Germany sixty-five years earlier, still occasionally used German.) He'd walked at fourteen months and recited his first poem at age three: *"Ich bin klein. Mein Herz ist rein."* ("I am small. My heart is pure.") At five, he tried to learn the word for *yes* in every language.

Why shouldn't such a superior child carry a gun? his father reasoned. He lobbied city hall for a special permit allowing his son to shoot birds in Chicago's parks. And since prominent men like Nathan Sr. typically got what they wanted, Nathan Jr. was soon walking around with his own little rifle.

Not long after the shooting incident, Paula quit. Mathilda Wantz, an eccentric thirty-year-old woman with lightning-quick mood changes and twisted morals, replaced her. She hid her perversity behind a mask of modesty and respectability. She smiled. She curtsied. She appeared so pleasant and hardworking that Florence Leopold, cloistered in her bedroom, gave her free rein over the household. Nathan nicknamed his new governess "Sweetie." And like dead birds and bloody crucifixions, she fascinated him. "She had a very great influence over me," he later said. "She displaced my mother."

For the next six years, Sweetie oversaw every aspect of Nathan's care—his schooling, his diet, his daily schedule. When they were alone, she slapped and pinched him. She even blackmailed him, once encouraging him to steal some stamps from another boy's stamp collection and then threatening to tell his parents if he didn't do exactly as she told him. Nathan kept all this to himself.

He kept darker secrets, too. Sweetie sexually abused both Nathan and his brother Samuel. In her dressing closet, she encouraged them to examine her body from head to toe. "Your mother wishes she had a figure like me," she told them. She bathed with Nathan in the same tub. And she rewarded his good behavior by allowing him to wrestle naked with her on her bed. "Many of the things she did to him have been forgotten or repressed," claimed Dr. Harold Hulbert, a psychiatrist who later examined Nathan. As for the incidents he *did* recall, Nathan detailed them factually and with little embellishment. He never expressed his feelings about them.

Around the age of nine, perhaps as a way to cope with the bullying at school and the abuse at home, Nathan began fantasizing. Lying in bed, he imagined a different life in which he transformed himself from a puny, picked-on boy into the strongest man in the world. Nathan became, as he called it, "a slave" who had saved the life of a king and earned his undying gratitude. The king would offer Nathan his freedom, which Nathan would refuse. He wanted only to serve the king. Sometimes the king would need someone to fight for him, and he always chose Nathan. Nathan would always win. Sometimes Nathan took on one combatant. Other times he'd vanquish a thousand soldiers with guns. When he wasn't fighting, he would lie at the king's feet, attached by a tiny gold chain.

Nathan called these evening revelries his "king-slave fantasies."

And like bird-collecting, they became a compulsion. He was building a sanctuary that allowed him to escape his reality. He dwelt in these fantasies—expanding them, changing them—well into his teens.

The summer before his twelfth birthday, Nathan was sent off to camp. He dreaded going. Just the thought of cabinmates and outdoor activities made him shudder. Once there, though, he experienced a new and powerful emotion: sexual desire. His male camp counselor, an attractive eighteen-year-old, consumed Nathan's thoughts. At night in his cabin, Nathan sank into his king-slave fantasy. But now the counselor was the king and Nathan his slave. It was the first time reality slipped into his fantasy world. It would not be the last.

One fall afternoon, after Nathan's return from camp, Florence made a surprise appearance in her son's bedroom. Pushing open the door, she caught Sweetie in the act of dumping Nathan out of bed. Florence was livid. Nathan had been suffering from a bad cold. He still had a fever and a cough. She fired the governess on the spot, apparently never knowing about the sexual abuse.

Nathan felt adrift without Sweetie. In his mind, she'd taken the place of his mother and was the only person in whom he could confide. "I was devoted to her," he later admitted.

That same year—1916—the family moved from their fashionable home on Michigan Avenue to an even grander mansion in Kenwood. At a time when Jews were excluded from many Chicago neighborhoods, Kenwood was a rare mix of Jewish and Gentile families. Still, the neighborhood did have its so-called "mink coat ghetto," half a square mile where the wealthiest and most socially prominent Jewish families in the city lived.

Nathan's parents enrolled him at the Harvard School for Boys (no relation to the Ivy League college), just one street over from their house. Unlike his previous school, Harvard had a student body made up of boys from rich families, Jewish as well as Gentile. Additionally, the school took academics seriously, and its students were educated with the goal of sending them to elite East Coast colleges like Harvard and Dartmouth. Many attended the University of Chicago, an excellent school just ten blocks from the Leopolds' house. Unlike so many other colleges across the country, the University of Chicago imposed no restrictions on the number of Jewish students it would admit. And because it was academically competitive with Ivy League schools, many of the city's richest families sent their children there. Its campus, which resembled the medieval colleges of Oxford and Cambridge, dazzled Nathan. He envisioned himself walking its quad, garnering dozens of scholastic awards, winning the admiration of professors, and earning a Phi Beta Kappa key.

Nathan excelled in his studies at the Harvard School. He was particularly good at languages—German, French, Italian—as well as philosophy. But he still didn't fit in. His classmates still teased him. They made fun of his shortness, his extreme intelligence, and his all-consuming interest in birds. They called him "flea" and "the crazed genius." They even printed a cruel speech bubble above his picture in the yearbook. It read: "Of course I am the great Nathan. When I open my lips, let no dog bark."

Their teasing humiliated him. It made him feel small and worthless. To compensate, he assumed an attitude of superiority and indifference. He made cutting, sarcastic remarks. And he sneered at what he considered his classmates' lesser intellectual abilities.

In the spring of 1920, fifteen-year-old Nathan, now a junior, had enough credits to graduate. Why spend his senior year as the butt of his classmates' jokes? he asked himself. Besides, there wasn't anything more he could learn from the school's teachers. He was more than capable of doing university work. And so he applied to the University of Chicago. After breezing through the entrance exams, he was accepted. He would start in the fall.

Preparation for his new college life included joining the university's Campus Club, a student social organization. Admittedly, Nathan couldn't have cared less about the dances and picnics the group threw. He'd be entirely too busy studying and bird-collecting to take part in such trivial activities. Still, it did seem like an intelligent choice to attempt *some* social life. He might make connections and meet up-and-coming young men who would later help advance his career. So Nathan suffered through a couple of get-togethers that included incoming freshmen, feeling both uncomfortable and disdainful.

* * *

On most Saturdays, Richard Loeb went "shadowing." The fifteen-year-old would walk along the streets of Kenwood, scanning the faces of passersby, searching for the perfect person to follow.

Should he follow that man in the pinstriped suit? Yes, he *looked* like a banker, but Richard's instincts told him the man was really a jewel thief.

Or maybe he should tail that woman in the park? Richard could see through her disguise. She wasn't homeless. She was a bank robber.

How did he know?

Because *he* was "the master criminal."

Eventually, Richard chose someone—a suspect—to shadow. For hours, he stalked that person. Keeping a safe distance so as not to be seen, he darted down alleys and hid behind trees. He watched his suspect's every move. He grinned if the person did something private like pick his nose or pee in the bushes. Not only did it prove the master criminal's extraordinary stealth (the victim hadn't noticed he was being watched), but he got to see something he shouldn't have. Richard *loved* seeing and doing things he shouldn't.

Naturally, the master criminal headed a gang of hardened no-goods. Richard conjured up this gang in his mind. He communicated with his imaginary criminals by using hand signals. He thumped his chest with his fist twice. He tap-tap-tapped three fingers to his chin, then cupped his ear. He might be signaling them to rendezvous at the hideout or beware of cops.

While he was shadowing, Richard's delusions ran free. Reality faded. He didn't hear the cars honking when he stepped, trancelike, into traffic. He didn't see the passersby staring when he waved his hands around. He was immersed in an alternate world. He'd been doing it since childhood.

Born on June 11, 1905, Richard was the third of Albert Loeb's four sons. Albert was the vice president of Sears, Roebuck & Company, the biggest mail order business in the United States at the time. One of the richest men in Chicago, he kept his family in regal style. His sprawling redbrick mansion on Ellis Avenue was, recalled one neighbor, "built to be important," and it dwarfed the homes of the other Kenwood elite. Stretching across three lots, its grounds held a greenhouse, a tennis court, a nine-hole golf course, and a fishpond. Inside, a staff of maids, valets, chefs, and chauffeurs satisfied the family's every whim. Growing up, Richard was fed, dressed, and driven to school by these servants. The cook baked his favorite cookies. The gardener let him dig for worms in the flowerbeds. But no one cuddled or sang to him. No one on the staff had time for that.

Neither did Albert Loeb, who was consumed by business.

Nor did Anna Loeb, whose days were taken up with charity work and social causes. Richard's mother cared deeply about him, as well as her other sons, but in those days, women of her social rank rarely took on the day-to-day tasks of child care. Instead, they employed governesses. And so, when Richard was four and a half years old, Anna hired Emily Struthers.

Miss Struthers took charge of all three Loeb boys—Richard, twelve-year-old Allan, and nine-year-old Ernest. (The youngest son, Tommy, would not be born for another five years.) But the older boys, already in school, needed her for very little. So the governess focused all her attention on Richard.

© © ©

Miss Struthers had definite ideas about how a boy should be raised. A strict disciplinarian, she expected Richard to "mind her to the minute." For the next ten years, she would dominate his every move. Her word was law, and her greatest desire was to remake him into her "ideal boy."

In the Loebs' book-lined library with the sun shining through the tall leaded-glass windows, Miss Struthers read him the work of Dickens and Shakespeare, as well as world histories and other books she considered the best. Every day, she accompanied him to school and back so she could consult with his teachers. She asked for extra work and more advanced studies. She was determined that Richard would excel in school . . . and life.

Richard often felt like Miss Struthers's prisoner. He wasn't allowed to play after school like the other boys. While they played baseball or fished in the lagoon at Jackson Park, he spent his free time at a big mahogany desk, Miss Struthers right beside him. She urged him to work hard, learn more, study, study, study. "I was kept under," Richard later said.

One afternoon when he was seven, he decided not to wait for her after class. Snatching at freedom, he raced down the street. He paid dearly for that delicious hour of play. Miss Struthers punished him by sending him to bed for the rest of the day.

Is it any wonder he began to chafe at her iron rule? Daily, his resentment grew. "To get by her," he recalled, "I formed the habit of lying." He lied about his grades. He lied about taking his big brother Allan's tie. He lied to a neighbor boy who had a lemonade stand. No, no, *he* hadn't stolen the boy's little cash register. Oh, no, he had no idea where it went. (Richard had taken and buried it.) Lying became both his pleasure and his art form. He lied by making false claims and omitting facts. He lied for no reason. He made up stories simply because he could. No one—not his parents, or his schoolmates, or even Miss Struthers—suspected him. He just smiled and oozed charm and people believed his every word. And he never felt guilty or remorseful.

He lied to Miss Struthers about his nightly reading, too. She insisted he retire with only literature of quality, but around the age of nine, Richard developed a passion for crime stories and detective novels. It had started by accident. While looking for something to steal from his brother's bedroom, he came upon a book by mystery writer Frank L. Packard.

Richard stole it.

And devoured it.

He found himself enthralled by Packard's story about a famous criminal who planned and executed breathtaking and elaborate robberies. Richard secretly bought and read the rest of the Packard series. He also read all the Sherlock Holmes books. But his favorite books were by Wyndham Martyn. They featured a character called Anthony Trent, Master Criminal.

To further feed his new obsession, he began sneaking out to the drugstore at night to buy crime magazines—*True Detective Mysteries, Master Detective, Black Mask*. Wildly popular, these and a dozen other publications like them hit magazine stands every month. Richard inhaled them.

Miss Struthers never suspected a thing. This made him feel superior, like Anthony Trent, Master Criminal.

At the age of ten, the "picturalizations," as Richard called them, began. Lying beneath his cotton duvet, he held his teddy bear close and let the images play across his mind: He saw himself in jail. Then the prison guards came. They tore off his clothes, threw him against the iron bars of his cell, and whipped him. Richard, however, felt no fear. He didn't feel pain, either, even as blood dripped down his back and puddled onto the floor. All he felt was gratification. People were looking at him as he was being punished, and he enjoyed their looking. He deserved their fascinated attention because he was a famous criminal.

Over the years, the picturalizations evolved. He imagined himself committing all sorts of crimes—setting buildings on fire, robbing banks. Before he drifted off into his fantasies, he would turn to his stuffed bear and say, "As you know, Teddy . . . ," as if he were telling it a bedtime story even as a teenager. In his imaginings, he became the "master criminal mind of the century," whose planning and carrying out of crimes confounded even the greatest detectives.

At first, picturalization was like being in another world, detached from reality. Sometimes, while drifting into it, he panicked, fearing that he might not find his way back. Soon, though, Richard didn't want to come back. His real life was not nearly as exciting as his fantasy life. Why struggle to keep them separate? Why not act on his compulsions?

Around the age of eleven, he began shoplifting. He took anything he could, it didn't matter what. He didn't steal because he wanted the item; he stole because of the thrill it gave him. Twice he was caught in the act, but he didn't feel ashamed of what he'd done. Rather, he felt ashamed of being found out. He berated himself. Wasn't the master criminal too clever to get caught? He didn't get in any trouble, though. A charming smile and a lie were enough to placate both shopkeepers.

Meanwhile, Miss Struthers kept pushing him in his studies. So advanced was he that in October 1917, just four months after turning twelve, he entered University High School near the campus of the University of Chicago. An academically rigorous prep school, it catered to the better families in the area, both Jewish and Gentile. But Richard's early admission wasn't enough of an achievement for the governess. Her ideal boy, she decided, would graduate from high school in just two years. And she would be by his side every step of the way.

Richard's teachers thought this was a bad idea. What purpose did it serve? The boy would have to carry a terribly heavy academic load. And then what? Did he plan to enter college at fourteen? Yes, he might be able to handle the coursework, but what would he have in common with the other students? He'd still be a child, attending classes with young adults. Such a situation might be harmful to his mental development, they warned Albert and Anna Loeb when the issue of early graduation was raised. Besides, the teachers added, Richard was a bright boy and a hard worker, but he wasn't a genius. Why not let him enjoy his school years?

Richard's parents seemed to have little opinion in the matter. Instead, they deferred to their governess.

Miss Struthers, of course, dismissed the teachers' advice. Richard, she believed, was bound to do something great with his life. An ambassador? A senator? That could only happen through constant hard work . . . and her aid.

Outwardly polite and obedient, her charge did as he was told. Miss Struthers coached him, sat with him, checked over his work, and kept track of his assignments. She urged him, as always, to study, study, study.

In the spring of 1919—one month before his fourteenth birthday— Richard received his high school diploma.

His voice hadn't changed yet.

But beneath his achievements and charm, Richard felt bitter and overworked. He envied his former classmates their freedom. And he daily dreaded going into his college classrooms. It was also clear that he was not ready for college work. Even though he managed to pass the university's entrance exams, he struggled with his classes that first quarter. Despite all Miss Struthers's help, he earned his lowest grades ever—straight Cs.

In June 1920, just days after Richard turned fifteen, Anna Loeb called Miss Struthers into her sitting room. She'd made a decision. Now that he was in college, he no longer needed a governess.

Miss Struthers fervently disagreed. If Richard was to succeed in college, her help was essential. In fact, she'd already put together a course of summer studies for him.

But Anna Loeb insisted. From now on, the governess would oversee six-year-old Tommy's education instead.

If she couldn't be with Richard, Miss Struthers declared, she would resign. She left the Loeb household that same day.

Richard felt torn about her going. She'd often made him feel like a prisoner. She'd pushed and nagged. He'd resented her and constantly lied to her. And yet, she'd provided a steadying presence. He'd held himself partially in check because of her. What would he do now that she was gone?

"I sort of broke loose," he later said.

The fifteen-year-old took up smoking and began carrying around a hip flask of gin. Despite being two or three years younger than most freshmen, he attracted girls. And, like Nathan Leopold, he joined the Campus Club. His charm made it easy for him to fit in. In truth, he didn't much like the group, but he liked being the center of attention. Miss Struthers had idolized Richard, and he missed her fawning focus. He tried to find it among his new acquaintances.

Whatever the other, older students considered smart and sophisticated, Richard would do. He felt he had to prove himself over and over—not just to them, but also to himself. He began going with them to a speakeasy on 65th Street, where he got drunk and lost his virginity. He didn't really care for sex—he found it far more enjoyable to lie about his sexual exploits than to actually engage in them. He loved putting one over on his new pals. They never knew he was lying—about the girls, about his grades. Many who considered him their friend would have been shocked to know his true opinion of them. Richard fooled people, used them for his purposes, and never felt bad about it.

❋ ❋ ❋

No one in their social circle remembered how the pair met. And neither Nathan nor Richard ever said. It was, however, in June 1920—perhaps at one of the dances or picnics thrown by the Campus Club—when someone introduced them.

Nathan, meet Richard.

Richard, meet Nathan.

The two young men had much in common. Both were Jewish. Both were sons of millionaires. Both dressed fashionably and expensively, wearing suits and ties to school and buying the latest serges and tweeds from Brooks Brothers. Both wore their hair slicked back in a style popular in the 1920s. Both were academically precocious. And both came from the exclusive Chicago neighborhood of Kenwood. In fact, they lived just two and a half blocks from each other— Nathan in the stately three-story Victorian on Greenwood, Richard in the imposing brick mansion on Ellis.

At that first meeting, Nathan took one look at Richard Loeb and immediately dismissed him. Loeb's build was too tall and muscular, his eyes too twinkling, his smile too sudden and attractive. Oozing charm, he tried to make everyone like him. He knew how to act and what to say. To Nathan's mind, Loeb was a faker and a show-off, the type of fellow Nathan looked down on. What were popularity and physical attractiveness compared to intellect? Nothing.

Richard didn't think much of Nathan Leopold, either. The fellow looked sinister with his stone-gray eyes and heavy brows. His smile was more like a smirk. And then there was his personality, or *lack* of it. Leopold rarely laughed. He came off as sullen and nervous and boringly serious. Why did everything that came out of his mouth have to sound so important? No, Nathan Leopold was entirely too dull for fun-loving Richard Loeb. He hoped never to socialize with him again.

Nathan hoped for the same.

But they kept bumping into each other—perhaps at Jackson Park or the neighborhood drugstore. Neither teenager ever provided any details of their budding friendship. But by the end of that summer, they were inseparable.

Their other friends didn't understand the pair's relationship. Nathan Leopold and Richard Loeb . . . *best friends?* How could that be? They had completely opposite personalities. What could possibly have drawn them together?

CHAPTER FOUR

THE SUPERMAN AND THE MASTER CRIMINAL

"What is happening to the youth of America?" asked a *Ladies' Home Journal* article in the fall of 1920. Across the nation, young people were rejecting what they considered the pretentious, outmoded, hypocritical lifestyle of their parents and grandparents. Their rejection sprang from deep disillusionment. Just a year earlier, World War I had ended. The bloody trench warfare had demonstrated the brutality and uselessness of war, and had left America's youth with a sense of unease. They began questioning the necessity of this so-called Great War and the sham idealism of their elders who had supported it. Their feelings were summed up in an article published in 1920 in the *Atlantic Monthly* magazine: "The older generation has certainly pretty well ruined this world before passing it on to us. Now my generation is disillusioned. . . . We have been forced to live in an atmosphere of 'tomorrow we die,' and so, naturally, we drink and are merry."

Drinking was illegal. At the start of 1920, the Eighteenth Amendment, which outlawed liquor, went into effect. Americans were no longer allowed to make, sell, or drink booze. But Prohibition only increased young people's frenzy to abandon traditional morality. Often shocking their parents, they seized the day and lived for the moment. The "new woman" of this postwar period began smoking in public, wearing makeup and short skirts, bobbing her hair, and speaking her mind. No longer was she the Victorian maiden sitting in a tearoom with her beau and her chaperone. Now she was a "flapper," listening to jazz music and going unaccompanied to illegal speakeasies and nightclubs, where a sense of hedonistic revelry gripped dancers doing the Charleston and the shimmy. Jazz music—what the *New York American* warned was "pathological, nerve-irritating, sex-exciting music"—pounded through their veins, much to the horror of their parents. Drinking copious amounts of bootleg liquor simply increased the pleasure of shattering conventions. Admitted one college student, "Defying the bluenose moralists was a gesture of intellectual respectability."

Young men and women defied conventions in other ways, too. Carousing in cars gave them a freedom and privacy their parents could never have imagined. New words like *petting* and *parking* entered the language. This was definitely *not* how their buttoned-up elders behaved. Declared one flapper, "Young America is enamored of life, real life, life lived in the raw, life lived at the highest pitch of excitement."

Nathan and Richard also felt that urgency. They enjoyed each day as if they would never enjoy another. Drinking. Smoking. Clubhopping. Driving in cars and picking up girls. They wanted to try everything *now*. And during that fall of 1920, together, they did.

Many nights, long after his family had gone to bed, Nathan would slip out the back door and into the garage. There sat the automobile his father had bought him, a flashy red Willys-Knight sports car with nickel trim and leather seats. Nathan would open the door and slide in behind the steering wheel. He'd sit a moment, straining his ears. Had Sven Englund, the chauffeur, who lived above the garage, heard him? When no sound came from Englund's rooms, Nathan would pop the hand brake and let the car coast silently down the driveway and out onto Greenwood Avenue. Only then would he start the engine and drive to the Loeb mansion.

Richard would always be waiting at the end of the driveway.

Nathan now admired his friend's good looks and seeming sophistication. Richard knew all about drinking, gambling, and picking up girls. In truth, Nathan didn't much care for that last activity. Girls, he believed, were inferior. Still, Richard seemed to enjoy it, so Nathan always went along.

As soon as he hopped into the car, Richard would pull out the flask of gin he frequently carried. The gin came from his father's liquor cellar, imported illegally and at great expense from Canada. Other Americans might have to swill homemade rotgut, but not Richard Loeb. After taking a swig, he'd pass it to Nathan. Nathan, who preferred his father's imported Irish whiskey, would take a gulp. And then, once again, they were off!

Chicago was their playground. Rich, young, and unsupervised—at a time when one didn't need an ID to get into a saloon, or a license to drive a car—the fifteen-year-olds could go anywhere, do anything.

Maybe they'd head over to the jazz clubs south of 65th Street to drink bootleg booze and shoot some craps. Richard used loaded dice. Would he get caught cheating? The possibility made it so much more exciting.

If the pair felt like listening to a band and ogling chorus girls, there was always the Friar's Inn, a basement speakeasy on Van Buren where patrons drank whiskey from coffee cups. Or, if they were feeling more adventurous, there was the Four Deuces, an establishment in the Levee District that looked like an office but was really a gambling parlor and brothel.

They could always pop into a dance hall. For a dime each, they could cut a rug with a couple of scantily dressed women. In these joints, Nathan usually did more drinking than dancing. Richard, though, loved getting out on the floor. He liked to see how far he could go before a girl slapped his face.

And then there was Colosimo's Café, owned by mobster James "Big Jim" Colosimo, located on South Wabash. It was a favorite of Richard's because of its duplicity. At one a.m., the lights in the front café would go out and the patrons would be escorted into a hidden back restaurant. This would enable the beat cop who walked by minutes later to report to his sergeant that Colosimo's had complied with the city's official closing hour. Sure, the cop knew about the second joint. So did his sergeant. In fact, everyone on the police force knew—the lieutenants and deputies and detectives, even the chief himself. The city aldermen knew, too, as did the mayor, William "Big Bill" Thompson, and the judges and most other officials and politicians. In Chicago, practically everyone was on the take. Colosimo, like the other leaders of organized crime outfits, paid plenty in "protection money" so they could go about their business—the bootleg business.

Bootlegging was lucrative in thirsty Chicago. Six thousand speakeasies freckled the city's South Side. And as business boomed, gangs began fighting for control of the city's booze distribution. Big Jim Colosimo got gunned down in his club by Johnny Torrio (owner of the Four Deuces), who'd joined up with Al Capone. Rival gangs roamed the streets carrying sawed-off shotguns and submachine guns. Gangland hits were common.

City officials tolerated them as a necessary evil. Sure, an innocent bystander got mowed down every now and then, but that was the price one paid to drink and dance, shoot craps, and listen to jazz.

For Richard Loeb, it was an intoxicating world of possibility.

For Nathan Leopold, it was intoxicating to be with Richard.

●　●　●

The Pere Marquette picked up speed as it left Chicago's Union Station, plunging into the darkness of a February night in 1921. For the next twelve hours, the train would make a slow curve northward along Lake Michigan's ice-thick shoreline. Its final stop would be Charlevoix, a small resort town in northern Michigan where the Loebs owned a baronial estate. Richard was headed there for a long weekend with his parents, and he'd invited Nathan along.

In their Pullman sleeper car, as the train rumbled along the tracks, Richard taught Nathan the finer points of cheating at cards. Naturally, Nathan learned quickly. They snickered at the thought of suckering Richard's father out of money.

Nathan leaned forward. He had a secret to tell.

Richard loved learning other people's secrets. What was it?

He had fantasies, Nathan admitted. About men. Sexual fantasies.

It was a shocking confession. In 1921, sexuality was considered a moral question, and same-sex relations were seen as acts of perversion. Homosexuality, it was believed, was nothing more than an immoral temptation that needed to be resisted. Those who did not resist were considered "reprobates," deserving of jail time (laws in those days made homosexuality illegal) or extreme psychiatric treatments like aversion therapy and lobotomy. For Nathan to reveal his sexuality was highly risky. If word got out, he could lose everything—his reputation, his place at the university, possibly even his freedom.

But Richard didn't recoil in disgust. He waited to hear more.

Nathan rushed on. Sure, he'd gone on a few dates with girls. He'd even had sex with a few. But he only went with them because he knew it was the thing to do. He'd never felt attracted to girls. Since adolescence, he'd longed for handsome men, like his summer camp counselor, and the models in the menswear advertisements, and . . . Richard. He admitted to having an intense crush on him.

Richard could feel the heat of Nathan's white-hot devotion. And he basked in it. Not since Miss Struthers had someone been so utterly and completely focused on him. He decided to share a secret of his own.

His college-student exterior was all an illusion, he told Nathan. In truth, he longed to live a life of crime. That was the reason he stole money from friends and family. That was why he shoplifted. It wasn't just for fun. It was because he was a master criminal. What did Nathan think of that?

Nathan thought it perfectly logical. Richard, after all, was a superman, Nathan told him. And so was he.

Nathan explained. He'd extensively studied the work of German philosopher Friedrich Nietzsche and his theory of the "superman." Nathan interpreted the theory this way: Men who possessed extraordinary physical or intellectual qualities were supermen, exempt from the laws that governed society. In fact, laws had only been made for ordinary people and didn't apply to supermen. Even murder, Nathan believed, was an acceptable act for a superman to commit. His only consideration was whether he got pleasure from doing the deed.

Richard liked Nathan's amoral attitude.

Later, when the lights went off, Richard slipped into his friend's bunk, and the young men had sex. The experience, Nathan later claimed, gave him "more pleasure than anything [I] have ever done." To repeat it, he would do anything—*anything*—Richard wanted.

❂ ❂ ❂

A few weeks after the pair returned from Charlevoix, Richard decided to change colleges. Going to the University of Chicago, he declared, was like going to a neighborhood high school. What fun was that? He wanted to get out from under his parents' watchful eyes, live on his own, and *really* experience life. He chose the University of Michigan in Ann Arbor. Not only did it have an undefeated football team, but it also had a reputation as a "party school." Richard looked forward to boozy bonfire parties and Big Ten games. Additionally, and perhaps just as importantly, the school had a less restrictive admissions policy for Jews than many other universities. And so, at the end of the 1921 spring quarter and with his parents' blessing, he applied. He easily got in.

Nathan, too, applied and was accepted. It hadn't taken much to convince his father to let him go. In truth, Nathan had been content in Chicago, but he hadn't wanted to be separated from Richard. In Ann Arbor, they would be sharing an apartment. The idea of living day to day with his lover must have thrilled him.

That summer the pair once again traveled to Charlevoix. They quickly established a relaxing routine. While Richard slept late, Nathan slipped out into the woods to collect birds. In the afternoon, they biked or boated, played golf or tennis. Richard taught Nathan how to shadow groundskeepers and livestock tenders, and they spent long hours at it. Nathan thought it a silly game for sixteen-year-olds, but he went along for his friend's sake. At night they played bridge with the Loeb family and won hand after hand. To Richard's delight, no one suspected them of cheating. Afterward, they visited the nearby dance halls and speakeasies. They shot dice at the illegal crap games behind the Charlevoix Inn and drove drunk through the dark and twisting country roads. After returning to the room they shared, they had sex.

One night, as Richard slid into Nathan's bed, the door opened. There stood Hamlin Buchman, a University of Chicago law student who was working for the Loebs that summer. Even in the dim light, Buchman could see that the two were naked. He quickly backed out of the room.

The teenagers were frantic. What if Buchman told someone? They'd be ruined, "despised by humanity," declared Nathan.

Years later, Nathan would admit that over the next few days the pair contemplated killing Buchman. They even put together the necessary supplies—chisel, rope, guns. But they never went through with it, although Nathan did confess to having daydreams about torturing the law student.

Buchman, however, believed they *did* try to kill him. Just days after he'd walked in on them, they asked him to go sailing. As the three swept across Pine Lake, Richard turned to Buchman. "Do you swim?"

"No," replied Buchman.

The teenagers smirked at each other. Then they tipped over the boat and, without a backward glance, swam away. They probably planned to report the tragic accident once they reached shore. What a shock it must have been when a dripping and furious Buchman appeared moments later.

Wait! Hadn't the law student said he couldn't swim?

Buchman clarified. He knew *how* to swim, he told them. He just didn't *like* to swim.

The teens burst into effusive apologies. Such a terrible mishap. Wasn't it lucky they all knew how to swim?

Convinced they had tried to kill him, Buchman went to see Richard's brother Allan. Eight years older than Richard, he often stepped in for their father. He listened to the law student's story.

Homosexual behavior *and* attempted murder? These were serious accusations. Allan called the teenagers into the study. Was there any truth to it?

Nathan and Richard denied everything. They accused Buchman of making things up. Probably, suggested Richard, to blackmail the family.

Allan believed the pair. As the teenagers smugly looked on, he fired Buchman on the spot and threw him out of the room.

An angry Buchman returned to campus. He told his classmates everything that had happened. Those boys, he said, "are not right."

Rumors spread. They soon found their way back to Nathan and Richard. The young men seethed. They longed for revenge. But since neither would be on campus that fall, they let it go.

Richard left for the University of Michigan first.

Unfortunately, a case of scarlet fever delayed Nathan's arrival in Ann Arbor for several weeks. When he finally got there, Richard treated him coldly. He barely spoke to him in public and was rarely home.

Nathan confronted him. What was going on?

Buchman's rumors about their relationship had found their way to Ann Arbor, Richard explained. To stop further spread, he suggested they quit being seen so often together. When they did go out together, they should treat each other politely but distantly. No longer could they act like best friends.

Nathan agreed. Any whiff of homosexuality, he knew, could ruin his future. But what about when they were alone together in the apartment?

Richard acted cold there, too. Later, he would tell people he'd gone along with this side of their relationship because he was curious, but that sex with Nathan had become abhorrent. Could part of this have been because they'd been caught? As rumors swirled, Richard might have realized that any pleasure derived from sex with Nathan was not worth the risk. Unlike Nathan, he didn't have any intense feelings about their relationship.

And Nathan's emotions were intense. He was, he admitted, even "jealous of the food and drink [Richard] took, because they came into closer intimacy with [him] than I could ever hope to reach."

His first semester, Richard rushed the Jewish fraternity Zeta Beta Tau (at that time, the traditional Greek system was closed to Jews, as well as African Americans, Asians, and Roman Catholics). Being a member of the fraternity was an indicator of social class and served to "filter out" those considered undesirable. Loeb certainly fit the Zeta Beta Tau mold. He came from a prominent family, was charming and wealthy. But he also had baggage, namely Nathan Leopold. "Nobody liked Leopold," recalled one frat brother. "Most people couldn't understand why Loeb hung around with him." Nathan was patronizing and conceited. Sometimes he even spoke of himself in the third person. And then there were those whispers about his being a homosexual. Did Loeb really want to associate with the fellow? They made a deal with Richard. They would accept him *if* he dumped Nathan.

It took Richard fifteen minutes to move out of the apartment and into the Zeta Beta Tau chapter house.

His actions devastated Nathan. The only reason he'd come to Michigan was to be with Richard. Now his best friend had abandoned him.

It wasn't the only loss he suffered that school year. In October, Nathan's mother, Florence, finally succumbed to the illness that had left her an invalid for so many years. Nathan returned to Chicago. As he stood at her graveside in the chilly autumn air, he gave no outward sign of emotion. His expression carried no hint of his thoughts. But he felt angry and further abandoned. And he blamed God.

God had taken away his mother when he needed her most. How then, he reasoned, could there be a God? Wasn't God supposed to help his children? Nathan had long suspected God was a myth. His philosophical studies had already forced him to question the existence of an immortal soul. Florence Leopold's death merely hardened the cynicism and mistrust he'd been developing about religious faith. There was no all-powerful entity to smite one for one's sins, or reward one for good behavior, he determined. God was nothing but a construct, meant to coerce ordinary people into conforming to society's rules.

"I realized that if I could kid myself into believing that there was a life hereafter, I would be happier," he later recalled, "but I felt I must be intellectually honest." He vowed to "cut out the emotional." He would become a "cold-blooded intellect."

Once back in Michigan, Nathan lost himself in his studies. He earned good grades. But he lived a solitary life, spending most of his free time alone. He salved his loneliness by reminding himself that the universe was nothing more than a mass of electrons, and the mind just a highly complicated reflex center. He could control his emotions because everything was mechanical. He saw no difference between right and wrong. "The only wrong I can do is make a mistake," he said, "and my happiness is the only thing in life that matters at all to me."

At the end of the spring semester of 1922, he transferred back to the University of Chicago.

CHAPTER FIVE

APART AND TOGETHER

For the next school year—fall 1922 through spring 1923—Nathan and Richard saw little of each other. Sometimes when Richard came home for a holiday, the two would sneak out and get drunk. But they weren't close anymore. They didn't share secrets. They didn't share each other's beds.

Nathan—who'd made it his goal to graduate from college early— was now a senior at Chicago. He'd always been an exceptional student, but that school year he applied himself with more vigor than ever. Was he trying to forget Richard? Or was he coming into his own, finally discovering himself, outside of his friend's dark influence? Whatever the reason, Nathan flourished academically. He was especially talented in languages, taking Latin, Greek, Russian, Sanskrit, and a course in Romance languages. He also took classes in philosophy (his major), sociology, and literature. He earned straight As.

He flourished socially, too. He joined a handful of clubs, including a literary society that sponsored dinners and lively book discussions. Because he could speak and write Latin and Greek, Nathan also joined the Classical Club. Through these groups, he made a circle of friends, both men and women, who admired his intelligence and achievements. He went to parties and dances. He even asked a few girls on dates because, as he later put it, "I knew I should."

He also took part in a Sunday-evening study group. In his bedroom, Nathan gathered with a handful of classmates to debate philosophical ideas, especially Nietzsche's.

Richard Loeb, Nathan told his study group one night, was a superman.

The others expressed doubt. What was Nathan's proof?

He cited Richard's handsomeness, as well as his brilliant mind.

Nathan's friends disagreed.

One of them, Arnold Maremont, snorted. "You don't know what you're talking about," he said. "Don't think brilliant, think glib. [Loeb] doesn't really know anything."

"You don't understand him," argued Nathan.

But Maremont insisted he did. He'd known Richard for years. Didn't Nathan see that the fellow was a liar and a cheat?

Nathan refused to listen.

At that moment, Maremont realized Nathan was "totally gullible as far as Loeb went." Nothing would ever change his mind.

Nathan stayed busy with birds, too. On Saturday mornings, he headed over to Wooded Island in nearby Jackson Park in hopes of adding new species to his collection. If he had an entire day free, he drove out to the forest preserves south of Chicago and the marshlands around Wolf Lake. He even began teaching a birding class and taking small groups of women or schoolchildren around the area. As if that weren't enough, he wrote papers about his hundreds of hours of field observations. These were published in some of the leading ornithological journals of the day, including the prestigious *Auk*. Nathan was making a name for himself in scientific circles.

That May, at the age of eighteen, he graduated with Phi Beta Kappa honors, just as he'd once imagined.

⊙ ⊙ ⊙

Anyone who knew Richard Loeb during his senior year remembered him being drunk, often before noon. His frat brothers were forever carrying him home from football games and parties and the late-night poker games he liked so much. They began to see the cruel streak beneath his personable exterior. He was especially feared during the fraternity's initiation for freshman pledges. Each member had a wooden paddle with which they struck the new members on the buttocks. Everyone went easy on the pledges—everybody, that is, except Richard. After winding up, he'd hit them so hard he'd send them clear across the room. "What a miserable son of a bitch he was," recalled one of those pledges, Abel Brown.

They started to see through his lies, too. "He lied like hell," recalled another of Richard's frat brothers. "About grades . . . girls . . . anything." Said another, "We had the line on him. We did not take him at his word."

Some even believed Richard was a thief. That year, stuff went missing. Little things. Cuff links. Pens. And Richard was alone in the house in the afternoons; all the others had classes. It seemed "fishy," recalled Abel Brown. Still, they never accused him. They didn't have any solid proof.

Meanwhile, Richard obsessed about crimes in the news. He would talk and talk about the latest robbery or murder. He would speculate about the criminals' motives, pose questions as if he were a detective, read long passages from the newspapers to his less interested frat brothers. Talking about these crimes left him breathless and excited, eyes glittering.

He didn't join any clubs or participate in extracurricular activities. Academics no longer interested him. Instead, he slid through school with ordinary grades, taking classes that sounded easy or fun. He graduated early—in three and a half years—but just barely. Weeks short of his eighteenth birthday, he became the youngest graduate of the University of Michigan.

Richard didn't have any plans for his future. He hadn't chosen or even thought about a career. After receiving his diploma, he hung around Ann Arbor for a few weeks, drinking, cheating at cards, and reading dime detective novels. He knew he had to do something or his father would cut off his allowance. He was mildly interested in history. Perhaps, he thought, he could take a graduate course or two at the University of Chicago. So in September 1923, he returned to his family's mansion on Ellis Avenue. He enrolled in just one class— American constitutional history.

Nathan was on campus, too. Busy as always, he'd been accepted into the University of Chicago's law school and was now enrolled in four courses. He planned to transfer to Harvard Law School the following fall.

Then Richard reentered his life.

❂ ❂ ❂

How could Nathan resist? Richard simply smiled in his charming way, and Nathan forgave him everything. Nathan was still deeply in love. He begged to resume their sexual relationship.

Richard acquiesced. "The actual sex," he later admitted, "is rather unimportant to me."

What *was* important was the control it gave him over Nathan.

It occurred to him that he really didn't like his friend that much. Leopold's superior and condescending attitude annoyed him. So did all that tedious prattling about birds and law and languages. Most grating was Nathan's constant harping about his philosophical beliefs. Supermen? Richard didn't give himself permission to break society's rules because he was some mythical superman. He broke them because he held conventional morality in contempt. He didn't care about right and wrong. It was as simple as that.

Still, he needed Nathan. What fun was there in breaking the law alone? Someone had to be there to admire his brilliant planning and flawless execution. The master criminal needed a witness. An accomplice.

And Nathan was willing to go along. He was up for anything as long as the master criminal made no mistakes in planning that might get them caught. *And* as long as they kept sleeping together.

Soon they were back to sneaking out at night, getting drunk and cheating at cards and dice. But now their adventures included other, more exciting activities. Sometimes they went to Jackson Park and, after breaking out Richard's gin, or the bottle of whiskey Nathan kept in his glove box, slowly drove along the secluded lanes, headlights dimmed. When they spied cars parked with late-night couples inside, Richard would grab one of the bricks he'd brought with him and heave it through their windshield. The act made him chortle.

One night, they picked the wrong victim. Seconds after Richard's brick smashed into the parked car, a man leaped from the backseat. He started shooting. Nathan sped away while Richard howled with laughter.

Another night, they sent a brick hurtling through the plate-glass window of a neighborhood drugstore. A burglar alarm went off, bringing two beat cops on the run. Richard flung himself into the Willys-Knight's front seat as Nathan peeled away from the curb, but not before one of the police officers fired. The bullet struck Nathan's car. How he explained the damage to the Leopolds' chauffeur is unknown.

Richard loved every second of the episode and began planning their next crime—robbing a family friend's wine cellar. He spent days devising the scheme, taking pleasure in considering every detail from all angles. He bought a chisel and wrapped its blade with adhesive tape, turning it into a heavyweight club. He bought a rope in case they needed to tie up servants. And he packed a loaded revolver in case the night watchman caught them. Then, on a night when he knew the family was out of town, he and Nathan slipped through the shadows to the mansion's back door.

Richard turned the knob.

It was locked.

He tried picking the lock.

No success.

Minutes crept by. How long could they stand there before someone noticed and called the police?

Finally, Richard called off the burglary. But he wasn't disappointed. The nervous tension, the fear, the rush of adrenaline had been exhilarating. He longed to experience that feeling again.

The pair took to stealing cars in the fall of 1923. By accident, they discovered that the key to Anna Loeb's Milburn fit other cars of that same make. They had a marvelous time riding off with the vehicles, then abandoning them miles from where they were taken. One night, while drunk, they took a car from a downtown garage. A truck began chasing them—obviously, someone knew they were not the car's rightful owners. Nathan hit the accelerator, careening around corners and roaring down streets. But the truck stuck close. At last, with no other choice, they flung open the doors and leaped while the car was still running. The Milburn smashed into a light pole.

Nathan ran down an alley and hid.

Richard hopped onto a passing streetcar.

Eventually, they met back in Kenwood. Breathless with excitement, Richard convinced Nathan to change his clothes (in case someone recognized them) and return to the scene of the crash. In the glare of police lights, they mingled with the crowd of gapers. What had happened? people wondered. Who'd caused the crash?

After each of these criminal adventures, Richard scoured Chicago's newspapers, hoping to see some mention of their misdeeds. But the city's dailies had bigger crimes to report on than broken windows and stolen cars. To get noticed, the master criminal needed to be bolder.

One chilly autumn night, Nathan parked the Willys-Knight five blocks from a vacant lot. Keeping to the shadows, carrying gasoline and matches, he and Richard moved toward an empty shack. They splashed gasoline around the floor and walls, lit a match, and dashed away.

Minutes later, they drove back to the scene. Richard needed, he admitted, the "thrill of watching it and talking with the crowd, sneering at their ignorant questions at the cause of the fire." He even offered suggestions as to what had happened. This gave him, he explained, "a great sense of satisfaction from the fact I knew the real solution to the mystery and no one else did."

The pair set at least two more fires that fall. But arson did little to sate Richard's appetite for crime. If anything, it left him hungrier.

It was time to do something even more daring, more dangerous. Was Nathan with him?

Nathan was.

◎ ◎ ◎

It was three a.m., November 11, 1923, when the teens parked on a side street in Ann Arbor. Autumn leaves crunched beneath their feet as they walked the two blocks to the Zeta Beta Tau chapter house. It had taken them six hours to drive from Chicago. None of the frat brothers knew they were coming.

Lights blazed from the house's living room windows. But not a soul stirred. The brothers had all fallen into bed after hours of celebratory revelry. Twelve hours earlier, the University of Michigan Wolverines had destroyed the Quantico Marines Devil Dogs 26–6, causing gin and beer to flow. Dancing had shaken the house's floorboards into the wee hours until, eventually, one by one, the brothers had staggered to the second-story study rooms. There they'd peeled off jackets, shirts, and trousers before climbing to the third floor and dropping onto their beds to sleep off their celebration. Obviously, the last man standing had forgotten to lock the doors and turn off the lights.

Nathan and Richard moved up the porch stairs toward the front door. Neither bothered to hide his identity. True, someone might recognize them and raise the alarm. But Richard figured he could lie his way out of the situation by claiming they'd driven up for the football game. If that didn't work . . . well . . . the teenagers had come prepared. Richard carried what was becoming his weapon of choice—a chisel with adhesive tape wrapped around its blade. He would use the tool's heavy wooden handle like a club, smashing any confrontational fraternity brothers over the head. Nathan, meanwhile, had a length of rope and a loaded gun in his jacket pocket. Both carried flashlights.

The front door creaked when they pushed it open. Cautiously, they stepped in. Empty bottles of liquor lay on tabletops and mantels. Ashtrays overflowed with cigarettes.

Richard inched across the floor and peeked into a small adjoining room. He knew from having lived in the house that weekend guests sometimes slept there on a cot. He was relieved to see that it was empty. He signaled for Nathan to follow him up the stairs. Slowly, ears straining, they crept to the second floor.

They switched on their flashlights. Clothes had been left in a tumble, draped over the backs of chairs and tossed onto the floor. Pockets had been emptied into careless piles on desktops. "We took everything we could get our hands on," Richard later admitted—coins, penknives, class pins.

The young men didn't worry about fingerprints. There was as yet no national repository of fingerprints for criminal identification. Even if there had been, neither had ever been fingerprinted. It would have been impossible to identify them.

Nathan found a wallet. He took out the bills.

Richard rifled through his friend Max Schrayer's desk. He took a medal Max had won for editing the school newspaper, along with some money and a watch.

The pair went from room to room like this, pocketing whatever caught their eye. A fountain pen. More money. A half-full bottle of gin. Nathan grabbed a portable Underwood typewriter before they hurried back to the car.

In the front seat, they counted their loot: $74 and an assortment of small items. Nathan asked if he could keep the typewriter.

Adrenaline coursed through Richard. Burglary! He'd planned and committed a seamless burglary. Perfect, even. No one would ever know who'd done it.

He knew word of the robbery would travel to the fraternity's chapter at the University of Chicago. He could hardly wait to hear the buzz.

Nathan drove them back toward Chicago. He was unusually quiet. What had he gotten out of the crime? A typewriter. It hardly seemed worth it, considering the risk. He looked at Richard sitting in the passenger seat. He demanded more from him.

Richard knew what *more* meant. In the past months, their sexual encounters had grown infrequent.

Why, demanded Nathan, was Richard holding him at arm's length?

Richard's pleasure at the burglary vanished. Why did Nathan have to be such a killjoy? Not for the first time, Richard wished he could get rid of Nathan. He was too clingy, too whining, too demanding. Still, Nathan knew Richard's darkest secrets. If Richard upset him, he might tell someone. And Richard couldn't risk that. The only way to be completely safe was to murder Nathan. He pictured shooting him. But no. If he killed Nathan, who would witness his grand criminal adventures?

Miles passed in silence. Nathan chain-smoked, his expression stony.

A month earlier, the two had had a terrible row. Later, Nathan claimed it was over plans for New Year's Eve, still months away. Whatever it had been about, it had caused such a rift that Nathan had sent Richard a long, emotional letter. "When you came to my house this afternoon, I expected either to break friendship with you or attempt to kill you unless you told me why you acted as you did yesterday," he'd written.

Richard had apologized, but things between them remained rocky.

What they needed were parameters, Richard realized. Rules that would allow each of them to get what he needed most from their relationship.

He had an idea, he told Nathan. What would his friend say to making a compact? Crimes for sex. One for one. They could even have a code: "for Robert's sake," which was a twist on the expression "for Christ's sake." When Richard made a request of Nathan using this code, Nathan had to do what he asked. Each time Nathan obeyed, they would have sex.

Nathan agreed to the deal.

The teenagers agreed on one more stipulation, too. Their compact would last until June 11, 1924—the day Nathan planned to leave for a summer trip to Europe.

Now both relaxed. A haze of cigarette smoke filled the Willys-Knight as they sped companionably along the deserted roads. It wouldn't be long until dawn. A few more hours and they'd be safely back in Chicago.

Richard began talking. He had an idea, he said. It had all been too easy. What they needed was to plot and carry out a more complex crime. It would be intricate, so flawlessly executed that not a single clue would be left behind for the police. No one would ever know how or why it was done. Only them.

What kind of crime did Richard have in mind? Nathan wondered.

Kidnapping. They could nab someone rich and make the family pay.

How much? asked Nathan.

That wasn't the important thing, explained Richard. What mattered was that demanding a ransom made the crime so much more complex. Think of all the details that had to be worked out—the delivery of the ransom note, the drop-off and pickup of the money.

Richard grew more excited as he spoke. It would take a master criminal to plan the perfect kidnapping.

Nathan was less enthusiastic. As a law student, he knew that Illinois's punishment for kidnapping was death. Richard's idea seemed too risky.

Not if they didn't get caught, Richard insisted. That meant, of course, they'd have to kill their victim. They couldn't have him identifying them later. What did Nathan say?

First-degree murder was, of course, also punishable by death. But Nathan didn't register that. All he could see was Richard's bright, eager expression, and he couldn't resist. Yes. They would kidnap and murder a boy "for Robert's sake."

PLANNING THE PERFECT CRIME

Weeks passed.

The holidays came and went.

A new year—1924—began.

So did a new academic quarter.

Nathan took another heavy course load—contracts, torts, criminal law. Every Thursday evening, he studied with four classmates at his house. They ate sandwiches and went over points of law. Nathan typed up their notes on his stolen Underwood typewriter. In his spare time, he went birding. And he began dating a slender, dainty philosophy student named Susan Lurie. He took her to teas and dances and bought her a book of poetry for her birthday.

Meanwhile, Richard attended a graduate seminar in history and hung out with fellow student Dick Rubel. The two of them and Nathan had a standing lunch date three times a week—one day at the Drake Hotel, where Dick lived with his parents; one day at Richard's house; and one day at Nathan's house. Richard also spent a lot of time at the Zeta Beta Tau fraternity house at the University of Chicago. When his brothers weren't looking, he swiped things. He dated lots of girls. He bragged about it.

And in between all these activities, as snow blanketed the campus, Nathan and Richard met to drink and scheme and plan the perfect crime.

Who should be their victim?

They decided on somebody rich, or from a rich family, somebody who could pay a big ransom. Nathan suggested kidnapping a girl, but Richard said no. Girls were harder to capture than boys because people kept closer tabs on them. They would grab a boy. Furthermore, it should be easier to lure him into their trap.

They'd kill their victim together. "Shared culpability" was what Nathan called it. But how? After batting around ideas, they settled on strangulation. They would wrap a rope around his neck, then each pull one end.

But that still didn't resolve the question of specifically *who* to strangle.

Could they murder one of their fathers? Richard suggested.

They considered the idea but eventually nixed it. As the victim's son, one of them would have to stay home and act bereaved while the other collected the ransom money alone. Where was the fun in that?

Nathan suggested they kill Hamlin Buchman. It would serve him right for spreading those rumors last year. But Buchman was taller than them, and athletic. He'd be too difficult to subdue.

What about Dick Rubel? Richard knew he'd be asked to be a pallbearer at his friend's funeral. The idea appealed to him. But Dick's father had a reputation as a cheapskate. He might refuse to pay the ransom.

No, they finally decided, it was better to kidnap someone smaller and younger, from a rich, doting family. Nathan suggested Armand Deutsch, grandson of Julius Rosenwald, the head of Sears, Roebuck &

Company. But Richard quickly rejected the idea. His father was vice president of the company, second-in-command. He didn't want to hurt his family's business. No, they'd go to the Harvard School for Boys and catch whoever was easiest.

It was the ransom part of the crime that most delighted Richard. It was also the hardest to work out. "We had several dozen different plans," Nathan later explained, "all of which were no good for one reason or another. Finally [Richard] hit upon the plan of having money thrown from a moving train after the train had passed a given landmark."

On several wintry afternoons, they walked the railroad tracks that led from the city, searching for a pickup point. It had to be an obvious landmark, something easily recognizable. They eventually chose the Champion Manufacturing Company, a large redbrick factory on the east side of the Illinois Central Railroad tracks.

Next they practiced the ransom drop. After rolling up a newspaper to simulate a wad of money, Richard climbed aboard the train and moved to the rear car. As the train passed the Champion factory, he counted to five, then hurled the newspaper out the window.

Success!

With a thump, it landed near 75th Street, where Nathan sat waiting in the car. He picked up the newspaper, then drove to the next train station to pick Richard up.

The pair practiced the drop three more times just to be sure they hadn't overlooked anything. It worked every time.

To make the drop even more complex and gamelike, they planned a series of relays. First, they would call the boy's father on the night of the kidnapping, telling him his son had been taken and to expect a letter the next morning. Second, they would send a letter by special delivery spelling out their ransom demands. This would arrive at the victim's home the morning after the kidnapping. The letter would also explain that the boy's father would be receiving a second phone call in the afternoon, telling him how and where to drop the money.

Now came the third—and most fun—part of the plan. That afternoon, they would call the victim's home again and instruct his father to get into a taxi already waiting outside (one they would, of course, send). The cab would take him to the corner of Vincennes and Pershing, where there was a trash can labeled KEEP THE CITY CLEAN. Inside the can, he would find a note they'd have planted earlier sending him to a drugstore on 63rd Street and instructing him to wait by the public telephone for yet another call from them.

In this call, they'd tell the boy's father to head over to the Illinois Central station and board the next train for Michigan City, Indiana. He'd have to hurry. They planned to leave him just enough time to follow the instructions. There'd be no time to contact the police.

Once he got on the train, he was to go to the rear car and look in the telegraph box. There he would find another previously planted note. This one would tell him to face east and look for the Champion factory. When he saw it, he should count to five, then throw the prepared ransom money out the window as far as he could.

All they had to do was pick it up and drive away.

⊛ ⊛ ⊛

Despite the low gray March sky, there were signs that spring was on its way. Green buds appeared on the branches of the tall trees that lined Kenwood's streets, and daffodils sprouted bravely in well-tended flowerbeds.

The kidnapping plan had grown, too. There were just a few last details to work out. One of those had to do with the killing itself. While they both still agreed on the method—strangulation—they realized they wouldn't be able to do this while the victim was conscious. He was sure to thrash and struggle, and Nathan didn't feel physically up to the fight. Should they knock their victim unconscious and stash him someplace while they picked up the ransom money? That seemed neither rational nor reasonable. What if someone found him while they were gone? What if he managed to escape?

Richard had a solution. He proposed they bash the victim over the head with a chisel and knock him out, maybe even cover his face with an ether-soaked rag for good measure. Once he was unconscious, they could drive out to some secluded spot and finish the job.

Nathan knew a place. Days later, he drove Richard out to the Indiana border. After turning onto a winding dirt road, he followed it deep into a tangled wilderness. Nathan parked. Remote and rarely visited, it was a good place for spotting birds . . . and burying a body.

The pair walked along a railroad track.

Richard wondered if they should bury the body beneath one of the low-hanging firs.

Nathan thought burying sounded like an awful lot of work.

They came to a culvert that ran below the tracks.

Nathan pointed. That spot would work perfectly. Not only would it save them from having to dig a grave, but the flowing water would hasten the decomposition. All they had to do was shove the body into the culvert.

◎   ◎   ◎

Spring was now in full bloom—green leaves, flowering blossoms, a soft breeze. On campus, spring-reveling students shed their overcoats and sat in the grass with books and friends. It wouldn't be long before the quarter ended. Nathan expected to receive his usual exceptional grades. He also expected to pass the Harvard Law School entrance exam. He intended to transfer there in the fall. And then there was his upcoming trip to Europe. He'd already made all the plans, booking his ship passage and hotel rooms. He still needed to stop in at Brooks Brothers for a few new suits, and his father recommended he be fitted for a tuxedo. But he had plenty of time to do that. His departure date was still five weeks away.

Not so for the kidnapping date. They'd chosen May 21—just fourteen days away—and there were still a few details left to deal with.

On May 7, 1924, Nathan walked into the Hyde Park State Bank. It was closing time and there were no other customers in the lobby. Nathan approached the teller. He asked about opening a checking account.

"Do you know anyone in the [area]?" asked the teller.

Nathan shook his head. "I don't know anybody."

The teller pushed an application card across the marble counter. He asked Nathan to write down his details.

Nathan wrote his name as Morton D. Ballard and gave an address in Peoria, Illinois. His occupation, he wrote, was a traveling salesman. He slid the card back to the teller, along with a $100 deposit.

The teller took them. In those days, it wasn't common practice to see any identification before issuing a bank account. Minutes later, he returned with a checkbook in the name of Morton D. Ballard.

Just after dinner that same day, Richard checked into the Morrison

Hotel with a suitcase full of books. After signing the register as "Morton D. Ballard, traveling salesman," he was escorted to room 1031. Richard waited a short time. Then, leaving his suitcase, he went back out to join Nathan.

Two days later, Nathan appeared at the Rent-A-Car Company on Michigan Avenue. He introduced himself to the clerk as Morton Ballard, a salesman from Peoria in town on business. He needed a car to visit some clients. Nathan showed the clerk his new checkbook. See? He was who he said he was.

The clerk had his doubts. The man standing in front of him looked too young to be in business. Did Mr. Ballard have a telephone number of a local acquaintance? The clerk would like to check his references.

Nathan nodded agreeably. He gave the clerk the phone number of a Mr. Louis Mason.

The clerk dialed the number.

In a nearby diner, the public telephone rang. Richard answered it.

"Is this Mr. Louis Mason talking?" asked the clerk.

"Yes," said Richard.

"Do you know anyone named Morton D. Ballard from Peoria?"

"I've known him for years," replied Richard. "He's a good man, thoroughly reliable."

Minutes later, Nathan left with a rental car. He drove it around the city before returning it. When he did, he mentioned that he'd be back in Chicago in two weeks and would need a car then, too. Was it possible the agency could provide him with an identification card so he wouldn't have to produce references again?

The clerk asked if Ballard had a Chicago address.

Yes, replied Nathan. The Morrison Hotel.

The clerk promised to send the card there.

Nathan thanked him and walked out.

*   *   *

On Saturday, May 17, just four days before the planned kidnapping, Richard strolled through his neighborhood. It was a sunny, warm day, and lots of kids were playing outside. One in particular caught Richard's attention: Bobby Asher.

Richard knew the boy. Besides living nearby, he was a friend and classmate of Richard's cousin Bobby Franks. He was tossing a baseball all by himself.

Richard noted how small the boy was for his age. He smiled. He offered to play catch with him.

The two threw the ball back and forth for a few minutes.

"You ought to come out to the university and see a real baseball game," Richard said.

"How would I get out there?" Asher asked.

"I'll give you a lift in my car."

"When?"

"How about next Wednesday [May 21]?" He could pick up the boy after school.

Asher drooped. "I have to go to the dentist that day."

"Well, maybe we could make it some other time," said Richard. He tossed the ball back to Asher and strolled away.

*   *   *

The birds had returned—warblers, orioles, bluebirds, and starlings—filling the wooded areas in and around Chicago with their song. Nathan had gone out a few times with his field glasses and gun. But between school and the kidnapping plans, he hadn't gotten in as much birding as he would have liked. And so, on Sunday, May 18, three days before the kidnapping, Nathan went out with a couple of fellow birders, George Lewis and Sidney Stein.

After visiting several bird habitats, the three ended up at Wolf Lake. Nathan spied some sandpipers. Wanting one for his collection, he ran toward them, stumbling and tripping across the uneven marshland in a pair of rubber boots that were a size too big for him. He fired three shots as the frightened birds took to the sky. He missed.

For another hour, he and the others searched along the lakeshore for the birds. At one point, they came close to the culvert Nathan had pointed out to Richard weeks earlier. But this day, Nathan was focused on birds, not bodies. He barely noticed the location.

The sun was already sinking, the shadows deepening, when the young men drove home. Nathan felt disappointed. He hadn't bagged a single bird.

❂ ❂ ❂

On the day before the kidnapping—Tuesday, May 20—Richard popped into a hardware store near his house. He bought a chisel and a length of rope.

Meanwhile, Nathan stopped off at a drugstore.

"Give me a pint of hydrochloric acid," he said, "and let me have a half-pint of ether, also."

The druggist looked at him. "What do you need it for?"

"An experiment," said Nathan. Technically, he'd told the truth. Tomorrow would be, for him, a groundbreaking experiment.

The druggist accepted the explanation. He disappeared into the back of the store and returned with two glass bottles. He gestured at one. "Be sure and keep it upright," he warned, "because it might leak out and burn your clothes." He tallied up the charges: seventy-five cents. The cheap price surprised Nathan.

That evening after dinner, he and Richard went up to his study. Under the watchful glass eyes of thousands of stuffed birds, the pair sat down to type the ransom note. They'd drafted it a few days earlier, using as a template a fictional ransom note published in the latest issue of *Detective Story Magazine.* But while the pair had borrowed its structure—a businesslike introduction followed by four numbered instructions—the wording belonged to them. With its advanced vocabulary, impeccable grammar, and literary style, their note, Nathan believed, was flawless.

Now all that remained was to type it. Nathan rolled a blank piece of stationery into his Underwood portable. As Richard read the draft, Nathan struck the keys. He'd never been a skilled typist. Rather, he pecked away using his index fingers. This made some of the letters darker than others. No matter. It still looked professional. Whoever received this letter wouldn't mistake them for brainless gang members.

They held off on an envelope. After all, they had no idea who would be receiving it until they'd chosen their victim. They would write the name and address by hand later.

⊚ ⊚ ⊚

On the morning of Wednesday, May 21, 1924, Chicagoans opened their morning newspapers to learn that baseball slugger Babe Ruth had joined the New York Army National Guard; President Calvin Coolidge had taken a chlorine-gas cure for his sore throat; and movie director Cecil B. DeMille's sweeping silent film *The Ten Commandments* was opening at a movie house in the city's Loop. Also in the news was a story about an attempted police raid on a bootleg brewery in the city. Tipped off by a "bought" cop, the gangsters had dumped the incriminating evidence—thousands of gallons of beer—into the sewer just before the police arrived. Within minutes, a five-foot-tall geyser of beer had spewed into the air from a manhole. It lasted for more than an hour.

In the Kenwood neighborhood, the Leopolds' chauffeur, Sven Englund, went downstairs to the garage and—as he did every weekday morning at seven-thirty—started Nathan's Willys-Knight. Englund drove it around to the side door and left it there, motor idling.

Moments later, Nathan got into it. He had a big day ahead, starting with an eight o'clock criminal law class, followed by a nine o'clock lecture on nineteenth-century French poets, and then another law class at ten. After that, he and Richard would commit murder.

Nathan put the car in gear. He sped off to campus.

In class, he found it hard to concentrate. He kept going over the plans in his mind. He couldn't find any flaws. They'd been making arrangements for months. What could possibly go wrong?

When his law lecture ended at eleven o'clock, Nathan headed out onto the quad. There, as planned, stood Richard, smoking and grinning. Together, they headed for Nathan's parked car. They drove to the Rent-A-Car Company.

While Richard waited in the car, Nathan went inside. Once again, he posed as Morton D. Ballard. This time, he rented a Willys-Knight similar to his own, but dark blue. Then he drove back toward Kenwood in the rental car while Richard followed in the red Willys-Knight. At a restaurant near campus, they stopped for lunch. Forty-five minutes later, they headed to the Leopolds' house. Nathan drove his own car and Richard followed in the rental. They pulled both cars into the driveway.

Noticing their arrival, Sven Englund came out of the garage. Was there something "Mr. Babe" needed?

Nathan explained that he had to get a few items out of his car. As Englund watched, Nathan transferred a large bundle wrapped in an automobile robe (a throw blanket specifically for cars) from his backseat into the rental car. Englund, who didn't know the car was a rental, thought Nathan was simply riding to school with his friend.

Nathan turned back to the chauffeur. His car's brakes squeaked, he said. "Can you do anything about it?"

Englund explained he could solve the problem by oiling the brake bands but warned, "You better be careful to use the emergency brake the first few times you stop after I do it, or you may run into somebody."

Replied Nathan, "I'd rather run into somebody than have squeaky brakes."

With that, he climbed into the passenger seat of the rental car.

And Englund pulled the red Willys-Knight into the garage. He got to work on its brakes.

The teens still had more than an hour until school let out. Richard drove to Jackson Park and parked by the golf course. The day had turned chilly and gray. The two chain-smoked and went over their plan again. Minutes passed. Finally, Nathan looked at his watch. It was time. He snuffed out his cigarette.

By afternoon's end, the teenagers would have kidnapped and killed a boy. And no one but the two of them, they believed, would ever know what had really happened.

PART THREE

TRACKING THE KILLERS

CHAPTER SEVEN

THURSDAY, MAY 22, 1924

On the morning after the crime, Nathan Leopold came out of his house and got into his car at his usual time—seven-thirty. No matter that he'd been out late the night before, or that his activities had been more strenuous than he was accustomed to. Nathan had an eight o'clock class, and he had no intention of skipping it.

There was, however, one event on his calendar he *would* have to cancel. He'd promised to take a group of high schoolers out birding. But he didn't have time for that today. And so, after his first class, he drove home and telephoned George Lewis. Would his fellow birder mind covering for him?

Lewis was more than happy to help.

Good thing, thought Nathan as he hung up. He and Richard still had so much to do. But first, he needed to zip back to class.

⊛ ⊛ ⊛

Three blocks away from the Leopold house, at around the time Nathan hung up with Lewis, the mailman rang the Frankses' doorbell. He had a special-delivery letter. Having been awake all night, a bleary-eyed Jacob tore open the envelope with shaking hands. Inside were two typewritten pages. They began:

Dear Sir:

As you no doubt know by this time your son has been kidnapped. Allow us to assure you that he is at present well and safe. You need fear no physical harm for him provided you live up carefully to the following instructions, and such others as you will receive by future communications. Should you however, disobey any of our instructions even slightly, his death will be the penalty.

Following this warning were the kidnappers' demands. First, they insisted Franks make no attempt to contact the police. Next they directed that he put together $10,000 in old bills—$2,000 in twenty-dollar bills, and the remaining amount in fifty-dollar bills. "The money must be old," they wrote. "Any attempt to include new or marked bills will render the entire venture futile." The ransom money should then be placed in a cigar box that was securely wrapped in white paper. "Have the money with you prepared as directed . . . and remain at home after one o'clock P.M. See that the telephone is not in use." They would call him at that time and let him know the next steps.

When Jacob finished reading, his friend Sam Ettelson, who had stayed with the Franks family all night, took the pages and read them.

Flora insisted on reading them, too. But when she got to the last line—"we can assure you that your son will be safely returned to you within six hours of our receipt of the money"—she fainted again, the pages of the ransom note fluttering down around her.

◎ ◎ ◎

That same morning, a millworker named Tony Minke decided to cut through the forest preserve around Wolf Lake on his way to a watch repair shop in the nearby Chicago neighborhood of Hege-wisch. Following a lonely path that ran alongside a single railroad track, Minke came to a water-filled channel that connected Wolf Lake with a shallower lake. A culvert had been built to allow the water to pass below the track. The millworker's steps slowed. He looked down into the channel. Something white floated in the murky water.

Minke inched down the embankment. Around him, tall grasses rustled in the chilly spring breeze. A bird called. Minke stared and stared. And suddenly his mind made sense of what he was seeing. He reeled. A foot! A foot was poking out of the culvert.

Minke scrambled back up to the path. He whirled around in a circle. He didn't know what to do.

The sound of an engine scattered the birds in the trees. Minke looked down the railroad tracks. Two gasoline-powered handcars rumbled in his direction. He waved frantically for them to stop.

One of the four signalmen on the handcars, Paul Korff, slammed on the brakes. What was the problem? Was someone hurt?

With a trembling finger, Minke pointed to the culvert.

"My God!" gasped Korff. He leaped from the handcar and plunged into the ditch's knee-deep water. Grabbing the bare foot, he pulled. The body scraped along the metal drainpipe, facedown, as the signal-man freed it.

A naked boy.

With the help of Minke and the other three signalmen, Korff carried the body to dry land. He turned it over, saw the wavy dark hair flattened to the head, the eyes, blank and half open.

The men saw the injuries, too—the bruised and swollen head, the two large wounds, deep gashes about an inch long. The men didn't know it, but there were two more such wounds on the back of the boy's head. Additionally, an odd copper color stained the boy's face and genitals. Scratches ran from his shoulder to his buttocks.

The men stood there, unable to speak, unsure of what to do next. Then one of the signalmen went to the handcars for a tarpaulin, and Korff began looking around. The boy's nakedness, so pitiful and vulnerable, bothered him. Where were his clothes? While the others wrapped the body, he searched through brush and thicket.

No shoes.

No trousers.

But wait . . . on the embankment just a few feet from the ditch lay a pair of horn-rimmed glasses. Korff picked them up and put them in his pocket.

Then the four signalmen and Minke climbed aboard the handcars and headed toward the Hegewisch railroad station a mile away. With them came the tarpaulin-wrapped body.

When they arrived, Korff called the police. His voice broke as he described what they'd found. The signalman had sons of his own. He imagined the grief of the child's parents.

Minutes later, a police car and squad wagon arrived. Sergeant Tony Shapino approached the handcar. He lifted a corner of the tarpaulin and peeked under it. It didn't take a medical degree to see that the child had been violently beaten.

Murdered, guessed Shapino.

He turned to the men. Why had the body been moved?

"We thought he might still be alive," Korff explained. When they realized he wasn't, well . . . Korff was a father himself. He couldn't be expected to just leave a child out there in the marsh, could he?

"Did you see anything else?" asked Shapino.

Korff nodded and handed over the eyeglasses.

The sergeant stuck them in his pocket and had the body moved to the police wagon. He escorted it to a nearby funeral home. There the mortician laid it out on a cold slab table in preparation for the coroner's autopsy.

Shapino almost forgot about the eyeglasses. He was already out the door when he turned back around and gave them to the mortician's wife.

Assuming they belonged to the boy, she placed them on his face. Then she stopped at the foot of the slab table and shook her head.

Who could have done such a thing?

And why?

❀ ❀ ❀

Richard stood in the sunshine, at the entrance to the law school, waiting for Nathan. Nineteen hours later, and he still felt powerful. He started whistling his favorite jazz tune, "Panama."

A little after eleven o'clock, Nathan appeared. As they set off across the campus, Richard could not stop congratulating himself. "I knew if we just put our heads together we could come up with a foolproof scheme!" he exclaimed. "Let's see them unravel this one." He suggested they celebrate by getting a card game together that night.

Nathan shook his head. He had to study. He'd missed out last night.

After retrieving the rental car from where they'd parked it the night before, they drove to the Leopolds' house. Last night, they'd washed away the more obvious bloodstains, swiping hurriedly at the dashboard and front passenger seat. Now, with soap and brushes, they began cleaning off the rest of the blood. It wasn't easy. There was still so much of it—on the floor, the backseat, the interior roof. They had to get rid of it all before returning the car to the rental company.

Sven Englund came out of the garage to watch. In all his twenty years with the Leopolds, he'd never seen Nathan do any physical work. Yet here he was with his equally rich and pampered friend, scrubbing away.

He asked if he could help.

Richard stopped rubbing at the bloodstains. He turned on the charm. He'd spilled some red wine, he told the chauffeur. He hoped to get it up before taking the car home.

Englund looked at them suspiciously.

Nathan, who'd been trying to clean the rugs in the backseat, stood. "We've been doing a bit of bootlegging. We don't want our folks to find out." He paused. "Don't say anything."

He turned to Richard. There were still some stains on one of the rugs, he admitted to his friend, but he didn't think anyone would notice.

The pair put down their scrub brushes and went into the house.

While Richard waited in the hallway, Nathan ran upstairs to his bedroom and dug out the other ransom notes from their hiding place. It was time to plant them. Richard climbed into the rental; Nathan climbed into his Willys-Knight. As Englund watched, they drove off.

They parked the cars near the KEEP THE CITY CLEAN trash can on Pershing Avenue. Nathan got out with the note that would tell Jacob Franks to drive to the drugstore on 63rd Street and wait for a call from the kidnappers.

Already there was a problem. The tape wouldn't stick to the can's slick metal surface. They couldn't risk its blowing away. If it did, Jacob Franks would never know what to do with the $10,000 in ransom money. They'd have to skip that step. Instead, when they telephoned Franks, they would send him directly to the drugstore. But they needed to hurry. The train they wanted Franks to be on would pull out of the station in less than an hour.

Leaving Nathan's Willys-Knight on Pershing Avenue, they drove the rental car to the 12th Street station. Before getting out, Richard put on a disguise—a black-rimmed pair of eyeglasses and a gray hat and overcoat of his father's. At the ticket booth, he paid seventy-five cents for a ticket to Michigan City. Then, note in hand, he boarded the train and made his way to the last car. He slipped the note into the telegraph box, arranging it so Jacob Franks would see it through the slats. After jumping off the train onto the platform, he looked around to see if anyone had noticed him. But the bustling passengers didn't give him a glance. Richard pushed his way out of the station.

As Richard was planting the note, Nathan went to a phone booth. He called the Yellow Cab Company and asked that a taxi be sent to the Frankses' house. After hanging up, he paused, collecting himself.

He had a second call to make, this one to Jacob Franks. He picked up the phone's receiver.

◉ ◉ ◉

Back at the Frankses' house, the entire family, as well as Sam Ettelson, waited for the phone to ring. Jacob Franks had spent the morning preparing the ransom money to the kidnappers' specifications. All he wanted now was to hand it over and get his son back. He didn't care if the kidnappers were caught. Only Bobby mattered.

Sam Ettelson had taken on the job of fielding the press. Somehow, reporters had found out about the kidnapping. One of them, James Mulroy, had been pestering him about the body of a boy found earlier that morning near Wolf Lake. Ettelson didn't believe it was Bobby. According to a description, the dead boy wore glasses. Bobby didn't. But Mulroy persisted. Finally, Ettelson agreed to send someone to the funeral home.

He got in touch with Flora's brother Edwin Gresham. Would Gresham mind driving out? If by some incredible chance it was Bobby, he should call the Frankses' house and say just one word: *yes*. Nothing more. After all, someone might be listening on the line. Chicago reporters were notorious for doing *anything*, even eavesdropping, to get a scoop.

That had been hours ago, and there had been no word from Gresham.

The phone rang.

Flora gasped.

Jacob leaped to his feet.

And Ettelson snatched up the receiver.

The voice on the other end identified himself as Mr. Johnson. "I am sending a Yellow Cab for you," he said. "Get in and go to the drugstore at 1465 East Sixty-Third Street."

"Just a minute," said Ettelson. "I'll let you talk to Mr. Franks."

Jacob Franks took the phone and listened as Mr. Johnson repeated his message. Then the caller hung up.

Franks stood there, clutching the receiver. What was the drugstore's address again? In his shock and fear, he'd forgotten it. He turned to Ettelson. Did he remember it?

The lawyer didn't.

The two men looked at each other in panic.

The phone rang again.

Ettelson grabbed at it, hoping it was the kidnappers.

It was Edwin Gresham.

"Yes," he said.

Ettelson hung up. He laid his hand on his friend's shoulder. "Jake," he said, "it looks to me as if the worst has happened."

Franks looked at him, confused. "What do you mean?"

"Your boy is dead," said Ettelson.

Franks stumbled backward. How could Bobby be dead? He'd just spoken with the kidnappers. They expected the ransom. They'd promised to return his son if he paid.

The doorbell rang.

The maid answered to find a Yellow Cab driver standing there. She didn't think anyone had called for a taxi, but she asked him to wait and hurried into the study to tell Franks and Ettelson.

Ettelson broke away from Franks and strode to the door. "Who sent you?" he demanded. "Where are you supposed to go?"

The cabdriver was taken aback by the lawyer's tone. "A Mr.

Franks called for the cab," he replied testily. "He didn't say where he wanted to go."

Ettelson hurried back to Franks. He told him what was happening.

Franks paled. He didn't know what to do. Maybe he should get in the cab anyway. Maybe—

His friend stopped him. Bobby was dead. Getting in the cab would be pointless. Besides, neither of them knew where the cab was supposed to go.

Franks wearily agreed.

And Ettelson returned to the front door. Maybe the driver knew something—*anything*—about the kidnappers' identity.

But the driver had left.

         ◉ ◉ ◉

The teenagers met back at the rental car. There was no time to lose. They planned to call the phone booth in the drugstore on 63rd Street where Franks would be from a nearby Walgreen's. From there, it would be a short drive to the drop-off spot. But as they stopped at an intersection by a newsstand, the headline on the early edition of the *Chicago Daily Journal* caught their eye: "Body of Boy Found in Swamp."

Richard pulled to the curb so Nathan could hop out and buy a copy. Huddled together in the car's front seat, they scanned the article. It was definitely their body. But it didn't appear that police had identified it yet.

"When are those damn papers printed?" cried Richard. He knew it was only a matter of time before the police figured out who the dead boy was.

"Hell, I don't know," replied Nathan. "Maybe a couple of hours ago."

Richard fumed. "That was some swell place you picked to leave him. They'd never find him, huh?" He laughed sarcastically. "Not for twenty minutes anyway."

Nathan ignored the barb.

"The game [is] up," said Richard sulkily. They might as well return the car.

But Nathan hesitated. "It [can] do no harm to call the drugstore," he pointed out. Maybe the body hadn't been identified yet. Maybe Franks was still following the drop-off instructions.

They headed to a public telephone and squeezed into the booth together so Richard could hear. Nathan called the drugstore on 63rd Street. Tense, they listened to the ringing on the other end.

At last, a man answered.

Nathan asked for a Mr. Franks.

A moment passed while the man on the other end looked around the store. There was no one there by that name, he finally said.

Nathan hung up.

Now what?

They decided to drive to a different phone and try the drugstore again.

They did, and got the same answer. Mr. Franks was not in the drugstore.

There could be just one reason that Jacob Franks had not followed their instructions. He knew the body found in the culvert was Bobby's. Despite Richard and Nathan's careful planning, the game had been foiled in less than a day.

There was nothing to do but return the rental car and go home.

© © ©

The pair drove Nathan's car back to Kenwood. Curious about what was being reported, they stopped at a drugstore kitty-corner to the Harvard School. It was hard to believe that a little more than twenty-four hours ago they'd been hunting for a victim there. Now they bought all the afternoon editions of the city newspapers, sat at the counter, sipped sodas, and read. Incredibly, the papers already had Bobby's name and the details of their ransom note.

Richard felt a jolt of excitement. This was *their* crime, although no one would ever connect them to it. This secret knowing, Richard realized, made the experience worth it. So what if they hadn't gotten to play the ransom part of their crime game? They hadn't done it for the ransom anyway. They'd done it for the thrill.

It was drizzling when they emerged onto the sidewalk. A familiar figure headed toward them—Mott Kirk Mitchell, a teacher at the Harvard School. The pair stopped him.

"Isn't it terrible what happened to poor Bobby Franks?" said Richard. He tried to keep his voice from sounding too excited. "He used to play tennis on our court all the time."

The three of them chatted about the murder for a few minutes. Then Mr. Mitchell hurried off to catch the streetcar, and the teenagers got back into the Willys-Knight.

After dropping Richard off, Nathan went straight home. He had dinner, studied for his law exams, and talked with George Lewis on the telephone.

Today's bird class, Lewis told him, had been swell.

Nathan was glad to hear it. By midnight he was asleep.

Richard, however, could not settle. Just up the street, a crowd of reporters and curiosity-seekers stood in front of the Frankses' house. Everyone sought details of the crime.

Richard left his house to join them. When he spied Alvin Goldstein, a reporter for the *Chicago Daily News* whom he knew from Zeta Beta Tau, he asked what Goldstein knew.

Goldstein described how he'd gone to the funeral home hours earlier and seen the boy's body.

Richard feigned sympathy. "Whoever committed the crime should be strung up," he said.

CHAPTER EIGHT

SEARCH FOR THE KILLERS

"We must and will clear up this murder," Chicago police chief Morgan A. Collins pledged at a press conference in the late-evening hours of Thursday, May 22. Already he'd dispatched several hundred officers to search the area around Wolf Lake, as well as around the Harvard School and the Kenwood neighborhood. And he'd called in typewriter expert H. P. Sutton to examine the ransom letter.

It appeared Collins had the investigation well in hand. But Chicago reporters were doubtful. It was no secret that Chief Collins presided over the most inept and unprofessional police department in the nation.

From top to bottom, the Chicago Police Department was mired in cronyism. Everyone—from the superintendent on down to the precinct captains—gave jobs to their friends in return for blind loyalty. Few of these hires had the skills or experience needed. Few had any aptitude for policing. And once hired, they received little, if any, training. The result was a police force largely made up of "dishonest, brutal, stupid men," noted a study of the department by the Illinois Association for Criminal Justice. Police officers commonly drank on the job and used excessive force on suspects. Many took bribes, turning a blind eye to gang killings and ignoring illegal drinking, gambling, and prostitution. And since promotions were given to those who paid for them, rather than earned on merit, few police officers had any impetus to excel at their job.

What did all this mean for the investigation into Bobby Franks's murder?

It meant the detectives in charge of the crime were simply not equipped to solve it. Most had never been trained to properly collect and mark evidence. They hadn't been taught how to conduct interviews and take statements. They didn't know the correct way to secure a crime scene, search a suspect's home, analyze blood spatter, or preserve fingerprints. Was it any wonder that the Illinois Association for Criminal Justice study found that 72 percent of all murders in Chicago went unsolved?

After the press conference, Collins returned to his office. The Franks murder was a high-profile case. If they could solve it quickly, it would help repair the police's reputation. But few tangible clues existed—just the pair of eyeglasses and the ransom note. Of course, neither of these had been fingerprinted at the time of discovery, and it was too late to do so now. Dozens of people had already touched the items. If any prints had been left, they'd long been obliterated.

Collins's telephone rang. He picked it up to hear the bullying, demanding voice of Robert Crowe, the state's attorney for Cook County.

Was the police chief close to catching the killers? If so, Crowe would bring them to trial as quickly as possible. "And they will hang!" he thundered.

Crowe had a flair for the dramatic. In court, he would often raise a fist high and beat at the air. He'd jut out his square chin and shake his head emphatically with every bullet-shot word of his impassioned pleas. His nickname among his fellow Republicans was Fighting Bob.

Robert Crowe had first been elected to the office in 1920, running as the law-and-order candidate and promising to close legal loopholes, restore morale in the police force, and reestablish respect for the law among Cook County's citizens. He jeered at reformers of the day who claimed that crime was the result of social and economic conditions: poverty, unemployment, and lack of education and adequate housing. What a "load of nonsense," he countered. Crime, he maintained, was deliberate. Criminals *chose* to break the law. Being poor or uneducated had nothing to do with it. The only way to end crime was to impose harsh sentences on wrongdoers. "There should be no sentiment about it," Crowe declared. "Persons whose existence means death and disaster to others who have done no wrong have no claim upon society for anything—not even for life itself." Crime would only subside when criminals realized society was serious about punishment. Arrest them. Prosecute them. Lock them away.

Hang them.

Crowe was a staunch advocate of capital punishment, the death penalty. In Illinois at this time, people convicted of the most serious crimes—such as willful and premeditated killing (first-degree murder), kidnapping for ransom, or killing a police officer—could be punished by death. And the method of execution was hanging. (The electric chair would not be used in the state until 1928.) It was true that most murder convictions did not result in death. Between 1870 and 1930, there would be almost 9,100 homicides in Chicago, and in only 100 of those cases was the death penalty imposed.

But Crowe believed it was a deterrent—it would make potential wrongdoers think twice before committing a crime. "Society should have no hesitancy in springing the trap every time the noose can be put around a murderer's neck," he said.

His thinking was in line with that of most Americans at the time. From the early 1920s to the 1940s, there was a national resurgence in the use of the death penalty. This was due, in part, to writings by criminologists who argued that it was a necessary social measure that saved innocent lives. And it would be decades before statistical findings and case studies would prove that the death penalty in actuality does nothing to reduce crime.

As the chief prosecutor in the county, Crowe had the job of working with police to put away bootleggers, gang members, murderers, robbers, rapists, and other criminals. In a city as lawless as Chicago, being the state's attorney was a tough job. And Crowe went about it ruthlessly. Within two months of his taking office, thirteen men were sentenced to death. Another twenty received long sentences in prison. "If the police can catch them, I *will* convict them," he often bragged.

Now he was just six months away from another election. The ambitious Crowe intended to remain in office. That was why he was pressing Chief Collins about the Franks case. It presented a huge challenge, as well as a huge opportunity. Chicagoans were already riveted by it—and State's Attorney Crowe would be at its center. But he couldn't prosecute until someone was charged.

He asked Collins if the police had any theories about the killers.

Collins's men were looking at a few theories. Perhaps the boy had been killed as an act of revenge against Jacob Franks. It was common knowledge that Franks had built his fortune as a pawnbroker. Maybe he'd gotten mixed up with criminals. Or maybe the losing players in the baseball game Bobby had umpired that day had roughed him up and accidentally killed him. While these theories seemed unlikely, police were following up on them.

Was it possible that Bobby had fallen victim to a child molester who had then tried to cover up his act by demanding a ransom?

This had been Collins's first thought. He'd already ordered "a general round-up of all persons suspected of being degenerates," he told Crowe. But so far, police had turned up nothing. Collins was also waiting for the autopsy report from the county coroner's office. Perhaps knowing the cause of those copper-colored stains on the boy's face and body would provide a clue. Yes, he would let the state's attorney know the minute they found *anything*.

As the sun rose on Friday, May 23, Sutton identified the kind of typewriter used to write the note: an Underwood portable. He noticed that it had a faulty lowercase *t* and *f.* And there was something else. "The man who wrote this letter was either a novice at typing or used two fingers. Some of the letters were punched so hard they were almost driven through the paper, while others were struck lightly or uncertainly."

Intriguingly, the note was flawlessly worded. No grammatical errors. No spelling mistakes. Only an educated person could have written it, he deduced.

Police suspicions now turned to the Harvard School faculty. Not only were the teachers educated, but they also had access to Bobby Franks. They knew his father was rich and able to pay a $10,000 ransom. To the average teacher, the sum was a fortune.

The city was still asleep when police rousted R. P. Williams, the school's athletic director, out of bed. He stumbled to the door dressed in his bathrobe.

Yes, he said, he had taken the Franks boys to an amusement park a year ago. Yes, Mrs. Franks had been worried because he hadn't gotten the boys home until after midnight. No, he had no idea who had killed Bobby Franks.

The police didn't buy it. They hauled Williams down to the Wabash Avenue station.

They also hauled in English teacher Mott Kirk Mitchell. Police suspected he was a homosexual. In those days, gay men were seen as an insidious threat. It was commonly believed that most were sexual predators who went undetected but posed a danger to society. Mitchell's English skills also made him a prime suspect. It didn't matter that he'd had friends over the night of the murder who could vouch for him. The cops refused to believe his alibi.

Police held both Williams and Mitchell for hours. Detectives grilled them, trying to get them to confess. While they were in custody, their homes were searched. Detectives didn't bother with a search warrant. In Williams's rooms, they found four bottles of what they believed to be some sort of liquid poison. Could Bobby Franks have been poisoned? That might explain the strange coloring around his mouth.

To the disappointment of the police, the bottles held nothing but a liniment for sore muscles. Williams was released.

They held on to Mitchell.

By midmorning, cops were crawling over the Harvard School. Other teachers, when questioned, speculated about their colleagues. They gossiped about one instructor who'd been overheard to say, "[Bobby Franks's] father has nothing but money. He would be good picking for someone."

A parent told investigators that her son had hinted at immorality at the school. "There are things going on I wouldn't tell you," he'd supposedly said to her.

Police immediately thought of Mitchell. They dug deeper into his affairs, discovering that he had a semiannual mortgage payment due the very day of Bobby's kidnapping. The amount was exactly $10,000.

Convinced the English teacher was their man, police dug up the sewers around his house, looking for Bobby's clothes. They found nothing. But they still did not release Mitchell from custody. Over the next four days, they questioned him again . . . and again. They beat him with a rubber hose and threatened to throw him out of a fifteenth-story window if he didn't confess.

Mitchell eventually did confess—to homosexuality, not murder. Despite having no evidence that the teacher had killed Bobby, police still considered him the most likely suspect.

Meanwhile, detectives got in touch with area opticians and asked them to check their records. Maybe one of them could trace the horn-rimmed glasses found near the body. With so many opticians and so many patient records, however, finding the owner of this particular pair of glasses was a long shot. Still, it and the ransom note were all the police had to go on.

* * *

"Get the story! Get the story!" was the frenzied cry heard that Friday morning in the Chicago newsrooms. The city had two morning papers, the *Chicago Daily Tribune* and the *Chicago Herald and Examiner,* as well as four afternoon ones, the *Chicago Evening Post,* the *Chicago Daily Journal,* the *Chicago Evening American,* and the *Chicago Daily News.* Competition among them was fierce.

Throughout the 1920s, Americans spent much of their spare time reading—books and magazines, but mostly newspapers. Newspapers published 36 million copies a day, or 1.4 newspapers for every household in the country. To feed America's hunger for news stories, most cities, like Chicago, had numerous papers (New York City boasted twelve), and many of these publications served up the daily news in a revolutionary way. They did not focus on important events of the day, such as President Calvin Coolidge's reelection bid or the soaring stock market. Instead, lurid, juicy stories—crime, scandal, celebrity gossip—were what made the front page. Stories were boiled down to their shocking essence. Headlines stood six inches tall. Every paper was fighting for readers' pennies (the average price of a newspaper was two cents), and they did it with blatant sensationalism.

"Wave a little blood around," advised Frank Carson, managing editor of the *Chicago Herald and Examiner.* "That's the bang that forces a reader at the newsstand to pick our paper out above the others."

Chicago's reporters would do anything to get the news. They flashed phony badges, broke into homes and offices, rummaged through trash, listened in on telephone conversations and through walls using stethoscopes, stole mail, lowered themselves into courtroom air ducts by rope, and impersonated firemen, gas meter inspectors, undertakers' assistants—*anyone* who could help them get the story. "The things we do for our papers," said Sam Blair, a top reporter for the *Chicago Herald and Examiner.* "We lie, we cheat, we swindle and steal. . . . We almost commit murder for a story. We're a bunch of lice."

They frequently uncovered clues and leads the police didn't.

And Chicago's finest encouraged that. Newspapers had far more re-
sources, and reporters were better sleuths. They knew how to question suspects and look at situations from different angles. The police
frequently shared detailed information with the press. Sometimes,
detectives let reporters sit in on interrogations and ask questions.
Jailers let them into cells, where they would chat with accused murderers. And some top reporters even carried a special note from
the chief of police instructing detectives, coroner's physicians, and
other law enforcement officials to provide the reporter with whatever he needed. It was a symbiotic relationship. The police solved a
crime and the newspaper got a scoop.

Hundreds of reporters were out on Chicago's streets, around
the clock, seven days a week. Each newspaper assigned a team to the
important news sites: the Cook County Criminal Courts Building, city
hall, police stations, the city morgue, the county hospital, train stations, and swanky hotels. One could always find a handful of reporters in and around these places. They'd call in to their newsrooms
with reports of petty burglaries and car crashes as they waited for
something bigger to happen. Most never waited long. This was Chicago, after all.

Now reporters swarmed over the Franks murder. A rich boy's
body dumped in the woods? Child-killers on the loose? A citywide
manhunt? It had all the makings of front-page fodder for weeks—
maybe even months—to come.

⊙ ⊙ ⊙

In the early-morning hours of Friday, May 23, with no solid leads
yet, an already impatient Robert Crowe decided to enlist the aid
of the press. Maybe the public could help crack the case. He called

all six newspapers and shared details of the police investigation. He encouraged them to run photographs of both the eyeglasses and the ransom note. He hoped somebody out there knew something.

◎ ◎ ◎

DID YOU SEE THE KIDNAPPING OF BOBBY FRANKS?

At approximately 5:15 Wednesday afternoon Robert Franks stood on the corner of 47th Street and Ellis Avenue. He started to walk south . . . intending to walk home. Somewhere between 47th and 51st Street on Ellis Avenue . . . he was kidnapped.

Someone living or walking along Ellis Avenue must have seen the kidnapping. A man or a group of men picking up a [14] year old boy, putting him in a motor car and driving away may not have seemed important Wednesday night, but this morning it has a great importance.

If anyone saw this kidnapping let them call Central 0100 and ask for the city editor. Every scrap of information will be traced with a view of learning the identity of the kidnappers.

(From the *Chicago Daily Tribune,* May 23, 1924, page 1)

◎ ◎ ◎

Hundreds of tips poured into the newspaper, whose editor passed them on to the police.

An anonymous caller pointed a finger at two suspicious men staying at the Sheridan Plaza Hotel.

A landlady claimed that the woman who rented her ground-floor apartment had told her all about the Franks case. The landlady also said she'd seen her renter packing a hammer in her luggage.

A psychic from Kansas sent a telegram. She'd had a vision: two men and a woman with red hair had committed the crime. "One of the men . . . is hiding. He's . . . somewhere in the southwestern part of [Chicago]. The Franks boy's clothes are there."

Both the press and the police followed up on every tip, no matter how crackpot. They led nowhere.

CHAPTER NINE

A MURDERER'S THEORIES; A CORONER'S INQUEST

When Richard came down to breakfast that Friday morning, he found several newspapers strewn across the linen-covered table. Banner headlines screamed:

KIDNAP RICH BOY; KILL HIM

(From the *Chicago Daily Tribune,* May 23, 1924, page 1)

KIDNAPPERS SLAY MILLIONAIRE'S SON

AS $10,000 RANSOM WAITS COLLINS ORDERS
ALL POLICEMEN TO LOOK FOR FRANKS BODY

(From the *Chicago Herald and Examiner,* May 23, 1924, page 1)

TONY MINKE, FINDER OF BOY'S BODY,
GIVES DETAILS OF DISCOVERY

(From the *Chicago Evening American,* May 23, 1924, page 1)

While Richard's mother and little brother chattered excitedly about the crime, Albert Loeb remained quiet. A recent heart attack had left him ashen and even more withdrawn than usual. Wordlessly, he buttered his toast as Richard sat down.

Anna Loeb continued talking. Imagine something this awful happening in their lovely neighborhood. It had to be the work of a madman. She confessed to feeling worried. What if the murderer was still prowling about? What if he was nearby?

Of course, Richard knew the truth—and it thrilled him.

At noon, he wandered over to the Zeta Beta Tau house, eager to hear what his frat brothers had to say about the murder. The place buzzed with theory and speculation. From the doorway of the dining room, he spied fellow student Howard Mayer, the campus reporter for the *Chicago Evening American*. Richard sat down at his table. Maybe Mayer had some information the papers hadn't reported yet.

Over steaks and fried potatoes, the two discussed the crime. Eventually, Richard volunteered his "theories" about what had happened.

"I don't believe the kidnappers would have met Mr. Franks [in person] at the drugstore," he said. "They merely would have left word for him there to meet some other place with the money."

Richard made a good point, Mayer admitted. It would have been too big a risk for the kidnappers to meet Franks face to face.

Richard had a suggestion. They should investigate his theory for themselves. "Why don't we make the rounds of the drugstores on 63rd and see if we can find out where word was left for Mr. Franks?"

Mayer hesitated. He hadn't finished his lunch yet. Besides, it was raining.

Just then Alvin Goldstein and his partner, James Mulroy, walked in. Only a year out of school, they were covering the crime for the *Chicago Daily News*. Richard waved them over and told him his idea. Mayer, he added, was reluctant to investigate. Were they game?

They were. Problem was, they didn't have a car.

But Mayer did. It took some convincing, but the three reporters finally climbed into the automobile with Richard. They sped off to 63rd Street.

Once there, they split up and began checking drugstores. By the time they'd scouted out several, it was pouring. Soaked and discouraged, Mulroy stayed in the car while Goldstein splashed across the street to check out a cigar shop, and Richard and Mayer hurried into the Van de Bogert & Ross drugstore.

The bell above the door tinkled, and the clerk looked up from his receipts.

Richard asked him if the store had received any calls yesterday for a Mr. Franks.

Yes, replied the clerk. There'd been two, on the public phone around two-thirty in the afternoon. But there hadn't been anyone in the store by that name.

Richard turned to Mayer. "You see? I told you we could find it, Howie. Now you have a scoop!"

He raced out onto the sidewalk and waved his arms to catch Mulroy's attention through the car window. "This is the place! This is the place!"

Mulroy and Goldstein came on the run. While the three reporters interviewed the clerk and then telephoned their editors, Richard wandered over to the soda fountain. He smiled at a girl sitting at the counter. By the time the cops arrived, he was sharing a milk shake with her.

Back in Mayer's car, Richard bragged, "This is what comes from reading detective stories."

Mulroy asked him if he'd known Bobby Franks.

Richard said he had. The boy had lived just across the street. He was Richard's second cousin.

What kind of kid was he? Mulroy wanted to know.

Richard looked out at the rain for a moment. Then he turned to the reporter. "If I were going to murder anybody," he said with a smile, "I would murder just such a cocky little son of a bitch as Bobby Franks."

◎   ◎   ◎

The little group drove the wet streets back to Kenwood. The reporters were headed over to Furth's Funeral Home on 47th Street for the inquest into Bobby Franks's murder. Did Richard want to come along?

He most definitely did.

Minutes later, Mayer pulled over to the curb, and the four dashed through the rain to the undertaker's canopied entrance. Although they planned on having their son's funeral service at home, Bobby's parents had had his body transferred here after the autopsy. In deference to their grief, the coroner had made the decision to hold the inquest here, too, instead of at the city morgue.

Richard and the reporters hurried into the funeral home's reception room. A handful of Bobby's schoolmates were there, as well as friends of the family, police, and other reporters—lots of them. Richard spied Jacob Franks and Sam Ettelson sitting in the second row. Franks looked gray and exhausted. Richard didn't feel a twinge of guilt.

At a table placed at the front of the room sat Cook County coroner Oscar Wolff, who was in charge of the inquest. After listening to the evidence, he would certify the cause of Bobby's death. Wolff's findings would become the county's official determination.

In Cook County, the coroner was elected every four years. Wolff,

like his predecessors, had come to the office with no special training. He was not a physician, nor did he know anything about police
work, pathology, or medical examinations made for legal purposes.
He was more concerned with staying in office than investigating
suspicious deaths. Wolff was, noted the *Chicago Daily Tribune,* "an
official as notorious for his ineptitude as he was for his association
with gangsters."

Problems in the coroner's office didn't end there. Because Wolff
appointed his staff, he hired men with political connections rather
than expertise. Woefully unqualified, these "coroner physicians"
knew little more than the basics of postmortem examinations. A
study of the coroner's office by the Illinois Crime Survey in the 1920s
declared that Wolff's physicians were "inexperienced [and their]
examinations incomplete and untrustworthy." One of these physicians, Dr. Joseph Springer, had conducted the autopsy on Bobby's
body. While Springer had graduated from medical school, he had
never received a license to practice.

Wolff called the inquest to order, and Dr. Springer stood. He reported on the two wounds to the boy's head, which had occurred
antemortem, or before death. He'd opened the forehead, he said,
to discover that those blows had smashed through Bobby's skull.
Springer deduced that some blunt object had made them. Next
he detailed the small scratches extending from the victim's right
shoulder to the buttocks. These had been made postmortem, or
after death. He speculated they'd been caused by dragging the body
along rough ground.

In his seat, Jacob Franks leaned forward. He cupped his ear to
hear better as Sam Ettelson laid a bracing hand on his shoulder.

Springer continued. More puzzling than the wounds had been

the copper coloring on the victim's face. Springer had opened the body to find a dark discoloration that went down the windpipe and into the right lung. The same coloring also stained the genitals. He couldn't tell what had caused this coloring. He had, however, found a wadded handkerchief in the boy's throat. This led him to ascertain that Bobby had died "from an injury to the head, associated with suffocation."

It was hardly revelatory. But considering Dr. Springer's lack of expertise, it was to be expected. He *had* removed various organs— the kidneys, stomach, and lungs, as well as a piece of liver and bowel—for later analysis by chemists at the city morgue. But all in all, he'd done a cursory job. When submitted, his official report was little more than a page long.

Despite this, no one questioned his work. Cook County had no minimum standards for autopsies at that time. How they were conducted was left entirely up to the coroner's physicians. As a result, there were years when "no complete autopsy, in the scientific sense of the term, was made, that is an autopsy in which the findings at the table are verified by further systematic microscopic and bacteriologic exam," noted the Illinois Crime Survey study. Forensics, of course, was still in its infancy. There was no such thing as DNA sampling yet, and minute traces of physical evidence like hair and fabric fibers were still impossible to identify.

Wolff now asked Springer if he had determined a time of death.

Springer had examined the body the very morning it had been found. Rigor mortis, he claimed, had not yet set in. This led him to believe that Bobby had died on the morning of May 22, just two to four hours before his examination. What time was that examination? Incredibly, Springer didn't include it in his report. And neither Wolff nor anyone in the room (or later in court) asked.

Springer also hadn't taken into account the water's effect on the body. It was commonly known that water is cooler than the air around it, slowing the process of decomposition. The onset of rigor mortis would have been delayed by the body's immersion in cold water, and qualified doctors in 1924 would have known that. They would also have known to look for other noticeable changes, such as wrinkling of the skin and livor mortis, a bluish-purple mottling under the skin of the lower body parts. All of this would have helped Springer make a more accurate determination. So, too, would have an examination of the stomach contents. But Springer had left that work for the chemists in the city morgue. (They would later report that Bobby's death had come five to six hours after a meal, correctly placing the time of death sometime between four-thirty and six-thirty p.m. on May 21.)

Coroner Wolff concurred with Dr. Springer's conclusions as to the cause and time of death. With authority, he added that the boy had not been sexually abused, ruling out the police's theory that a "pervert" had killed Bobby.

Reporters took down every word.

Afterward, Richard followed Howard Mayer into the funeral home's reception room, where Jacob Franks was speaking with reporters. No, he couldn't imagine why Bobby had been killed. "The kidnappers could have had everything I own for the return of my boy," he said as Richard listened.

❋ ❋ ❋

Nathan didn't have time to read the newspapers until late Friday afternoon. With only a few days left in the academic quarter, he needed every spare moment to study both for his finals and for the Harvard entrance exam. So he was shocked when he finally opened the *Chicago Daily Tribune* to find a photograph of the horn-rimmed glasses beneath the words "Whose Spectacles Are These?" He skimmed the article. The glasses, he learned, had been found near the body. Detectives believed they belonged to the murderer. They were calling them "the best clue to his identity."

Nathan knew at once that those glasses were his. He hurried upstairs to his room, where he went through his drawers and the pockets of his suits, looking for his glasses. He searched without much conviction. He was sure he wouldn't find them.

How could it have happened? He didn't even wear the glasses, not really. Months ago, suffering from headaches caused by eyestrain, he'd gone to an optician, who had prescribed reading glasses. Nathan had worn them for a few weeks. But when the headaches had stopped, he'd stopped wearing the glasses. He hadn't put them on in months.

He thought a moment. The glasses must have been in the breast pocket of one of the old suits he wore when birding. Knowing he'd be mucking about at Wolf Lake with a dead body, he had chosen to wear one of these suits the day of the crime. Since he didn't use the glasses anymore, he hadn't even known they'd been in the suit's pocket. Now they were in the hands of the police.

He telephoned Richard.

"Hey, Dick," he said. "I think you better get over here. Something's come up. . . . No, it's not too serious. But we better talk it over."

Richard arrived within the hour. "This had better be important," he grumbled.

After handing Richard the newspaper, Nathan explained what he believed had happened.

Richard exploded. "How in hell could you be such a stupe? Look, can they trace them, do you think?"

Nathan didn't think so. "There must be a jillion pairs like them in the city."

Still, he was uncertain about what to do next. Should he forget about the glasses and hope the police never connected them to him? Or should he go in and claim them?

"I have got all the alibi in the world for their being found there," he said. "I go birding out there all the time. Hell, I've been there—right at the same spot—half a dozen times in the last couple of weeks . . . I was out there last Sunday."

Richard shook his head. "Make 'em come to you," he said. "Then if wurst comes to sausage, you can be so surprised that the glasses are yours. [That's] the time to tell your story about losing [them] birding."

Nathan agreed. It seemed like sound advice.

Then Richard told him about his afternoon, how he'd led the reporters to the Van de Bogert & Ross pharmacy, his attendance at Bobby's inquest, and listening in on Jacob Franks's interview with the press.

It was Nathan's turn to lose his temper. What was Richard playing at? Was he trying to get them caught? He *had* to stop involving himself in the investigation.

But Richard shook his head. What was the fun in that?

                ❂ ❂ ❂

Richard still felt like celebrating. And who better to celebrate with than his sometimes girlfriend, Patches Reinhardt? A dark-haired flapper who wore fringed shimmy dresses and an Egyptian band over her bobbed hair, Patches was wild, impetuous, and up for anything. She was also "half in love" with Richard, she later admitted.

When he telephoned and asked her out for that night, she quickly accepted.

He took her to the Edgewater Beach Hotel, a lavish and popular resort. They drank whiskey and danced to almost every song. When the band left at midnight, Richard and Patches strolled along the boardwalk to an all-night waffle shop. The day's rain had cleared, and stars now twinkled over Lake Michigan. Richard sparkled, too, with charm and good humor. He was so attentive and romantic that Patches wondered if he was finally and truly falling for her.

CHAPTER TEN

SATURDAY, MAY 24–SUNDAY, MAY 25, 1924

It was just past midnight on Saturday morning when Robert Crowe held a meeting of all the law enforcement officials working on the case. The investigation, he declared, was a mess. No one knew which leads to pursue or what information to collect. If someone uncovered helpful details, no one else on the case would learn about them because there was no overall director. How could they track the killers this way? It was time for some coordination and communication.

Crowe divided the investigation into areas of responsibility. Lieutenant John Farrell would follow up on the theory that "mental defectives" had committed the crime. Sergeants William Crot and Frank Johnson would focus on the kidnapping angle. Sergeants Charles Egan and Philip Moll would delve into Jacob Franks's background, on the theory that revenge was a motive. And Lieutenant Michael O'Grady would follow up on a tip about a gray car, a Winton, being spotted in Kenwood the day of the kidnapping. Their findings would be submitted to Chief Collins, who in turn would share them with the state's attorney.

Did everyone understand his assignment?

The officers did. They got back to work.

● ● ●

Members of Nathan's study group noticed a change in him that Saturday afternoon. The sullen and superior teenager seemed lighter, happier, more talkative. Arnold Maremont asked why he was in such a good mood.

Nathan laughed. If he were to be struck by lightning and die that very moment, he would not regret it, he replied. "I already have experienced everything that life has to offer."

His good mood spilled over into the evening. That night, he and Susan Lurie, along with Richard and his date of the moment, Lorraine Nathan, went to a jazz club. In the smoky basement lounge, they danced and drank. And they bumped into Abel Brown, a fellow law student.

Brown introduced the foursome to his companion.

Richard smiled and shook the man's hand. Then he said, "You've just enjoyed the treat of shaking hands with a murderer."

Brown took the remark as proof of Richard's "madcap sense of humor." He didn't give it a second thought.

● ● ●

At two the next morning, Nathan parked his car on the corner of 51st Street and Cottage Grove Avenue. He lit a cigarette. Richard should have been here by now.

At last, the car door opened and Richard slid into the passenger seat. Wordlessly, Nathan put the car in gear and drove to Jackson Park. Earlier, they'd learned from newspaper accounts that an expert had identified the make of the typewriter used for creating the ransom note, as well as its faulty lowercase *t* and *f*. The Underwood had to go.

Nathan stopped on the bridge near the golden statue of Columbia and lifted the typewriter from the backseat. He handed it to Richard. With a pair of pliers, Richard twisted off the tips of the keys. Then he stepped from the car onto the bridge and tossed them into the water.

They drove farther on. Once again, Richard got out. This time he dropped the typewriter into the harbor. With barely a splash, it disappeared into the dark depths.

All that remained was the bloodstained automobile robe.

Nathan drove to a secluded spot along South Shore Drive. After gathering dry sticks and twigs, Richard struck a match. The pile flamed. Nathan tossed the robe on top. The two watched as the evidence went up in smoke.

On the drive back to Kenwood, Nathan brought up the idea of an alibi. What if the police *did* connect him to the eyeglasses? He would need proof of his whereabouts on the night of the crime. "It seems unlikely [police] will put two and two together," he said, "but it is best to be prepared."

Richard agreed. Together, the pair concocted this story: On May 21, after morning classes, they'd lunched at the restaurant at Marshall Fields. Then they'd gone birding in Lincoln Park. They'd also done some drinking before heading to the Coconut Grove for dinner. Afterward, they'd picked up a couple of girls named Edna and Mae. They hadn't bothered to learn their last names. The four of them had driven around a while, but when it became clear the girls wouldn't do more than kiss, they'd dropped them off in Jackson Park. It was after one a.m. when they got home.

They argued about how long to use the alibi if they were

questioned. Nathan wanted to use it until he left for Europe in June. But Richard thought that would be a dead giveaway. After all, he reasoned, people didn't remember things for very long. If they gave the police detailed accounts of their whereabouts on the day Bobby was kidnapped, it would look suspicious.

They finally settled on using it for seven days from the time of the crime. After that, they'd say they couldn't remember their exact actions on May 21.

◉　◉　◉

Jacob Franks couldn't sleep anymore. Night after night he lay awake, racking his brain. Who could have killed Bobby?

A thought struck him around the same time that Nathan and Richard were destroying evidence. Bobby *knew* his murderers. He must have. That was how they'd lured him away. More importantly, that was why they'd killed him—because he could have recognized them, and they were afraid.

Another thought quickly followed, and this one chilled Jacob: "[If] Bobby knew them, I must know them."

Bobby's killers weren't strangers.

Bobby's killers were friends.

◉　◉　◉

The promise of summer was in the air that Sunday morning. Lilacs and hyacinths bloomed. The trees lining Kenwood's streets were blurred with leaves, round and full. The sun dazzled.

Two police officers knocked on the Leopolds' front door. When the maid answered, one of them asked to speak with Nathan Jr.

He was still in bed, the maid explained. He'd been out late.

The police said they'd wait.

Minutes later, Nathan came downstairs in his pajamas and robe.

The police told him they'd gotten his name from the game warden of the forest preserve that encompassed Wolf Lake. They understood that Nathan frequently visited the area to watch birds.

Nathan nodded.

"Then I'd appreciate it if you'd accompany us to the police station for questioning," one of the officers said.

Nathan balked. He couldn't possibly go now. He had a date, he explained. He was taking a girl to lunch.

The police expressed regret for troubling him. But in the hope of turning up clues, they were speaking with anyone who frequented the forest preserve. It was routine, they explained.

Nathan grudgingly agreed. After dressing, he followed the police officers in his car to the Ewing Avenue station. There, Captain Thomas C. Wolfe took over.

"I hear you're in the [Wolf Lake] area quite a bit," the captain said amiably.

"That's right," replied Nathan. "I go out [there] two or three times a week."

"Well, that's just why I called you in," said Wolfe. "I figured you'd know a lot of people who go out there for nature study. Would you give me a list of names of the people you know who go there?" This, too, he stressed, was routine.

Nathan wrote down some names, including George Lewis and Sidney Stein. He also wrote and signed an official statement. In it, he detailed his movements the previous Sunday. "On May 18 [my companions] and I drove along a road to the forest preserve and out to May's shack between Wolf and Hyde Lakes [the location of the culvert where Bobby's body was found]. We arrived about 6:30 . . . walked east to the ice house, back to the railroad track and left by the same road about 7:20 or 7:30." The reason for the trip, he concluded, was "the observation of birds."

Wolfe thanked the teenager and apologized for getting him out of bed.

Nathan apologized for not being more helpful.

They shook hands. Later, Wolfe would claim Nathan's answers were "so ready and his demeanor so innocent that [I] regarded him without any suspicion." Wolfe filed away the statement and forgot about it.

On the drive home, Nathan thought about how the police hadn't seemed to even come close to suspecting him. Maybe it had all been for the good. He'd told them he'd been at Wolf Lake last Sunday. Now if the glasses *were* traced to him, "I have an insurance policy . . . A police captain as character witness no less!"

Nathan's afternoon was a relaxed one. He drove Susan Lurie out to a country inn on the Des Plaines River, where they rented a canoe. As he paddled lazily, she strummed the ukulele she'd brought along. Sunlight sparkled on the water, and Nathan pointed out a blue heron at the river's edge. A bit farther on, they beached the canoe to sit in a grassy glen. Susan pulled out a book of French poetry and read "the liquid verses to me," recalled Nathan. He lay back and gazed at the cloudless blue sky. "It could not have been a lovelier day."

❧ ❧ ❧

Grief pervaded the Frankses' house that same afternoon. Before the fireplace in the family's library, Bobby's closest friends and relatives gathered around the small white coffin, which stood half open. It was hard to look down on the boy's battered and waxen face; harder still to be burying him on such a lovely spring day.

The funeral service began. Two readers from the Fifth Church of Christ, Scientist recited scripture and led the mourners in prayer and hymns. (The Frankses had converted from Judaism to Christian Science years before.) Through it all, Flora Franks remained quiet, her eyes lowered. She'd said her goodbyes earlier that day when she'd sat alone beside her son's casket, sobbing for hours. Now her expression looked distant.

Once the service ended, the undertaker closed the casket and prepared to move the body. A group of Bobby's school friends chosen as pallbearers shuffled to the front of the room. Flora stood and walked toward them. She ran her hands hungrily over their young faces. Just four days ago, her son had been with them, alive and happy. Now he was being carried out the front door to a waiting hearse.

On the sidewalk a crowd of people had gathered. Silently, they lowered their heads and removed their hats as the coffin passed. There were sobs and murmured prayers.

Richard was there, too. It had been a lucky break. He'd been returning from the drugstore with the latest newspapers at the very moment Bobby's casket was being carried out of the house. Of course he stopped to watch the procession make its way down the steps and into the street.

The funeral procession, guarded by six police officers on motorcycles, made its way to Rosehill Cemetery and the Frankses' mausoleum. "I will lift up mine eyes to the hills," recited one of the readers as the body was placed inside the granite vault.

"Mrs. Franks, assisted by her son and daughter, stood for a long time at the [mausoleum] door looking down at the coffin where her boy lay," reported the *Chicago Daily Tribune*. "She trembled, turned away and went back to the car where she gave way to her grief in pitiful little moans." Jacob Franks tried to comfort her, but "he too was on the verge of breaking down."

● ● ●

Later that night, while his wife lay crying upstairs, Jacob Franks went into the library. The scent of roses and lilies of the valley hung heavy in the air. Jacob hadn't had time to read any of the cards that accompanied the dozens of floral arrangements the family had received. Now he went from one to another. So many people had sent condolences.

He came to a small wreath of tiger lilies. Peering at the handwritten card, he read: "Sympathy from Mr. Johnson."

Jacob froze. Was his son's murderer taunting him? Or was this the work of some heartless prankster? Either way, someone was playing a cruel game.

CHAPTER ELEVEN

INTERROGATION

The start of a new workweek, Monday, May 26, found Chicago police darting all over the city, following tips and tracking down leads. After Jacob Franks handed over the mysterious wreath and card, two detectives spent the day questioning florists in the Kenwood area. They eventually learned that a man had bought the arrangement late Saturday afternoon from a flower shop just blocks from the Frankses' home. The shop's owner described him as wearing a black-rimmed pair of eyeglasses and a gray hat and overcoat. It wasn't much to go on. Still, police hauled in and interrogated dozens of people. But they learned nothing more. They speculated that the glasses, hat, and overcoat had been a disguise. After all, the weather had been warm on Saturday—too warm for hats and coats. The identity of the wreath sender remained a mystery.

●　●　●

For Nathan, the beginning of the new week was a "dizzying merry-go-round." He took his finals, lunched with Richard and Dick Rubel, and studied at home with his group. He even squeezed in some time for birding. Bobby's murder, and his part in it, faded into the background.

Richard was busy, too, lunching at the Zeta Beta Tau house, where he tossed out more of his "theories," and repeatedly walking past the Harvard School and the Franks house. He read every newspaper, too, closely following the investigation. He laughed at the police's theories. Obviously, they were grasping at straws.

⊙ ⊙ ⊙

RAID DOPE RINGS FOR FRANKS SLAYERS

Evidence that cocaine addicts at the behest of a well-informed "mastermind" slew young Robert Franks has been in the hands of the police for several days, it became known last night. This developed when it leaked out that State's Attorney Crowe and Chief Collins . . . have ordered a general search of dope fiends, expecting . . . to single out those who acted in the murder conspiracy. The haunts of dope fiends are well known. Said State's Attorney Crowe, "We shall . . . try to find [a drug user] who was sufficiently well acquainted with the habits and movements of the Franks family to have contrived a kidnapping plot. . . . Dope will be found at the bottom of it."

(From the *Chicago Daily Tribune,* May 28, 1924, page 1)

⊙ ⊙ ⊙

On the morning of Wednesday, May 28, Jacob Weinstein, a Chicago optician, finally found the receipts he'd been looking for. He'd spent the last thirty-six hours going through store records trying to match the horn-rimmed glasses discovered at the crime scene to one of his customers. He'd traced the frames and discovered that only three pairs of glasses with those particular hinges had been sold in the city. One of them had been purchased by Nathan Leopold Jr.

* * *

It was Thursday afternoon, May 29, and Richard wanted to drink and play cards. "Come on, Nate," he'd said when he'd telephoned. But Nathan couldn't. He had a birding class. He was in his room getting ready when the maid came to his door. Two gentlemen wanted to see him. They were waiting in the library.

Nathan went downstairs.

The men introduced themselves as Detective Sergeants William Crot and Frank Johnson of the Chicago Police Department.

"What can I do for you gentlemen?" asked Nathan.

Crot asked the teenager if he wore glasses.

"I do, but I don't have them at the moment," replied Nathan.

"Did you lose your glasses?" asked Johnson.

"No."

Johnson pressed. "Have you got them?"

"No, but I'm sure they're around here someplace," Nathan replied.

"I'll have to ask you to come downtown," Crot said.

"This is mighty awkward," replied Nathan. "I was just on the point of leaving to meet my bird class. . . . They'll be waiting for me."

The class would have to wait. Crot and Johnson escorted Nathan to their car. They didn't read him his rights. Unlike they are nowadays, law enforcement officials weren't required to do this. But as a law student, Nathan knew them—the right to remain silent, the right to have an attorney present. Curiously, over the course of the next three days, he would not invoke them.

The detectives drove him downtown, but they didn't go to the police station. Instead, they went to the LaSalle Hotel.

State's Attorney Crowe waited in a suite of rooms on the sixteenth floor. He'd chosen the hotel over his office for the same reason he had not sent uniformed officers to the Leopold house. The son of an important businessman warranted special treatment. He didn't want to risk the ire of Nathan Sr. by causing the family any notoriety. At the hotel, they could talk privately without the press spotting them. Besides, Crowe didn't really think the teen was involved. Not a Leopold. He just wanted to hear Nathan's explanation for why his glasses had been found at the culvert. (He might not yet have realized that Captain Wolfe had spoken to the teenager the previous Sunday.)

Crowe greeted the teenager and showed him the glasses they'd found near the body. Were they Nathan's?

"They sure look like mine," Nathan answered. "If I didn't know mine were at home, I'd almost think they were."

"Yours are at home?" said Crowe.

"Yes," lied Nathan.

Crowe nodded. The best way to clear up the matter was to have the teenager produce his eyeglasses. He had Crot and Johnson drive him back to his house.

Mike Leopold was there when they arrived. After Nathan explained to his older brother what was happening, Mike helped with the search. So did the Leopolds' servants. They emptied drawers and peeked behind furniture. They looked under sofa cushions and in the glove box of Nathan's car. All they found was the empty eye-glass case.

"This place where they found the body is right where you go looking for birds," Mike finally said. "You must have dropped them out there and never noticed."

Nathan agreed that was probably what had happened.

Still, Mike was concerned. Maybe they should call a lawyer. No, he didn't think Babe had done anything wrong, but this was a serious matter—a murder investigation.

"Look," Mike said to the detectives, "Samuel Ettelson is our next-door neighbor and a friend of the family. Let me get him on the phone. He'll be able to straighten this out in a jiffy."

The detectives agreed, and Mike made the call.

But Ettelson wasn't home. According to his maid, he was at the Frankses' house.

Mike hung up and turned to the detectives. He insisted they drive over to the Frankses' so he could talk to Ettelson in person.

Again, the detectives agreed.

Minutes later, Ettelson came into the Frankses' entrance hall to meet them, followed by Jacob Franks. The grieving father shook Nathan's hand, his grip weak.

Little did Jacob Franks know that he was holding the hand of one of his son's killers.

Nathan felt no guilt, only a sense of urgency. He hoped Ettelson could get rid of the detectives.

Mike explained the situation.

Jacob Franks appeared confused by the story.

Ettelson faced the detectives. "There's been some mistake here," he said. "I've known this boy all my life; I know the whole family. It's a fantastic coincidence. You tell Mr. Crowe it's all a mistake. I'll take the responsibility."

"There," Nathan later recalled thinking, "the whole business [will] be settled with no more inconvenience than the loss of an afternoon with my bird class."

But one of the detectives took Ettelson aside. He whispered something that changed the attorney's mind. Ettelson nodded to him, then walked over to the Leopolds. "The thing is absurd, of course," he said to Mike. "But the officers feel they are duty bound to take Babe back downtown to Mr. Crowe. . . . Perhaps that would be the better thing to do."

Deflated, Nathan got back into the police car, and Mike followed in his. They returned to the suite at the LaSalle Hotel.

The police escorted Nathan into the bedroom, where the questioning would take place, while Mike took a seat in the living room. He felt sure his kid brother would quickly clear up the confusion.

Nathan felt sure, too. He still had an airtight explanation for why his eyeglasses had been found at the scene. So what did the police actually have? Nothing but a pair of eyeglasses.

Nathan's inability to produce his glasses, however, had given Crowe an excuse to hold him. There was something about Nathan that rankled the state's attorney. Perhaps it was the teenager's smooth, ready answers, or his air of superiority. And so Crowe and two assistant state's attorneys, Joseph Savage and John Sbarbaro, now waited for Nathan. Crowe had decided his questioning would no longer be routine.

After offering the teenager a seat, he asked, "Do you know where the body of Robert Franks was found?"

"Yes, sir," replied Nathan. He claimed he'd read it in the papers.

"Are you familiar with that spot?"

Nathan said he was. He and his birding companions had passed right over the culvert the weekend before the body was found. No, he hadn't known his glasses were with him. He hadn't worn them in months.

"How do you think you lost the glasses?" asked Savage.

They'd probably fallen out when he stumbled, Nathan replied smoothly. "I had a pair of rubber boots that didn't fit me [and] my stumbling [that Sunday] was greater . . . than normal."

Savage handed Nathan the glasses. "If you put your glasses in your pocket, you would put them in what pocket?"

"My breast pocket," said Nathan.

Savage asked him to put the glasses there now and demonstrate how he might have lost them by tripping.

Nathan did. Pretending to stumble, he fell to all fours on the floor. The glasses stayed in his pocket. He did it again. The glasses stayed put.

Savage asked him to take his suit jacket off, lay it on the floor, and then pick it up by its hem.

When Nathan did this, the glasses tumbled out onto the hotel's plush carpeting.

As Crowe watched this demonstration, his suspicions grew. Losing the glasses wasn't as easy as they'd thought. And there was something else: If Nathan really *had* lost his glasses at the culvert on the weekend before the murder, why weren't they dirty? Wouldn't they have been mud-spattered after lying on the ground for days? And yet, according to signalman Paul Korff, they'd been clean when he'd found them. Crowe's gut told him the teenager was lying. But he needed proof. He directed the detectives to search the Leopold house.

⊙ ⊙ ⊙

It was almost ten p.m. when the detectives searched Nathan's bedroom and study. With Nathan Sr.'s consent, they rifled through closets and drawers, turning up two items: a Remington .32-caliber automatic repeater and a letter to a boy named Richard Loeb. Neither item linked Nathan to the Franks murder, but the gun was illegal. The teenager had never applied for a permit. And the letter was highly suspicious.

Dated the previous October, it indicated that the pair had argued. About what wasn't clear. But it was serious enough for Richard to consider breaking off their relationship. Nathan hoped he wouldn't but recognized that it was Richard's decision. "I do want to warn you that in case you deem it advisable to discontinue our friendship, that in both our interests extreme care must be taken," he wrote. In other words, rumors about their homosexual relationship were sure to surface if they suddenly stopped spending time together. "Therefore, it is . . . expedient . . . to observe the conventionalities such as salutation on the street and a general appearance of at least not unfriendly relations on all occasions we may be thrown together in public." He went on to beg Richard for an answer by the next day. In fact, Richard didn't even have to speak with him directly. He could simply leave a message with the maid—"Dick says yes" or "Dick says no." Nathan ended the letter by promising to keep private "our confidences of the past" no matter his friend's decision. He ended with: "I am (for the present) as ever, Babe."

It seemed obvious to the detectives that the teens were lovers. They returned to the hotel and handed over the letter to the state's attorney.

The letter only heightened Crowe's suspicions. So Nathan Leopold was a homosexual, it seemed. Could the teenager have murdered Bobby for sexual motives? The state's attorney wanted to talk with Richard Loeb. He didn't believe the son of wealthy, prominent Albert Loeb was in any way mixed up in the Franks murder, but he could use Loeb to get information on Leopold. All he had to do was hint at publicly revealing the boy's homosexual secrets, and the Loeb boy, he felt sure, would talk.

◦ ◦ ◦

Savage's and Sbarbaro's questions now came at Nathan in rapid succession. When one paused, the other would jump in. Hoping to knock the teen off balance, Crowe walked in and out at various times, hurling a few questions of his own.

Nathan remained unruffled.

"What did you do on the twenty-first?" asked Savage.

"Gee, I don't know," said Nathan. He lit a cigarette and leaned back in his chair.

A smart kid like him? Crowe's men jabbed at his academic record. They'd heard he was some kind of genius. A straight-A student. Surely a brilliant guy could remember what he did a week ago.

Nathan shrugged. He said he had to go to the washroom.

On his way, he passed Mike, who was still waiting in the living room.

"How are things going?" asked Mike.

"Fine," said Nathan. He meant it.

Another round of questions began the moment he returned. What had Nathan been doing the day of the kidnapping? Who was he with? Where had he gone?

Again, Nathan claimed he couldn't remember.

Really? He couldn't recall any details about the day a neighbor child was kidnapped and murdered? Come on. He must have *some* idea of what he'd done.

Nathan walked across the room to an open window and looked out at the lights of the city. Should he use the alibi he and Richard had concocted? They'd agreed to use it within a week of the crime. It had now been eight days since the murder, but seven days since they'd tried to get the ransom. With shock, he realized they'd left a big hole in the planning of their alibi. Was he one day past the agreed deadline, or not? He had no choice. He had to use the alibi.

Haltingly, so it wouldn't sound rehearsed, Nathan began to talk. It was embarrassing, he admitted, and it involved a friend. He hadn't said anything because . . . well . . . he hadn't wanted to get his pal mixed up in this.

Crowe's men pressed. What was his friend's name?

Nathan acted hesitant. Did he really have to say?

Savage and Sbarbaro pressed harder.

The teenager lit another cigarette. Outwitting his interrogators seemed so easy.

Acting resigned, he gave them the name: Richard Loeb. "We played hooky," he said. Then he told them the alibi, every detail.

What were the girls' names? Savage wanted to know.

"Edna and Mae," replied Nathan. "I don't know their last names."

Crowe's men peppered him with questions. Could he describe the girls? Exactly where did he pick them up? Did the girls do more than kiss them? Where did Nathan and Richard drop them off? What birds did they see in Lincoln Park? What did they order for dinner at the Coconut Grove? What time did they get home? Did any family members see him when he came in? What were the names of the girls again? And was he driving his own car?

"Yes."

A Willys-Knight?

"Yes."

"What is the color of your car?"

"Red."

Nathan remained cool.

He didn't know that Richard had already been picked up and was at that moment in a different room at the hotel.

❋   ❋   ❋

The muscle in Richard's cheek twitched. No, he and Leopold did not have a sexual relationship, he told Crowe, although there had been rumors. "That was three years ago when this rumor started . . . and so we were very careful never to be seen alone together in public . . . purely and simply on the advice of my brother, who had told me to be careful and to—not to see too much of Leopold, and if I did to be sure there was somebody else around."

"Wasn't that an intolerable condition to exist, two fellows that were very friendly and wanted to be together and could not be together without the world suspecting they were [homosexuals]?" Crowe asked.

"No."

Crowe didn't buy a word of it. In fact, he'd begun to wonder if Richard was somehow involved in the crime, too. He asked the teenager what he'd been doing on the twenty-first.

Richard claimed he couldn't remember. "That was more than a week ago," he said. It was, he figured, too late to use the alibi.

⊕ ⊕ ⊕

Nathan felt comfortable. He was in a rhythm, answering questions quickly and confidently even as Crowe's men jumped from subject to subject in an attempt to catch him off guard.

"Did you read the works of [Robert Louis] Stevenson?"

"Yes, *Treasure Island.*"

"*Kidnapped*?"

"Yes."

"What languages do you know?"

"I've studied fifteen languages and speak six fluently: English, German, French, Italian, Spanish, and modern Greek. I can order breakfast in any Greek restaurant."

"What is your idea about the existence of God?"

"I do not believe there is a God."

"If you die, what becomes of you?"

"Your ashes return to ashes and dust to dust."

"Is there any difference between my death and the death of a dog?"

"No, sir."

"Have you read the ransom note that was published in the newspapers?"

"Yes."

"Could you compose such a letter?"

"Without any trouble whatsoever."

"Do you own a typewriter?"

"Yes, a Hammond Multiplex."

"Can you type?"

"Fairly well. No doubt I could have typed the ransom note. I have the skill. But of course, I didn't."

❂ ❂ ❂

It was around midnight when Detective Sergeants Crot and John-son returned yet again to the Leopold house. They came to pick up Nathan's Hammond Multiplex typewriter. They also took the oppor-tunity to search the second-floor study, where Nathan kept his bird collection. They found a can of ether, a bottle of strychnine, and a bottle of arsenic.

Nathan Sr. explained that they were part of his son's ornitho-logical equipment. He was unfailingly polite to the detectives. He earnestly believed that the sooner the police got their answers, the sooner his son would be released.

❂ ❂ ❂

At four a.m. Crowe's men ended their interrogation. Nathan felt re-lieved. He was ready for bed. The police, however, did not take him home. Instead, they drove him to central headquarters and stuck him in a cell with two other men. "Drunks, they looked like. Or bums," recalled Nathan. Sitting gingerly on the edge of the cot and hoping he didn't catch lice, he thought about his situation.

He knew Crowe could keep him in custody for seventy-two hours. "I hadn't been taking criminal law all year at school with-out learning that," he later said. Within those three days, Crowe had to either bring charges against him or release him. That was Illinois law.

Nathan did the math. He'd already been held twelve hours. That left sixty more. If he stuck to his story, he'd be home by Sunday night.

❂ ❂ ❂

Richard's poor memory had only heightened Crowe's suspicions. How could Nathan remember every detail of their whereabouts on May 21, and Richard recall none? Crowe's instincts told him the two had been up to something else that day, something they didn't want to reveal. But what? He decided to keep Loeb in custody, too. He had officers take the teenager to the police station at 48th and Wabash. They put him in a cell by himself.

CHAPTER TWELVE

ANOTHER DAY IN CUSTODY

MILLIONAIRE'S SON ON THE GRILL

NATHAN LEOPOLD JR. NEW SUSPECT

Nathan Leopold Jr. . . . 19 year old student marvel, son of a millionaire, and connected with some of the wealthiest families in Chicago was held this morning in the office of State's Attorney Robert Crowe, where he was being questioned about the murder and kidnapping of [14] year old Robert Franks. Leopold . . . was charged with the ownership of the eyeglasses which were found . . . near the culvert in which the body of young Franks was discovered last Thursday. . . .

Richard Loeb . . . who was a companion of young Leopold, was also taken to the state's attorney's office. . . .

(From the *Chicago Daily Tribune,* May 30, 1924, page 1)

● ● ●

After a couple of hours of sleep and a shower, Nathan met with a handful of reporters who had been allowed to visit him in his cell.

Between bites of a ham-and-egg sandwich, he talked about the one scrap of evidence connecting him to the murder. "There's no question in my mind the glasses are mine," he admitted. "They must have been in the suit I wore the last time I went there and dropped from my pocket." He stirred some cream into his coffee with a pencil before adding, "It's queer, but I have been following the Franks case all along, and from the first I had a feeling that those glasses were mine."

Reporters found Nathan intellectually dazzling, a prodigy. In its afternoon edition that day, the *Chicago Daily News* reported that he was a new type of educated young man: intellectually gifted and financially well off, but morally and emotionally bankrupt. That was because he'd told them that he drank, smoked, and caroused. He'd also admitted that he did not believe in God. "His conduct, like his thinking, is independent of conventions and taboos," the newspaper continued.

From that very first interview, the press saw in Nathan a new kind of danger. He had been sent to the most prestigious schools with the expectation that education would improve him. But instead he had been "contaminated with moral miasma," a reporter for the *Chicago Herald and Examiner* would write. Higher education had taught him to "scoff at God."

The reality that he was a killer, however, seemed unlikely to the press. The teenager had a logical explanation for his glasses having been found near the body. His possible guilt, noted the *Chicago Daily Tribune* the next morning, was "too silly to discuss."

The suspect's families found it ridiculous as well. "The affair will so easily straighten itself out," said Anna Loeb.

Nathan Sr. also gave a statement to the reporters gathered on his doorstep. "While this is a terrible ordeal to my boy and myself to have him under suspicion, our attitude will be one of helping the investigation rather than retarding it."

Neither family felt the need to hire a lawyer for their son. As Nathan Sr. said, "I probably could get my boy out . . . but there is no need for this technical trickery. The idea that he had anything to do with this case is too absurd to merit comment."

◉ ◉ ◉

On May 30, Howard Mayer awoke to the ringing of the telephone. Who could be calling at seven a.m.? He stumbled out into the hallway and picked up the receiver.

It was his editor at the *Chicago Evening American,* who'd just gotten an anonymous tip. "Get over to the Loeb mansion—pronto!" he told the cub reporter.

Mayer, who hadn't yet heard that Nathan and Richard were in police custody, threw on some clothes and raced to Ellis Avenue. He arrived just in time to see a police car pull up. Detective Sergeants Crot and Johnson had come to search Richard's bedroom.

When Mayer asked what was going on, Johnson told him both Loeb and Leopold were suspects in the Bobby Franks case.

"That's impossible!" exclaimed Mayer.

"No, it's not," countered the detective. "They're telling different stories. These boys are in deep trouble." He went on to explain that Leopold had said he'd gotten drunk and picked up girls on the day of the kidnapping. Loeb, however, claimed he couldn't remember a thing.

Mayer, who'd known both teenagers in college, thought he understood why their stories didn't mesh. Richard, naturally, didn't want to ruin his reputation or shock his parents by admitting he'd been out drinking and carousing. But now was not the time for Richard to worry about social position, Mayer thought. He decided to help.

After the police left the Loeb mansion, Mayer drove to the state's attorney's offices in the Criminal Courts Building. He'd learned from Johnson that Nathan had been taken there from jail. The six-story stone behemoth took up almost an entire city block and teemed with people. Mayer approached a police officer at the front desk. He asked to see Nathan Leopold.

Because Mayer was a reporter, the officer allowed it. He led Mayer to a guarded conference room on the first floor. Inside, Nathan sat smoking. The cop left the two alone.

"I'm telling the truth, Howie," said Nathan as soon as the door closed. He said he and Richard really had been out with some girls the night of the murder.

"That's not [Richard's] story," Mayer replied. "According to the police, he can't recall what he did that night."

Nathan felt sucker-punched. He realized Richard wasn't using the alibi because he thought it was too late. But he *had* to use it. He had to corroborate Nathan's story.

He begged Mayer to get a message to Richard. "Tell him to remember what happened on Wednesday. He'll understand."

Mayer agreed. He asked the police officer if he could speak with Richard.

Loeb, however, wasn't in the building. He was still at the police station at 48th and Wabash. Mayer headed there. Yet again, police allowed him to be alone with the suspect.

Richard sat, head bowed, in his cell. But when he saw Mayer, he walked to the bars.

"Dick," pleaded Mayer, "if you want to clear yourself, you have to tell the truth."

"I don't want to talk at this time."

Mayer told him he had a message from Nathan.

Richard's fingers clenched the cell's bars. "What did he say, Howie?"

"He said to tell the truth about the two girls. Tell the police what you did with them. You can't get into any worse trouble than you are now. He said you'd understand."

Richard *did* understand. Nathan had used Mayer to deliver a message that broke the police security around the two. Now their alibis would match seamlessly despite their being held separately. Richard grinned. Would Mayer mind asking his interrogators to return?

Mayer didn't mind at all. As he walked away from the cell, he felt relieved that he'd helped.

❧ ❧ ❧

On that same Friday, *Chicago Daily News* reporters Alvin Goldstein and James Mulroy were trying to trace the Underwood portable that had been used to type the ransom note. They knew Leopold had been brought in for questioning, so they began their search at Nathan's friend Arnold Maremont's house. They asked the student if he had any study notes typed by Leopold.

Maremont handed over a stack, and the reporters rushed them across town to H. P. Sutton, the typewriter expert who'd worked with the police earlier. Sutton agreed that these study notes and the ransom note had been typed on the same machine.

But where was that machine now?

Police returned to the Leopolds' house to search for it. But if Nathan had ever had an Underwood portable, it was gone.

❂ ❂ ❂

SEEK GIRLS' STORY

State's Attorney Robert Crowe has the spectacles that prove Nathan Leopold Jr. was at the culvert where Robert Franks' body was found. Leopold has an alibi corroborated by Richard Loeb and needing only the confirmation of two girls, Edna and Mae, to give preponderance to his claims to having been else-where when Robert was kidnapped and killed. The police are seeking the girls' whereabouts.

Both youths had been drinking the afternoon of Wednesday, May 21, on the lake front of Grace Street, left there about 5 p.m. . . . and the drinking continued far into the evening. Both told that to different questioners without having time to consult. . . .

Because of drink he had taken, Richard was more hazy about the story than Nathan. He had a flask of Scotch, Nathan a flask of gin when they started out that morning; more gin was purchased later, he related. His father objects to his drinking . . . so when he did go home [on the night of the murder] it was long after his household was darkened and all asleep.

Richard attributed the fact that he and Nathan had been talked about—their names coupled—to a former law student at the University of Chicago, a poor student who sought employment in Charlevoix, Mich., and who started the rumor because of enmity toward them both.

He said he had not seen his boy chum wear glasses for at least a month; Nathan didn't say he had worn them during that period, he only claimed to have carried them in his pocket. Several fellow students were called in and questioned on this point; none gave important information.

(From the *Chicago Daily News*, May 30, 1924, page 1)

◦ ◦ ◦

Late that Friday night at the Criminal Courts Building, State's Attorney Crowe met with his team in his office. The investigation was stalled. The teenagers now had corroborating alibis. The eyeglasses could indeed have been lost while Nathan had been out birding. And while the Underwood portable typewriter seemed to have belonged to Nathan, they could not find it.

It was almost midnight. The teenagers had been in custody for almost thirty-two hours. Crowe worried about holding the pair much longer. "They've got wealthy parents. We've either got to book them or release them."

A police officer knocked on the conference room door. Could somebody come out and talk with the Leopolds' chauffeur? The guy had been sitting out in the waiting room for hours.

Assistant State's Attorney Bert Cronson went out to talk with the chauffeur. He shook Sven Englund's hand and asked what this was about.

"Master Babe's" innocence, replied Englund. He told Cronson about fixing the brakes on Nathan's car the day of the Franks murder.

Cronson didn't understand.

Englund explained. Nathan couldn't have driven the dead boy's body out to Wolf Lake that day because . . . *he didn't have his car!* It had been in the Leopold garage all day. Nathan was innocent.

The chauffeur didn't know that Nathan had lied to investigators and told them he'd been driving around all that day in his Willys-Knight.

Cronson tried to grasp the timeline. "Then when you finished, [the pair] took the automobile and left?" he asked.

"Oh, no," said Englund. "I worked on the car all day. It never left the garage."

That didn't make sense to Cronson. The teenagers had said they'd driven around in Nathan's car. But Englund was saying the car hadn't left the garage. Was the chauffeur sure of the date?

"Very sure," said Englund. He remembered it because his wife had taken their sick daughter to the doctor, who'd given them a prescription with the date on it—May 21.

And how long had the car remained in the garage? Cronson wanted to know.

Until late in the evening, Englund replied.

It took all Cronson's self-control not to sprint down the hall to Crowe's office. He asked the chauffeur to wait, then walked back to the state's attorney's office. He told Crowe what he'd learned.

Crowe smacked his fist into his palm. "I think we've got them."

PART FOUR

CONFESSIONS

CHAPTER THIRTEEN

"I WILL TELL YOU THE *REAL* TRUTH"

State's Attorney Robert Crowe entered the interrogation room. Despite the late hour—it was now one a.m. on Saturday, May 31— Richard Loeb looked fresh and alert. So far he'd easily deflected the detectives' questions.

But they were about to get much rougher.

Assistant State's Attorney John Sbarbaro leaned across the table and glared at Richard. He might as well stop pretending and confess. They knew the truth. He and Leopold hadn't been out birding and drinking on the twenty-first. They hadn't picked up any girls and driven around. In fact, they hadn't gone anywhere in Leopold's car because it was in the garage all afternoon.

Richard looked up. "Who told you that?"

"Englund," said Sbarbaro.

Richard went pale and the muscle in his cheek began to twitch. He said something, but it was garbled. He coughed.

Sbarbaro poured him a glass of water.

Richard gulped it, coughed again, and in a voice barely above a whisper said, "My God! He told you that?"

"Yes, he did," said Sbarbaro.

Richard lit a cigarette with shaking hands, then turned to stare out the window. He said nothing. Minutes passed.

Sbarbaro was silent, too.

Richard sighed. He turned to look Sbarbaro in the eye and said, "I will tell you all."

@ @ @

In another room, Assistant State's Attorney Joseph Savage and chief of detectives Michael Hughes pressed Nathan. They told him what Englund had said.

The chauffeur had his date wrong, Nathan insisted. He and Richard had used his car. Sure, Englund had fixed his brakes. But that was a different day. He was positive.

The interrogators could get nowhere with him.

At four a.m. Crowe walked into the room. He grinned at the unruffled nineteen-year-old. "Well," he said, "your pal has just confessed. Told us the whole thing."

Nathan laughed. "Do you think I'm stupid? I'm not going to believe that. Anyway, it's impossible. There's nothing to confess." He sat back in his chair and calmly lit another cigarette.

Crowe took off his glasses. Nonchalantly, he polished each lens with his handkerchief. While he hadn't heard Richard's entire confession yet—obtaining the teen's full statement had been left to John Sbarbaro—Crowe did know the most important details.

Nathan watched him and took a drag on his cigarette.

Crowe put his glasses back on. "Oh, yeah, Mr. Wise Guy? Who told me about the car from the [rental] agency? Who told me about Morton D. Ballard and his bank account at the Hyde Park Bank and his registering at the Morrison Hotel?"

Only Richard could have known those details.

Crowe didn't push Nathan. He simply and unemotionally recited all Richard had told him.

And the truth sank in. Richard had indeed confessed.

Nathan crushed out his cigarette and lit another. He listened intently to Crowe.

"[Richard] says he was driving the car, that you were riding in the back seat. That you struck the fatal blow," said Crowe.

Nathan flashed with anger. That was a lie.

What should he do?

He thought a moment. The fat was in the fire. He was sunk. But he'd be damned if he'd take more than his share of the blame. He exhaled smoke. "I will tell you the *real* truth," he said.

◎　◎　◎

It was 4:20 a.m. Nathan scanned the faces of the men sitting around the interrogation room table—Savage, Hughes, and a stenographer, E. M. Allen, who would be taking down every word in shorthand. Robert Crowe was not present. He'd decided to let his assistant hear Nathan's full confession. He would ask questions later.

"Now, Nathan," said Savage. "I just want you to go on in your own way and tell us the story from the beginning, tell us the whole thing."

Nathan lit a cigarette and began. His voice was matter-of-fact as he told about the long months of preparation and planning; told about the day of the kidnapping and the problem of getting a victim. Bobby Franks had been chosen "by pure accident," he explained. They'd set out simply "with the idea in mind of getting a boy that day." It was Bobby's bad luck that he happened to be on the street. Richard had lured him into the rental car by asking about a tennis racket.

"I was sitting at the driver's wheel," said Nathan. "Robert was on the front seat [with me], Dick was in the rear seat. . . . As soon as we turned the corner, Richard placed his hand over [Bobby's] mouth to stifle his outcries, with his right hand he beat him over the head several times with a chisel specially for the purpose."

He paused and drew on his cigarette, confident and composed. He continued. "[Bobby] did not succumb as readily as we had believed. Richard seized him, [and] pulled him into the back seat. Here he forced a cloth into his mouth. Apparently, the boy died by suffocation shortly thereafter. . . . We [then] drove to Gary [Indiana, twenty-five miles from Chicago], being a rather deserted place. We even stopped to buy a couple of [hot dogs] and some drinks for supper." They ate in the car.

The image of the teenagers enjoying hot dogs while the body of a dead child lay in the backseat jarred Savage. He broke in with a question. Where had the pair bought the food?

"On Calumet Road," replied Nathan. "The body was covered with an automobile robe." He smoked a few moments before going on. "We drove up and down the road until dark, then proceeded . . . to the prearranged spot for the disposal of the body. We had previously removed the trousers and stockings of the boy, leaving the shoes and the belt by the side of the road concealed in the grass."

Nathan gave no reason for partially undressing the body. And neither Savage nor Hughes asked. The teenager went on with his story.

"Having arrived at [Wolf Lake] we placed the body in the robe, carried it to the culvert where it was found. Here we completed the disrobing; then in an attempt to render identification more difficult, poured hydrochloric acid over the face and body."

Savage asked for clarification. "What kind of acid was that you say you used?"

"Hydrochloric," said Nathan. "There was a faint discoloration."

This, then, explained the copper-colored stains on the body's face and genitals.

Nathan continued. "Then I stepped into the water, took the feet of the body while Dick took the head end . . . and when it struck the water, pushed it in, gave it a shove as far as I could. . . . At first I thought it was rather doubtful whether it would fit at all, but . . . it was not hard at all. . . . [I] used my feet to push it in as far as I could."

"And then?" asked Savage.

"We gathered up all the clothes, placed them in the robe and apparently at this point I lost my glasses. I carried the robe containing the clothes back to the automobile."

❂ ❂ ❂

Meanwhile, in another interrogation room just two doors down the hall, Richard was telling his version of events to Assistant State's Attorney John Sbarbaro, Captain William Shoemaker, and a second stenographer, F. A. Sheeder.

"Calling your attention to the twenty-first day of May," said Sbarbaro, "just tell us in your own words if you know of anything unusual relative to the disappearance of Robert Franks."

Richard began. "On the twenty-first of May, Leopold and myself . . ."

"What is his full name?"

"Nathan Leopold Junior . . . and myself intended to kidnap one of the younger boys from Harvard School. . . . The plan was broached by Nathan Leopold, who suggested that as a means of having a great deal of excitement, together with getting quite a sum of money."

"And adventure, as you would say?" asked Sbarbaro.

"Yes," agreed Richard. His voice, too, was matter-of-fact as he now tried to pin most of the responsibility for the crime on his best friend. "We turned down Forty-Eighth Street and turned the car around, Leopold getting in the back seat. I drove the car, then . . . parallel to where Franks was, stopped the car, and while remaining in my seat [leaned across], opened the front door and called to Franks. . . . I told him that I would like to talk to him about a tennis racket; so he got [into the front seat of] the car. . . . Just after we turned off Ellis Avenue, Leopold reached his arm around young Franks, grabbed his mouth and hit him over the head with the chisel. I believe he hit him several times. I do not remember the exact number. He began to bleed and was not entirely conscious. . . . At this point, Leopold . . . grabbed Franks and carried him over the back of the front seat and threw him on a rug in the car. He then took one of the rags and gagged him by sticking it down his throat."

The teen leaned forward in his chair, seeming to relish telling the details. He, too, told about stopping on a deserted country road to partially undress the body and hide the shoes and belt. But he provided a reason for it. "We did this in order that we might be saved the trouble of too much undressing him later on," he explained. Afterward, they drove around waiting for dark. At one point they stopped at a sandwich shop.

"Leopold got out and purchased a couple [of hot dogs] and two bottles of root beer," said Richard.

If Nathan had repeatedly struck Bobby before pulling him into the backseat, wouldn't his clothing have been bloodstained? Would Nathan really have walked into a roadside restaurant in that condition? Or had Richard been the one spattered in blood, which might explain why he had remained in the car? Unfortunately, neither the assistant state's attorney nor the police captain asked.

Richard went on with his story. Once at Wolf Lake, "Leopold carried the feet, I carried the head. We deposited the body near the culvert, and undressed [it] completely. . . . The boy was quite dead. . . . We knew by his eyes; and then when . . . we poured hydrochloric acid over him we noticed no tremor . . . not a single tremor."

The teenager seemed almost proud when he said this. He paused to drink from the cup of water in front of him before continuing. "Leopold put on his hip boots . . . and took the body and stuck it . . . headfirst into the culvert. It . . . was still not pitch black, so we were able to work without a flashlight."

"And then what did you do?" asked Sbarbaro.

"I went to the opposite side of the culvert, where the water runs out . . . and I washed my hands which had gotten very bloody through carrying the body."

"The head had bled very freely?"

"Yes . . . quite freely . . . [and] the robe was quite saturated with blood. We then left, taking the robe we used as [well as] the clothing of young Franks, and we started homeward."

❧ ❧ ❧

Nathan's and Richard's stories matched up from this point.

"Around 9 p.m. [Leopold] stopped to call up his folks and tell them he'd be detained," Richard told his interrogators. Then they drove back to Chicago to "a drugstore somewhere in the neighbor-hood where I looked up the address of J. Franks and the telephone number, and at the same time, Leopold printed the address on the envelope [of the ransom letter]."

"From there I spoke to Mrs. Franks and told her that my name was George Johnson," Nathan told his interrogators, "and that her boy had been kidnapped but was safe, and that further instruc-tions would follow. In passing Fifty-Fifth Street, we mailed the letter." They'd attached special postage to the envelope guaranteeing that it would be delivered the next morning.

They went to Richard's house from there. After sneaking into the basement, they opened the furnace door. Flames danced inside. "[We] destroyed the clothes," confessed Richard. "The robe was placed in a little hiding place near the greenhouse at my house."

"We intended burning the robe [but] it was too large to fit in and could have caused an awful stench," confessed Nathan. "We left [it] hidden in some bushes there."

While still at the Loebs', they "proceeded to get a pail, soap and brush, and to the best of our ability in the dark to try and wash out the car of bloodstains," admitted Richard.

There had been blood—lots of it—on the back of the passenger seat and on the backseat carpet. It had soaked through the floor-boards beneath and spattered the rubber boots worn by Nathan.

"We washed the more obnoxious bloodstains from the car," ad-mitted Richard.

But it was dark and late and they "didn't want to be monkeying around too much," explained Nathan. They decided to give the car a more thorough cleaning the next day.

Then they'd headed to Nathan's house. After parking the rental car a block down the street, they went inside and had a drink with Nathan Sr. He soon went to bed. Alone in the living room, the teens had a few more drinks and played cards. It was around midnight when Nathan drove Richard back to his house in his red Willys-Knight.

"On the way home, we threw the chisel out of the car . . . someplace between 48th and 50th [Streets]," said Richard, who'd taken the weapon from the rental car earlier.

"He threw the chisel out," said Nathan.

And then what happened?

"He took me home," concluded Richard.

"I went to bed," concluded Nathan.

● ● ●

It was almost dawn when police escorted the teens into Robert Crowe's office, where the state's attorney waited. Their confessions had been typed up. Now a stenographer read them aloud, beginning with Richard's.

When he finished, Nathan turned to Crowe. "I have some corrections," he said. He proceeded to pick apart Richard's statement. Most were little quibbles—the rental car company was at 14th Street and Michigan Avenue, not 16th Street. The hardware store where the chisel had been purchased was between 55th and 56th, not on 47th. The hip boots worn while shoving the body into the culvert were not his brother's, but his own. And he had dropped off Richard at home at one o'clock in the morning, "not ten thirty as he seems to think."

"No, I never said that," argued Richard. He glared at Nathan. "I said I *went* to your house at ten thirty."

Nathan ignored him. "The entire kidnap and murder scheme was Mr. Loeb's idea," he explained to Crowe. "It was his plan and it was he who did the act."

Crowe motioned for him to quiet down. He asked the stenographer to read Nathan's confession.

He'd barely finished when Richard erupted. "There are certain corrections that Leopold has made . . . such as the boots being his and not his brother's . . . which don't amount to a damn. . . . However, I would like to say this . . . He had the method of the killing very well conceived and planned out as evidenced by the ether in the car. . . . The boy was supposed to be etherized to death, and he was supposed to do that, because I don't know a damn thing about it, and he does. He has . . . chloroformed birds and things like that and he knows ornithology. I don't know a damned thing about that."

Who struck Bobby Franks with the chisel? asked Crowe.

"He did," shouted Richard, pointing at Nathan. "He was sitting up in the front seat. I said, he was sitting up in the front seat. I mean, *I* was sitting up in the front seat. That is obviously a mistake; I am getting excited."

Had Richard just made an inadvertent slip? Nathan leaned back in his chair wearing a smug expression and lit another cigarette.

Richard continued, raging directly at his partner. He felt betrayed by Nathan's use of the alibi. If he hadn't used it, Richard believed, the chauffeur's story would never have tripped them up. They would have gotten away scot-free. "You told the stories you shouldn't have told," he cried.

Nathan said nothing, although he was fuming, too. Why had Richard confessed? If he'd just stayed quiet, it would have been the chauffeur's word against theirs. Crowe didn't have any other hard evidence.

Richard never explained why he'd confessed. But psychiatrists who later examined him believed he'd been compelled to do it. He'd *wanted* credit for the crime. He hungered for the attention he'd get.

Right now, though, he was angry and shouting. "I tried to help you out!" he hollered at Nathan. "I thought you, at least, if worse came to worst, would admit what you had done and not try to drag me into this thing in that manner."

"Those are all absurd dirty lies," Nathan hissed at his partner. He turned to Crowe. "He is trying to get out of this mess. . . . I was driving the car. I am absolutely positive."

He turned back to Loeb, his tone mocking. "I am sorry that you . . . stepped into everything and broke down and all that. I am sorry, but it wasn't my fault."

Then Nathan turned to Crowe. "All [he's said] are lies."

Crowe interrupted their argument. The boys still did not have lawyers, but the state's attorney knew it was only a matter of time before they did. And he foresaw that these lawyers would claim that Nathan and Richard had spoken under duress, that the police had beaten the confessions out of them. And so he had a few last questions to ask them.

"Now listen, boys," he said.

"Yes?" replied Nathan.

"You have been treated decently by me?"

"Absolutely," answered Nathan.

"No brutality or roughness?"

"No sir," said Nathan.

"Not one of you have a complaint to make, do you?"

"No sir," Nathan said again.

"Have you, Loeb?"

"No," said Richard.

That was all State's Attorney Crowe needed . . . for now.

CHAPTER FOURTEEN

MURDERERS' FIELD TRIP

Outside Crowe's office, rumors spread that the case had been solved. More and more reporters gathered at the Criminal Courts Building. They crammed into the hallway, notebooks at the ready. Photographers set up a forest of camera tripods. The air felt electric.

At six a.m. on that same Saturday, Robert Crowe stepped from his office. Flashbulbs popped. Questions rang out.

Despite his rumpled shirt and the dark smudges under his eyes, the state's attorney looked triumphant. "The Franks murder mystery has been solved," he announced. "The murderers are in custody. Nathan Leopold Jr. and Richard Loeb have completely and voluntarily confessed. . . . The Franks boy was kidnapped out of a spirit of adventure and for ransom. The kidnapping was planned many months ago, but the Franks boy was not the original victim in mind. . . . He was beaten with a chisel, strangled and then [an] attempt was made to disfigure him with acid."

Pandemonium erupted as reporters dashed for telephones in order to call their newsrooms with the scoop. Within minutes of the announcement, the *Chicago Herald and Examiner* began churning out an extra morning edition carrying the banner headline "How Franks Boy Was Killed Is Told." Within ten minutes of the edition's hitting the newsstands, it had sold 100,000 copies.

The press rushed to the Frankses' house, too.

Jacob answered the door. Flora, who'd become a pale, listless recluse since her son's murder, rarely left her bedroom. In a voice that held a bitter edge, Jacob said, "Young Leopold has said that he is an atheist. Now perhaps he will realize there *is* a God, that God alone would have caused him to drop those glasses and lead the way to my son's murderers." He couldn't understand, he went on, why the teenagers had done it. For the adventure of it? He shook his head. The youths were either insane or fiends. "The law must take its course," he added.

Across the street, reporters found two private bodyguards at the front gates of the Loeb mansion. Neither parent would speak to the press. Albert Loeb was still convalescing, and Anna was too distraught. She could be seen from the sidewalk in a second-floor window, pacing back and forth as she waited for further news of her son. Eventually, Richard's older brother Allan spoke to the *Chicago Sunday Tribune.* "There is no truth to this report," he said angrily. "Just lies, lies, lies! He is innocent and merely confessed to get sleep. It can be repudiated when it comes to trial."

Three blocks away at the Leopold house, Nathan Sr. stepped out onto the front porch. Tearfully, he denied his son's guilt. "Impossible, ridiculous, Nathan—my boy, my boy—I can't believe it . . . I won't believe it." He tried to smile as reporters gathered around him.

Others who lived in the neighborhood spoke with reporters, too.

Salmon Levinson, whose son Johnny had been the teenagers' first choice as their victim, was still in disbelief. He'd dined with the

Loebs just weeks earlier, he told reporters. Richard had "delighted us by his charming personality. I regarded him as one of the finest youths I have ever known. . . . I can hardly think it possible that he and young Leopold contemplated harm to my boy."

Dick Rubel—who didn't yet know he'd been on the teenagers' victim list—refused to even consider their guilt. "That's a damn lie," he shouted. "I'm Dick Loeb's best friend, and he couldn't have done it."

And one acquaintance, speaking anonymously, blamed the murder on the teenagers' lack of religious training. Both families were members of the Sinai Congregation, a Reform temple on 47th Street. But they rarely attended, and the boys had not been formally educated in Jewish principles. "Though the father of 'Babe' Leopold is a devout Jew, he failed to make religious influence a part of his son's training," said the acquaintance. "[This] would have made all the difference in the world in that young man's development." As for Richard, his mother was a Catholic who had only reluctantly agreed to have her sons brought up in the Jewish faith. Was it any wonder they'd come to this?

Indeed, Chicago's Jewish community (as well as Jewish communities across the country) reacted with shock at the identity of the killers. "The fact that the murdered boy had been Jewish was painful enough, another example of the endless persecutions inflicted on Jewish people," wrote historian Hal Higdon. "But to learn that the killers were also Jewish was an embarrassment that the Jewish community had to suffer together. It would be inaccurate to suggest that Jews shared the *guilt* of Leopold and Loeb. More accurately, [they] shared the *anguish* of the Leopold and Loeb families, that their children could be capable of such a crime."

Meyer Levin, a University of Chicago student who decades later would write a bestselling novel about the case, recalled that around Jewish families' dinner tables "there was one gruesome note of relief in the affair. One heard it uttered only amongst ourselves—a relief that the victim, too, had been Jewish. Though [the religious] aspects were never overtly raised in the case . . . we were never free of the thought that the murderers were Jews."

However, that very morning, the *Chicago Daily Tribune* did raise the issue overtly, pointing out to readers that the importance of this case lay in the fact that "it concerns a particular people. The three principals in the tragedy . . . the Franks boy, Leopold and Loeb are all Jews."

The mayor of Chicago, William Dever—who counted Albert Loeb among his closest friends—obviously feared an antisemitic backlash in which the public might hold the whole Jewish population responsible for the crime. And so that Saturday afternoon, in his first public comments on the murder, he congratulated the detectives for their "efficient and vigorous work." Then, in a carefully worded way, he called for citizen restraint. "I have the deepest sympathy for the parents of all three boys. I know Mr. Loeb, whom I regard as a man of splendid character and attainment. It is sad that such a tragedy should be visited upon these people and it invites the sympathy of *all.*"

Chief Justice of the Cook County Criminal Court John R. Caverly, a short, gray-haired man with rimless glasses, spoke with the press, too. As the judge who would be hearing the case, he promised to move quickly, and expected to go to trial within thirty days. That the defendants' parents were rich pillars of the community made no difference to his timetable.

Some reporters wondered if the teens could be tried as juveniles.

According to Illinois law at the time, persons under twenty-one were considered minors. They couldn't vote, sign contracts, or marry without parental permission. Their guardians were legally responsible for all their actions and decisions.

Caverly patiently explained that Illinois law set the age of criminal responsibility at fourteen. At that age, a person was deemed by the state to be capable of committing a crime and, therefore, completely responsible for it. It did not matter that Leopold and Loeb were minors. They would be prosecuted to the fullest extent of the law.

What might the boys' punishment be?

Nathan and Richard had both confessed to first-degree murder, as well as kidnapping. For the crime of murder, Illinois's statutes called for death, or a term of not less than fourteen years in prison. Kidnapping, too, carried the death sentence, or a term in prison of not less than five years. The only way the teenagers could get a lesser sentence was to prove to the court that they were insane.

Would the boys hang?

That remained to be seen.

◉ ◉ ◉

Crowe had kept the murderers sitting and waiting in the interrogation room while he spoke with the press. They were still there two hours later when—without breakfast or a wink of sleep—he had them put into two separate cars and taken on a field trip to the sites involved in the murder. The state's attorney wanted to strengthen his case by corroborating the teenagers' confessions. He also expected the families' lawyers to come charging in at any moment, now that the news of their confessions was public.

A long procession of police cars followed by reporters and photographers wound its way through the city's streets to the Rent-A-Car Company on Michigan Avenue. Flanked by police officers, Nathan went inside.

Did the clerk recognize the teenager?

He did. He handed over the rental contract signed by Mr. Ballard.

Next they visited the diner where Richard had waited to be called as Ballard's reference.

Nathan eyed the lunch counter. "Let's eat!" he suggested.

Ignoring him, Detective Hughes asked the diner's owner if she recognized either youth.

She pointed at Richard. She remembered him waiting near the phone booth for almost an hour.

Richard went pale. His knees buckled and he crumpled to the floor.

Nathan looked on contemptuously. Either Richard was a weakling who couldn't take the pressure, or he was faking it. Whatever the reason, Nathan disdained his behavior.

Police officers helped Richard back to the car. Rather than making him continue on with them, they took him to the Hotel Windermere. This, too, was Crowe's idea. To prevent the teens' families (and their lawyers) from talking with the pair, he would keep them on the move. The strategy was simple, he'd told Detective Hughes earlier. "Shuffle them here, there, all over town, out into the country, from one hotel to another, while the boys talk and talk and talk."

Nathan went on to the hardware store, where the clerk was unable to identify him as having purchased a chisel recently. (This was because Richard had bought it.) At the drugstore where Nathan had

Richard, around age six, dressed as a cowboy. New-school psychiatrists would later point to this ordinary childhood game as evidence of "excessive aggression."

Seven-year-old Richard rests his head on governess Emily Struthers's shoulder.

Although just thirteen when this picture was taken in 1918, Richard was already a sophomore at University High School. He would graduate the following year at age fourteen.

Taken while on a birding expedition to Michigan in June 1923, this is the earliest known photograph of Nathan Leopold. Here, the eighteen-year-old is feeding flies to a Kirtland's warbler in its nest. A day after this picture was taken, Nathan killed the warblers for his collection.

Montages of photos like this one appeared regularly in Chicago's newspapers. Pictured here are the teenagers' palatial homes. Above, the Loeb mansion. Below, the Leopold house.

An ad for a Willys-Knight touring car, the same make of vehicle rented by Nathan and Richard for the kidnapping and murder.

The victim: Bobby Franks in 1924, age fourteen.

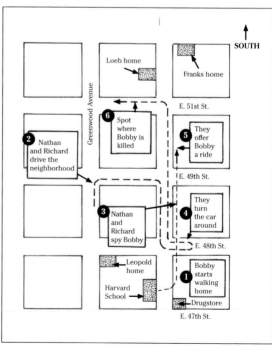

The route the killers took through their Kenwood neighborhood on May 21, 1924.

Bobby's father, Jacob Franks (left), with his brother-in-law Edwin Gresham (right), who identified Bobby's body.

Dear Sir:

As you no doubt know by this time your son has been kidnapped. Allow us to assure you that he is at present well and safe. You need fear no physical harm for him provided you live up carefully to the following instructions, and such others as you will receive by future communications. Should you however, disobey any of our instructions even slightly, his death will be the penalty.

1. For obvious reasons make absolutely no attempt to communicate with either the police authorities, or any private agency. Should you already have communicated with the police, allow them to continue their investigations, but do not mention this letter.

2. Secure before noon today ten thousand dollars, ($10,000.00). This money must be composed entirely of OLD BILLS of the following denominations:
$2,000.00 in twenty dollar bills
$8,000.00 in fifty dollar bills
The money must be old. Any attempt to include new or marked bills will render the entire venture futile.

(2)

3. The money should be placed in a large cigar box, or if this is impossible in a heavy cardboard box, SECURELY closed and wrapped in white paper. The wrapping paper should be sealed at all openings with sealing wax.

4. Have the money with you prepared as directed above, and remain at home after one o'clock P.M. See that the telephone is not in use.

You will receive a future communication instructing you as to your future course.

As a final word of warning - this is a strictly commercial proposition, and we are prepared to put our threat into execution should we have reasonable grounds to believe that you have committed an infraction of the above instructions. However, should you carefully follow out our instructions to the letter, we can assure you that your son will be safely returned to you within six hours of our receipt of the money.

Yours truly,
GEORGE JOHNSON
GMR

The ransom note received by the Franks family on May 22, 1924.

Detectives gather around the culvert where Bobby Franks's body was found, May 23, 1924.

The eyeglasses found at the culvert that eventually led police to Nathan.

Cook County State's Attorney Robert Crowe in 1924.

This picture montage of Bobby's funeral shows (top) a grieving Flora Franks clinging to her brother Edwin Gresham; (middle) an inset photo of Bobby; and (bottom) the dead boy's casket being carried from the house by his friends who acted as pallbearers.

Nathan during the early hours of the state's attorney's interrogation, May 29, 1924. Less than thirty hours later, he would confess to killing Bobby Franks.

Richard during the early hours of the state's attorney's interrogation. He would be the first to confess to the murder.

purchased the hydrochloric acid, however, the druggist did remember him. Who could forget such an unusual order?

The procession drove past the lot on Drexel Boulevard where the teenagers had watched the group of boys playing baseball, then stopped at the Leopold house to pick up the hip boots Nathan had worn while shoving the body into the culvert.

At Jackson Park, Nathan pointed out the places where Richard had dumped the typewriter keys and then the machine. Detective Hughes immediately called for divers to search the lagoon. It would take them six days to find the battered Underwood in the murky depths.

The car carrying Nathan continued along South Shore Drive. When it neared the secluded spot where he and Richard had burned the robe, he piped up. "Pull in here. . . ." He pointed to a pile of ashes.

Police sifted through them. They found a remnant of the robe. It was bloodstained.

And from then on, Nathan told them whatever they wanted to know.

"I knew, I suppose, that [the police] were building their case," he later explained about that day. "Making it absolutely airtight. But it struck me as a waste of effort. The harm—all that could possibly be done—had already been done. We had admitted our guilt. . . . What did it matter how many witnesses [the police] did or did not assemble? I didn't think ahead to a possible trial. I didn't consider the possibility of there being more than one punishment. We had confessed; we would be hanged."

Reporters, however, had a different take on Nathan's chatter. It was about "egotism and precocity," declared Orville Dwyer in the *Chicago Daily Tribune*. Nathan Leopold liked showing off.

Next the group headed east into Indiana, looking for the place where the killers had left Bobby's shoes. It took a while—Nathan had forgotten the exact location—but finally he shouted, "Stop here!"

He climbed out of the car and walked along the side of the road, kicking at underbrush, finding nothing. He and the detective continued searching. But the weather had turned cold and gray. Rain threatened. It was decided to take Nathan to the hotel, too.

They had one last stop—the Hyde Park police station. One of the detectives there held out an object. Could Nathan identify it?

He nodded. It was the chisel Richard had used to bash in Bobby's head. It still had the adhesive tape wrapped around its blade and was stained with blood. He wondered how they'd found it.

A night watchman had seen it thrown from the car, a police officer explained. He'd picked it up, noticed the blood, and turned it in.

Some master criminal Richard was, Nathan must have thought.

Later, as the killers slept in separate rooms at the Hotel Windermere, a suitcase that had been packed by one of the Leopolds' servants and delivered to the state's attorney's office was brought over by a police officer. It contained a pair of silk pajamas and a change of clothes for each teen. Mike Leopold had also included a deck of cards, magazines, and some candy for his kid brother. It was, noted one police officer, like the care package sent to a kid who is away at camp.

At one a.m. police rousted the pair out of their comfortable beds. It was time to move again, this time to the Wabash Avenue police station near the Loop, where they would remain in separate cells until daylight.

© © ©

The boys' confessions made the front pages in New York and California and dozens of places in between. Some newspapers, like the *Washington Post* and the *New York Times,* sent their own top reporters to Chicago. "The case is one of the most remarkable ever to win the interest of an eager public," claimed the *Post*'s editor. It was too juicy a story to rely on secondhand reports. Out-of-town reporters, like their Chicago counterparts, led with the lurid and sensational, as this lengthy headline published on the front page of the *New York Times* on June 1 proves:

TWO RICH STUDENTS CONFESS TO KILLING FRANKS BOY IN CAR

SONS OF WEALTHY CHICAGOANS HIT HIM WITH A CHISEL AND THEN GAGGED HIM.

THEN DISPOSED OF BODY

YOUTH'S CLOTHING, WHICH THEY STRIPPED FROM HIM, BURNED IN HOME OF ONE SLAYER.

LONG PLANNED SUCH CRIME

ONCE THOUGHT TO KIDNAP ROSENWALD'S GRANDSON— CHAUFFEUR UPSET THEIR ALIBI.

It seemed everyone, everywhere, wanted to know about the murder.

CHAPTER FIFTEEN

"IMPALING A BEETLE ON A PIN"

Late that same Saturday, in an apartment building on Chicago's South Side, a doorbell rang. Ruby Darrow woke with a start. Who could be at the door at this hour? She glanced over at her still-sleeping husband, Clarence.

The bell rang again.

With a sigh, Ruby climbed out of bed, pulled on her robe, and moved sleepily down the hall. She knew it would be legal business.

When she opened the door, she found four men on the threshold. Ruby recognized one of them, Jacob Loeb. He was the former president of the Chicago Board of Education. He was also, she knew from the newspapers, the uncle of one of the teenage murderers.

Loeb pushed past her into the apartment. "We've got to see Clarence Darrow. Is he here?"

Ruby nodded. But he was sleeping. He couldn't be disturbed.

Loeb ignored her. He charged down the hall to the Darrows' bedroom and barged in.

Darrow sat up in bed. The rumpled sixty-seven-year-old lawyer ran a gnarled hand over his face as Loeb dropped to his knees beside him. "You must save our two boys," he pleaded. "Get them a life sentence instead of death. That's all we ask. . . . We'll pay anything, only for God's sake, don't let them hang."

Why did Jacob Loeb, as well as the Leopold family, want Darrow to represent *both* teens, rather than hiring two separate lawyers?

Since the pair had committed the crime together, they would be tried together. That was Illinois law. In addition, it made no legal difference who had killed Bobby Franks. Intent to kill—to which Nathan and Richard had both admitted—carried the same maximum penalty: death. Both could be hanged if found guilty. This left the families with just one practical option: hire the very best criminal attorney to defend *both* their sons. And Clarence Darrow was the best.

Throughout the 1910s and into the early 1920s, Darrow had defended a hundred people who were facing the death penalty. He'd saved all of them from the gallows. His clients came from every part of society—Black, white, working class, and upper class. Just five years earlier, he'd gotten Emma Simpson, a wealthy socialite charged with first-degree murder for shooting her husband, off on a plea of insanity. Simpson had spent six weeks in a psychiatric hospital before being allowed to resume her life in Chicago. Jacob Loeb must have hoped Darrow would do the same for Nathan and Richard.

But Darrow hesitated. He ran his hand over his face again, thinking. He wanted both to help *and* to stay out of it. The crime had been shocking, and the public and the press were already against the teenagers. Keeping them from the gallows would, he knew, be a tough fight. And he was "very weary," he later recalled. "I had grown tired of standing in the lean and lonely front line facing down the greatest enemy that ever confronted man—public opinion."

While Darrow often defended the rich and well positioned, his sympathies lay with the poor and oppressed. In his lengthy legal career, he'd defended union leaders against the federal government and had traveled across the country fighting for the voiceless. He was a master orator, a ruthless cross-examiner, and a brilliant strategist. He almost never took notes during a case—and he never forgot a fact. And despite his reputation, his opponents often underestimated him. Seeing the rumpled, homespun Darrow "drawl before a jury box is a notable scene," wrote Chicago journalist Ben Hecht, "the great barrister artfully gotten up in baggy pants, frayed linen, and a string tie, and 'playing dumb' for a jury as if he were not a lawyer at all, but a cracker-barrel philosopher groping for a bit of human truth."

Darrow possessed a deep compassion for those who faced loss, despair, or persecution. "Not only could I put myself in one's place," he wrote in his autobiography, "I could not avoid doing so."

This compassion seeped into his law practice. Every day, the bench outside his office would be filled by "men in overalls, their arms in slings; by women huddled in shawls and threadbare clothes, wan-faced, waiting for Darrow," recalled a friend. Darrow would step out of his office at day's end, see the long line, sigh, and offer an understanding smile. While his dinner grew cold at home, he would invite these people in, one by one, to hear their cases and offer advice. He never asked for a dime. He once estimated that a third of his cases were pro bono.

Above all, he hated capital punishment. He claimed that the death penalty was "the State laying its bloody hand upon some poor forlorn individual who it had earlier betrayed by neglect and oppression." And so his most ardent and strenuous fights were against what he saw as a barbarous practice, cruel and utterly useless in deterring crime. In his autobiography, he wrote, "No client of mine had ever been put to death, and I felt that it would almost, if not quite, kill me if it should ever happen."

For this reason, Clarence Darrow slowly nodded at Jacob Loeb. He would defend the teenagers, "to do what I could for sanity and humanity against the wave of hatred and malice, that, as ever, was masquerading under its usual nom de plume: 'Justice.'"

⊙ ⊙ ⊙

It was Sunday, June 1, and State's Attorney Crowe had another full day planned for the killers. After changing into their fresh and fashionable Brooks Brothers suits, the teenagers were once again hustled into separate police cars.

Crowe invited a handful of reporters to ride along with Richard and Nathan. This was not surprising. As usual, it was tit for tat. Reporters would promise to write favorably about the Chicago police and their ongoing battle against crime. In return, they were given access to prisoners. The practice provided the newspapers with titillating tidbits and inside scoops that increased readership, while the police department's less-than-stellar reputation was boosted by good press.

Today, however, Crowe wanted more than good press; he saw the reporters as an insurance policy. He'd already heard that the families had hired Clarence Darrow, and if anyone could get the confessions declared inadmissible in court, it was Darrow. But what if the teenagers told reporters something incriminating and they wrote about it? Then it would be harder for the young men to deny guilt in court.

The procession's first stop was Daley's Restaurant for breakfast.

Nathan and Richard were seated at the same table. They angrily refused to utter a word to each other.

Sulky and irritable, Richard glared at his partner in crime. His meal grew cold.

Nathan ignored him. He joked with the police, flirted with the waitress, and ordered a second helping of scrambled eggs. He gulped down a jelly doughnut and a second cup of coffee, too, before they finally returned to the cars.

In Nathan's car, Wallace Sullivan, a reporter from the *Chicago Herald and Examiner,* asked him about the murder. Whose idea was it, his or Loeb's?

Nathan, who was chain-smoking in the backseat, grew angry at his friend's name. "It was all Loeb's idea," he declared. "Loeb . . . enticed the boy into the car and it was Loeb who struck him on the head. . . . I could not—I would not have been physically able to strike the blow. . . . Loeb knew this, too. . . . My repugnance to violence is such that I could not have killed [Bobby]. . . . He thinks that by proving me the slayer he will eventually be free."

Then Nathan's dark mood passed as quickly as it had come. Pointing out the window at the South Shore Country Club, he said disdainfully, "Aren't golf players nuts?"

Asked what he thought of the ransom note, Nathan turned boastful. "It was concise and well-phrased. It instilled terror. And it certainly impelled action."

He bragged about the preparation for the crime, too. "We even rehearsed the kidnapping . . . carrying it through in all details, lacking only the boy we were to kill."

Then he looked at James Doherty, the *Chicago Daily Tribune* reporter. "It was just an experiment. It is as easy for us to justify as an entomologist in impaling a beetle on a pin."

In case that hadn't shocked the reporters, he added, "Making up my mind whether or not to commit murder was about the same as making up my mind whether or not to have pie for dinner."

The car came to a stop. They were back on that Indiana road where the teenagers had left some of Bobby's clothes. Detectives had found the boy's shoes the day before, not long after Nathan had left.

The car carrying Richard pulled up behind them. Richard climbed out, took a rake from a police officer, and began dragging its prongs through the sandy soil. He soon turned up Bobby's blue-and-white belt. Nearby, police found its gold buckle, as well as the murdered boy's class pin.

When it was time to move on, Wallace Sullivan climbed into Richard's car.

"Nathan said you killed Bobby Franks," said Sullivan. "Is it true?"

"No," snapped Richard. He didn't say another word.

Miles passed.

At last, Richard began to speak again. "This thing will be the making of me. I'll spend a few years in jail and I'll be released. I'll come out to a new life. I'll go to work and I'll work hard and I'll amount to something, have a career."

Police Captain William Shoemaker corrected him. The state's attorney wanted both teenagers hanged. Surely he knew that.

Richard shrugged. He knew. He fell silent again.

How did he feel about the crime? asked another reporter.

It didn't bother him, Richard replied. "I could have carried the secret in my mind the rest of my life. It didn't bother me much. A thought or two at times. That's all."

Had Richard been dominated by Nathan? Had Nathan made Richard do it?

"Well, I wouldn't say that," Richard said slyly. "Of course, he's smart. He's one of the smartest and best-educated men I know. Perhaps he did dominate me . . . maybe I just followed along."

◉ ◉ ◉

Later that day, Chicagoans devoured the evening editions of the newspapers along with their dinners. They learned from the *Chicago Daily News* that Nathan Leopold was having "an 'experience' that seems to bring him no regret, worry or alarm." To him, Bobby Franks's murder was a "marvelous opportunity to study his own reactions. And with a sense of detachment, he watches—as a scientist might—his own lack of emotion."

They learned from the *Chicago Herald and Examiner* that Leopold was "undoubtedly the brains of the combination." His knowledge and intelligence simply "swept the other boy along."

Other newspapers painted Nathan as a "detached, philosophical killer." They reported on his atheism and his "intellectual anarchism." They detailed his belief in Nietzsche's theory of the superman, and how he saw himself as above society's laws and traditional moral concepts. In their narrative, Richard Loeb became a thrill-seeking follower who'd fallen for Nathan's delusions of superiority. Nathan became the manipulative monster who had managed the whole crime. "A thirst for knowledge is highly commendable," Nathan was quoted as saying, "no matter what extreme pain or injury it may inflict on others. A six-year-old boy is justified in pulling the wings off a fly, if by doing so he learns that without wings the fly is helpless."

Chicagoans were both repulsed and fascinated by the murderers. They wanted to know more. They wanted to know everything.

Newspaper sales spiked, and special editions were rushed into print if any especially riveting disclosures emerged. The *Chicago Herald and Examiner* ran as many as eight articles a day on the murder. And all six papers began adding special photograph sections that included pictures of *everything*—the culvert where the body was found, the charred remains of the automobile robe, the Dew Drop Inn, where the murderers bought hot dogs. A map even appeared of the route the killers took on the day of the crime. Hundreds of Chicagoans drove it for themselves.

❂   ❂   ❂

While the teenagers were out driving around with the police and press, Clarence Darrow arrived at Crowe's office. With him came Jacob Loeb, as well as the Leopold family attorney, Benjamin Bachrach. Tidy and trim, dressed in an expensive suit and silk tie, Bachrach presented a startling contrast to Darrow's uncombed hair and wrinkled seersucker jacket. Bachrach, too, was a celebrated criminal attorney. But unlike Darrow, his client list was a who's who of Chicago's rich, powerful, and famous. Over the years, Bachrach had successfully defended politicians and professional athletes, socialites and CEOs, against charges of embezzlement, arson, murder, conspiracy, and more. He had expected to act as Nathan's lawyer. But after the teenager confessed, Bachrach realized he needed more legal firepower and happily joined forces with Darrow.

The lawyers demanded to see the teenagers.

Crowe told them the boys weren't there. And no, they would not be allowed to see the boys when they returned to the Criminal Courts Building.

Darrow protested. His clients had the right to an attorney.

But Crowe had the upper hand. It was Sunday. The courts weren't open. It would be impossible for Darrow to find a judge who would compel the state's attorney to hand over the accused. Crowe had the pair to himself for a few more hours. And he intended to use that time wisely.

＊ ＊ ＊

Midafternoon, the police cars returned to the Criminal Courts Building, where Crowe had another surprise waiting for Nathan and Richard. Upstairs in his office were three psychiatrists: Dr. William Krohn, author of a highly regarded textbook on mental diseases; Dr. Hugh Patrick, professor of nervous and mental diseases at Northwestern University Medical School; and Dr. Archibald Church, head of the department of nervous and mental diseases at Northwestern University. Crowe expected Darrow to attempt to get his clients off by pleading insanity. So he'd decided to beat Darrow to the punch by rounding up the city's foremost "alienists," as authorities on mental illness were sometimes called back then. Crowe felt confident that after an examination, these alienists would find the teenagers completely sane.

It was a good bet. All three were "traditionalists." They believed that disorders of the nervous system and mental diseases were mostly hereditary and signs of degeneracy. And the medical standard for insanity was the same as Illinois's legal standard—simply: Did the accused know the difference between right and wrong at the time of the act? If he did, he was sane.

Crowe had Nathan and Richard brought into his office. The room was crowded—not only were the three doctors present, but so were his assistants and several detectives. The psychiatrists got right to it. They wanted to hear how the teenagers had committed the crime.

Each repeated what he'd said in his confession.

Nathan added that Richard had always been the natural leader.

Richard smiled. "Well, I'll leave it to you gentlemen to decide who has the brightest mind here," he said smoothly. "I'll leave it to you to judge who has the dominating mind."

Nathan scowled at Richard's manipulative charm.

Dr. Church addressed Nathan. "When you made this plan to do the killing you understood perfectly your responsibilities in the matter."

"Yes," agreed Nathan.

"And you knew about the legal consequences of criminal acts like kidnapping and murder?"

Nathan nodded. "Yes."

The former law student must have known that everything he said would be used against him in court. But he must not have thought it mattered. "What could a lawyer do now?" he would later say. "A lawyer couldn't make [the facts] unhappen. . . . I just didn't think any further on it."

Richard told the doctors he knew the difference between right and wrong. Yes, he knew he'd done wrong in kidnapping and killing Bobby Franks. And yes, he understood the consequences of those actions.

"Was there a moment when [you] considered abandoning the idea, or giving up on committing the crime?" asked Dr. Krohn.

"No," replied Richard. "[I] do not want to be called a quitter."

Krohn pushed harder. Could Richard have stopped himself from doing it, or had it been an undeniable compulsion?

Sure, he could have stopped, replied Richard. He simply didn't want to.

Dr. Patrick jumped in with a question. What was their reason? If they knew right from wrong, understood the consequences, and had the self-control to stop themselves, then why had they done it?

"I don't know," said Richard.

But Nathan had an answer. "The thing that prompted [us] to do this thing . . . was sort of pure love of excitement . . . doing something different. . . . The money consideration only came afterwards, and never was important. The getting of the money was a part of the objective, as was also the commission of the crime; but that was not the exact motive. [The ransom] came afterwards."

Crowe asked a question. "You wouldn't take ten thousand dollars out of my pocket if I had it?"

"It depends on whether I thought I could get away with it," said Nathan. He lit a cigarette and leaned back in his chair.

◉　◉　◉

Later that evening, alone in his office, Robert Crowe went over the case. He had the confessions. He had evidence and witnesses corroborating those confessions. And he now had consensus from the psychiatrists: Neither teen showed the slightest signs of mental illness. They were self-possessed, coherent, rational, and lucid. They'd planned the crime for months, meticulously, thus ruling out temporary insanity. It seemed impossible that the teenagers would escape the gallows. The evidence was overwhelming.

Still, one thing nagged at the state's attorney: motive. Crowe knew that if the case went to trial, he would need a more solid reason for the crime than thrills and excitement. A jury might not understand that.

But they *would* understand killing for financial gain. Crowe went back through the confessions. The teens had intended to split the ransom money. They'd also agreed not to spend any of it for a year, and not in Chicago. Nathan had considered going to Hawaii with his half; Richard had planned to hold on to his share so he could "have something [incriminating]" on Nathan.

Crowe thought for a while. Yes, that was it. If this case went to trial, he would focus on the ransom as the crime's motive. The ransom . . . and maybe something darker.

◎ ◎ ◎

The sun was setting by the time the police escorted the teenagers out into the courtyard of the Criminal Courts Building. Nathan waved to the crush of reporters and photographers before walking over to a blue Willys-Knight parked on the cobbled pavement. Was this the car the pair had rented for the kidnapping?

Richard said he couldn't be sure.

But Nathan bent down to examine the passenger side. "Yes, this is the car," he said. "I know it by the scratches on the front door."

Reporters begged the teenagers to get in.

Good-naturedly, Nathan climbed in behind the steering wheel.

But Richard refused to slide into the passenger seat. "Not with him."

A camera flashbulb popped, and Richard stumbled backward.

"Poor fellow, he's weak," said Nathan contemptuously. He smiled for the cameras.

Later, the teenagers were taken to separate restaurants for dinner.

At the Golden Diner, Richard picked at his food. He seemed preoccupied and worried.

Meanwhile, blocks away at the Weiss Restaurant, Nathan ordered the house specialty—herring—then regaled his police escorts with a long list of unusual foods he'd tried over the years. "I presume you've never eaten seaweed or bamboo shoots," he said. "You evidently haven't been to Hawaii."

At a nearby table, a woman pointed at him, then whispered in her husband's ear. They both turned and stared.

Nathan got up and walked over to their table. "I beg your pardon, madam, but I'm not Nathan Leopold. I've been embarrassed several times today by being mistaken for him." Smiling innocently at the startled couple, he returned to his herring.

One of the police officers elbowed the other. "How'd you like to be able to lie like that?"

CHAPTER SIXTEEN

DARROW FOR THE DEFENSE

On Monday, June 2, Clarence Darrow finally got access to his clients. It hadn't been easy. Crowe had wanted more time for his psychiatrists to examine the teenagers further. But Judge John Caverly had refused him. After reminding Crowe of the boys' legal rights, he ordered the state's attorney to relinquish control of them. He then remanded them to Cook County Jail, where both their attorneys and their families would be able to visit them.

There was no question of the teens' being released on bail. Illinois law denied bail for defendants charged with offenses punishable by life imprisonment or execution. It also denied bail for those who were obviously guilty (as evidenced here by their confessions).

Caverly's decision disappointed Crowe, but he consoled himself with the fact that he'd gotten what he most wanted from the teenagers. He'd gotten them to talk . . . and talk . . . and talk.

Now it was Clarence Darrow's turn.

He met with Nathan and Richard together in the lockup room of the Criminal Courts Building. Darrow had on a suit jacket that looked as if he'd slept in it. His wrinkled shirt wore egg stains from his breakfast, and his hair was a bird's nest; one especially unruly lock kept falling over his right eye.

Nathan could not believe that *this* was the famous Clarence Darrow. "Could this scarecrow know anything about the law?" he later recalled thinking. "He didn't look as if he knew much of anything."

Their first meeting was brief, but Darrow's advice was firm. "Be polite. Be courteous. But don't give Crowe any more help. Just keep quiet and refuse to answer questions."

They understood. When the jail clerk, who was filling out their inmate forms, asked Nathan to list his religion, the teen replied, "We cannot talk without advice of counsel."

⚬ ⚬ ⚬

A smell permeated Cook County Jail—an institutional smell, old and irretrievably unclean. As Nathan's jailer escorted him to the sixth floor (the sixth and seventh floors were where prisoners under the age of twenty-one were held), he could hear the shouting, coughing, and low conversation of those locked up in the rows of small cages. Nathan stepped into cell 604 for the first time. Its back wall and floor were made of granite, its door of iron grating. Two cots hung from the walls like bunks, filling half of the ten-by-five-foot space. On each cot were a mattress made of straw, a blanket, a sheet, and a towel. At the back end stood a toilet, as well as a small washbasin with running water. (The showers, Nathan would learn, were on the first floor next to the guardroom.) There was no place to hang or stow belongings. He would have to make do with stacking items on the floor. There was no lamp, either. The only light came from a barred window high up near the cell's ceiling, or from the single electric bulb hanging just outside the cell. Nathan would be forced to sit close to the grating to read by it.

This cell would be his living room, dining room, and bedroom until his trial ended. How long would that be? He glanced over at his cellmate, twenty-year-old Thomas Doherty, who was charged with extortion. Nathan didn't say a word to him. Instead, he sat on the edge of his cot. "Waiting," he later remembered thinking, "for . . . what?"

Meanwhile, Richard was led to cell 717 on the seventh floor. It was identical to Nathan's. As his jailer rattled the door's lock, Loeb bit his lower lip. After stepping inside, he looked around. "It could be worse," he said. He offered a cigarette to his cellmate, accused robber Edward Donker.

Around five p.m., a jail attendant arrived at Nathan's cell with a covered and soggy cardboard plate. Nathan peeked beneath the lid. It was some sort of meat, potatoes, and vegetables all mixed together. This couldn't be dinner. It was entirely too early. The teen wasn't accustomed to dining before seven or eight p.m. Besides, he'd only been given a spoon to eat with. He set the plate on the cot and waited for the rest of the silverware. Minutes passed before it dawned on him: the spoon was it. Nathan felt revolted, not only by the meal but also by the unmannerly way he was expected to eat it. He refused to sink that low. Instead, he gave his food to his cellmate, who gobbled it down gratefully.

A few hours later, the attendant reappeared. He had a far more appetizing dinner for Nathan, and he had one for Richard, too. Sent by their parents from a nearby restaurant, these meals would continue to arrive three times a day for the duration of their sons' stay in the Cook County Jail.

That first night behind bars, Nathan—filled up with a tasty

meal—fell asleep early. But Richard read the newspapers until al-most midnight. He reveled in every word written about him, and the fact that he was, indeed, a famous criminal.

◉ ◉ ◉

On Thursday, June 5, just two weeks after the discovery of Bobby Franks's body, a grand jury of the Criminal Court of Cook County voted to indict Nathan and Richard for kidnapping and murder. Now that they'd been officially charged with the crimes, they could be brought to trial. Neither Nathan nor Richard attended these pro-ceedings. Illinois law did not require it.

◉ ◉ ◉

As the wheels of justice turned, the teenagers adjusted to life in Cook County Jail. Always comfortable in social situations, Richard mingled easily with the other inmates. He played baseball with them in the prison yard, shared his cigarettes and his newspapers. He started using their lingo, talking about how he might "get the rope" or "get the street." And even though he loved fashionable, well-tailored clothing, he wore his gray prison uniform proudly. It made him "one of the boys." In many ways, Richard liked prison. For years he had "picturalized" about being in jail, beaten and stared at by strangers because he was a famous criminal. His real-life incarcera-tion felt like the fulfillment of that fantasy.

Nathan, on the other hand, acted disdainful toward the other in-mates. He kept his distance and spoke to no one in the prison yard. Grumbled one inmate, "He better lay off the ritzsie stuff . . . or he'll find himself in a hell of a situation."

Each teenager blamed the other for their predicament.

If only Nathan hadn't used the alibi.

If only Richard hadn't confessed.

But as the days in jail passed, they found it hard to stay mad at each other.

"What the hell's the use?" Richard said to Nathan one day in the prison yard. "We're both in for the same ride so we might as well ride together, Babe."

"Yes, Dickie," replied Nathan, "we have quarreled before and made up. Now, when we are standing at the home stretch of the greatest gauntlet we will ever have to run, it is right we should go along together." He stuck out his hand. "Shake."

And just like that, they were friends again.

⊙ ⊚ ⊙

On June 6, newspapers printed the teenagers' confessions in full. Readers were shocked and horrified. But above all, they were bewildered. Why had the boys done it? The public seemed unable to accept Nathan's explanation that it had been done for "a pure love of excitement." There had to be something more.

In churches across the city that following Sunday, June 8, preachers blamed Nathan's atheism, as well as his college education. The Reverend Alva Vest King of the Roseland Presbyterian Church told his congregation that the "only cure for youthful crime and bobbed hair is the thorough training of the children in the principles of Christian religion."

And the Reverend Simon Long of the Wicker Park Lutheran Church preached the saving grace of the death penalty from his pulpit. "Capital punishment is God's last act of love to save man from eternal punishment."

The *Chicago Sunday Tribune* reprinted an article by Dr. S. M. Melamed that had originally been published in the *Daily Jewish Courier,* a Yiddish-language newspaper that was the voice of Orthodox Jewry. In it, Melamed lambasted the killers' families for abandoning Jewish values. "If the parents of these two had given the children a Jewish education . . . if they had interested them in Jewish problems . . . if they had been consciously Jewish with Jewish souls, they would certainly not have devoted their entire time to pleasure and good times," Melamed wrote. He also blamed the families' wealth. "I always feared for the rich Jews who had no Jewish ideals."

Unfortunately, these comments fed into a common antisemitic trope that went back generations. During the 1920s, many non-Jews perceived moneymaking as the immigrant Jew's way of accumulating power and prestige at the expense of Christians. The public became preoccupied with the extraordinary wealth of the Leopolds and Loebs. In article after article, the press trumpeted the teenagers as being the sons of "Jewish mercantile millionaires."

That same Sunday, the *Tribune* ran two articles, side by side, tracing the genealogy of the Leopolds' and Loebs' "two Jewish fortunes," and noting that they had a combined wealth of $15 million (approximately $245 million nowadays). The articles listed the German Jewish forebears of both families, along with their intermarriages with other rich Chicago Jewish families. Reporters concluded that the city's wealthy Jews formed a mysterious and elite clan and asserted that Nathan was "related to every branch of a little royalty of wealth which Chicago has long recognized." The article's meaning was clear. These rich, connected families formed a type of "Jewish Mafia."

Antisemitic articles like these were commonplace, and they inflamed the public. Many people became convinced that the families would flex their wealth and "Mafia" ties to get their sons off. Rumor spread that they planned to buy off witnesses and bribe the judge. It was also rumored that they would mount a million-dollar defense. Wasn't that why they'd hired the famed Clarence Darrow? Under a banner headline that trumpeted "Millions to Defend Killers," the *Chicago Daily Tribune* quoted the state's attorney: "The fathers of these boys have an estimated combined fortune of $15 million and we suppose it will be millions versus the death penalty."

The suspicion that "Jewish wealth and influence" would be used to free Nathan and Richard was a point of heated debate being waged in Chicago and across the country. "Can a rich man be convicted?" asked *Forum* magazine in an article with the same title.

Many Americans thought not, with good reason. A look at the records of those convicted of murder and sentenced to death in Cook County between the years 1870 and 1930 shows that in Chicago, at least, death row was a destination for the poor. Ninety-eight men received the death penalty in that time. In seventy-two of the cases, their employment was listed as "outside [the] labor force," "unskilled laborer," or "factory worker." Obviously, these were not men of economic means. Only one offender was listed as a professional, a doctor found guilty of criminal abortion. He managed to save himself from the gallows, however, by using his wealth to push his death penalty conviction all the way to the Illinois Supreme Court, where his charge was reduced to manslaughter. He then appealed the manslaughter charge, ultimately reducing his sentence to time served—five years.

And then there was the 1922 case of Walter Krauser and Bernard Grant.

On a cold December morning, just seventeen months before the murder of Bobby Franks, Krauser and Grant—who were living in a festering slum behind Chicago's stockyards—held up an A&P grocery store on Halsted Street.

Krauser, almost nineteen at the time, already had a long police record of petty thefts and break-ins. He waved his gun in the store manager's face while seventeen-year-old Grant rifled through the cash drawer. Neither teen planned to shoot anyone, but simply to grab the money and run. They didn't know that Ralph Souders, an off-duty police officer who was moonlighting as store security, was in the back room. Hearing the commotion, Souders raced to the front of the store, lunged at Krauser, and grabbed for the gun. In the ensuing struggle, the weapon went off. Souders was killed, and the teenagers fled. Hours later, police picked up the pair after the store manager identified Krauser from mug shots. By nightfall, both had confessed.

They were charged with first-degree murder. Too poor to hire an attorney, they were forced to make do with a court-appointed one. In those days, there was no public defender's office, and their lawyer—eager to end the trial so he could collect his small fee as quickly as possible—barely defended them. A jury found both teens guilty and sentenced them to hang. They currently sat on death row.

The *Chicago Sunday Tribune* reminded its readers that Grant and Krauser "had no means to make a spectacular fight; no fancy lawyers to help them escape the [death] penalty; and no social position with which to impress the court." Without wealth and influence, they'd never stood a chance.

The innuendo and accusations eventually drove the Leopold and Loeb families to issue a joint statement. They assured the public that "in no event will the families of the accused boys use money in an attempt to defeat justice."

While the statement helped calm public concern, it wasn't entirely true. By hiring Darrow, the families *were* mounting an extraordinary defense, one the average American could never afford. The legal bills for medical examinations and expert testimony, not to mention Darrow's fee of $30,000 (there was no reason for him to work pro bono this time), would eventually come to over $100,000 (about $1.5 million nowadays).

Crowe stirred the pot of public opinion another way, too—by providing a scandalous secondary motive he'd concocted for the crime. Nathan, he claimed, wanted the ransom money to indulge in his homosexual lusts. "If [I] had not fastened the crime on these two defendants," Crowe told reporters, "Nathan Leopold would be in Paris or some other of the gay capitals in Europe, indulging his unnatural lust with the $5,000 he had wrung from Jacob Franks."

Assistant prosecuting attorneys told reporters that along with the hard evidence, "there was the suspicion that . . . Leopold was a profound student of perversion."

Perversion was a word associated with homosexuality at the time. And the message was clear: homosexuality was a crime against nature—one that naturally led to committing further crimes against humanity.

Richard was spared, however. The state's attorney hadn't hinted that he was homosexual—perhaps because Richard's mother was Catholic.

Now the press scurried down new paths of investigation. They published articles with titles like "Weeping Girls Mourn Plight of Richard Loeb." The *Chicago Daily Tribune* told readers, "It is an easy thing to locate girls who knew Dickie, but girls who were fond of Nathan Leopold . . . are not so easy to find."

Richard collaborated in the characterization of his best friend as the true homosexual. In front of reporters, he flaunted his attractiveness to females. "Girls?" he told them. "Sure, I like girls. I was out with a girl on Friday night after the [murder] and with another one on Sunday night."

The *Chicago Herald and Examiner* called in a physiognomist—a pseudoscientist who claimed he could determine a person's mental traits simply by "reading" his or her face. After studying photographs of the accused teenagers, the physiognomist concluded: "Nathan with his brooding Semitic looks, large nose, hooded eyes and sensual lips mesmerized the less intellectual, more socially popular, better-looking Loeb—an all-American type and fraternity man whose mother was not born Jewish."

⊙ ⊙ ⊙

HYPNOTISM MAY PLAY ROLE IN LOEB DEFENSE

Two university students whose names are withheld, told of Leopold . . . demonstrating his skill in hypnotism and the power of suggestion . . . and in one instance put a student under his influence and caused him to drink some unpleasant tasting fluid, one thought it was soap suds, the other remembered it as castor oil; the subject believed it wine. Leopold also used his tricks of hypnotism as aids in his hobby of studying birds, his classmates said, and he was able to fascinate birds, compelling them through his will and wiles to remain still as he made his observation. This fact might figure importantly in the defense, Loeb setting forth that he was in a state of complete suggestion, acting automatically at the command of Leopold.

(From the *Chicago Daily Tribune,* June 10, 1924, page 1)

Newspapers painted Nathan as perverted, ungodly, cold-blooded, manipulative, and Jewish. He had coerced Richard into homosexual and criminal acts through his mesmeric powers.

Surely *this* explained why the teenagers had committed such a terrible crime.

◉ ◉ ◉

It was just one hundred steps from the Loebs' front gate to the Frankses' circular driveway. But to Anna Loeb it must have felt like a hundred miles. What could she say? And yet she felt compelled to go see Flora Franks. They were friends. They were neighbors. And because Albert Loeb was Flora's cousin, they were family, too.

Three times Anna made the journey.

Three times she steeled herself for Flora's anger and accusations.

Three times she struggled to keep her own grief in check.

Twice the Frankses' maid turned her away. Flora could not, or would not, see her.

But the third time, at last, Anna was admitted into the living room.

Flora looked like a gray ghost, hovering by the window.

What Anna said went unrecorded. But she must have spoken from her own broken heart.

When she had finished, Flora stared at her in confusion. "But I'm sure Bobby will be coming back pretty soon," she said.

It seemed that Flora did not grasp the truth, that her son was dead.

But Anna did. Neither of their sons was ever coming back.

CHAPTER SEVENTEEN

SEARCHING FOR INSANITY

June 11 was a red-letter day for the teenagers. It was Richard's nineteenth birthday. It was the day Nathan would have sailed for Europe. And it was both boys' first appearance in court. Today was their arraignment. They would enter their pleas—guilty or not guilty.

The idea of being the center of so much attention excited Richard. He wanted to radiate the good looks and charm of a master criminal. And so he carefully slicked back his hair with pomade and dressed in a brand-new suit and tie. Did he look handsome? he asked the guard.

In his cell one floor below, Nathan also paid close attention to his appearance. He didn't care about photographers so much as showing the world he was an ordinary guy. He'd read what newspapers had been writing about him. "I've been pictured in the public mind as the Svengali, the man with the hypnotic eye, the mastermind and the brains," he would complain. "I've been made out to be the man who schemed, planned and executed the thing. I've been described as the devil incarnate. But [Richard] on the other hand, seems to have won the sympathy of the public." Today, he hoped to win some of that sympathy back.

As usual, Clarence Darrow didn't seem to care how he looked. He arrived in the courtroom wearing a rumpled shirt and a crooked tie. Benjamin Bachrach, well dressed as usual, was already at the defense table. Beside him sat his younger brother, Walter, a recent addition to the defense team. All three lawyers shuffled papers and waited for their clients to be brought across the walkway from the county jail.

Others waited, too. Robert Crowe and his assistants—Joseph Savage, John Sbarbaro, Thomas Marshall, and Milton Smith—sat at the prosecution table.

At the bench, Judge Caverly poured himself a glass of water.

Two rows behind the defense table sat Nathan Sr., looking confused. He repeatedly cupped his ear because he couldn't hear. When reporters asked him for a comment, he muttered, "Why come to me? What did I do? Why come to me?"

Neither of Richard's parents sat in the courtroom. They'd chosen to isolate themselves at their estate in Charlevoix, and had asked Jacob Loeb to take their place in court. He settled beside Nathan Sr.

Just feet away from these two men sat Jacob Franks. Crowe had told Franks he didn't need to come to court that morning. No evidence would be given, no witnesses heard. But Franks refused to miss a moment of the proceedings. He felt he had to represent his son. It was a father's duty.

And then there were the spectators, packed into every available space.

The women sat on the right side of the courtroom, the men on the left. Leaning against the walls and filling the jury box were dozens of reporters, notebooks at the ready, while behind the judge's bench dozens of photographers formed a solid line.

Judge Caverly motioned for the clerk to open the door to the walkway. A gasp ran through the courtroom as the teenagers entered. Handcuffed and flanked by deputy sheriffs, they appeared poised even as the flash of many cameras momentarily blinded them. Then their guards pulled them down the aisle to the judge's bench. Darrow joined them there.

The clerk read the indictments. Judge Caverly looked down at them. How did each youth plead to the charge of kidnapping? Guilty or not guilty?

Richard spoke first. "Not guilty, sir."

"Not guilty," said Nathan.

And to the charge of murder?

Again, they both pleaded not guilty.

At the prosecutor's table, Robert Crowe jutted out his chin. Pleas of not guilty could mean just one thing: Darrow planned to mount an insanity defense. But the state's attorney doubted it would work. He stood and asked that the proceedings begin on July 15.

Bachrach countered. That was a little more than a month away. The defense needed more time.

The judge granted them two additional weeks. He set the trial date for August 4.

Next he addressed when he would hear motions—issues that the judge would rule on ahead of time. A motion, which both the prosecution and the defense could present, might keep certain evidence out of the trial, or disallow certain people from testifying, or dismiss a charge altogether. These motions would set the boundaries for the trial before it began. They were important, and could profoundly change the course of the trial.

Caverly looked down at his calendar, silently counting out the days while the attorneys waited. At last, he ordered all the parties to return to court on July 21. "All motions will be heard and decided upon that day," he said. He banged his gavel. Court was adjourned.

As the crowd filed out, Darrow pulled aside Walter Bachrach. Darrow had an important and secret errand for the lawyer. The American Psychiatric Association's annual meeting was taking place in Atlantic City, New Jersey, the following week. He wanted Bachrach to travel there and persuade some "new-school" psychiatrists to examine Nathan and Richard.

What did Darrow mean by *new-school*?

Less than twenty years earlier, Sigmund Freud, a Viennese doctor, had developed a new method of treating mental illness, as well as a theory explaining human behavior. He called it psychoanalysis. Freud believed that all people have unconscious thoughts, feelings, desires, and memories. One's psychological problems, he claimed, are a result of conflicts between the conscious and the unconscious mind. To understand and treat mental illness, these conflicts needed to be not only talked out but also experienced. This was done by redirecting emotions to a substitute (usually the therapist) in a phase of analysis called transference neurosis. By doing so, repressed emotions and experiences, unconscious thoughts and motivations, could be made conscious. Patients gained insight into their behavior. And eventually their mental illness was cured. In 1924, the ideas that a person's behavior was rooted in unconscious forces, that mental illness was treatable, and that psychoanalysis could bring relief were still revolutionary concepts. But there were eminent psychiatrists in the United States who had seized on this "new school" of thought.

It was these doctors Darrow sent Walter Bachrach to hire. Money, obviously, was no object. It was imperative that the defense counter Crowe's traditionalist doctors.

In the meantime, Darrow had already engaged two psychiatrists—Drs. Harold Hulbert and Carl Bowman—to examine the teenagers. With luck, they'd turn up some useful psychological maladies.

© © ©

LEOPOLD, LOEB TRIAL SET FOR MONDAY, AUG. 4

By Maurine Watkins

Yesterday was a big day for the Messrs. Loeb and Leopold, those two young collectors of sensation, for it brought them a new experience: court arraignment for the murder of Bobby Franks—whom they killed as they'd crush a beetle. Then, too, it was an anniversary: the nineteenth birthday of Dick Loeb—and hundreds came to his party!

But it was a big day in itself to Mr. Nathan Leopold Jr., that gentleman who first won fame because "he loved the birdies so." How it must have delighted his egocentric soul—Your pardon, Leopold!—his egocentric mind, to know the crowd had been gathering before 7 o'clock that morning . . . just for a chance glimpse [of him].

"The Master [Leopold]" entered accompanied by his dutiful friend. . . . Still poised and self-possessed . . . both were carefully groomed, and Dick wore a brand new suit for the "party." His brown eyes searched the crowd. . . . But the "hypnotic" eyes of Nathan sought no one. He swept the crowd with a glance; just a mob, important only because they wanted to see him.

"Nathan Leopold and Richard Loeb . . . do you plead guilty or not guilty?"

"Not guilty, sir!" their voices, clear and unfaltering, rang out above the courtroom. . . . (They never forgot the "sir"—millionaires are bringing etiquette to our courts!)

(From the *Chicago Daily Tribune,* June 12, 1924, page 9)

The reporter's sarcasm obviously hit its mark. For decades afterward, Nathan would profess his hatred for both the *Tribune* and Maurine Watkins.

*   *   *

Drs. Bowman and Hulbert arrived at the county jail on Saturday morning, June 14. Carl Bowman, a precise middle-aged man, was chief medical officer at the Boston Psychiatric Hospital. A highly regarded physician, he believed that the answers to questions about a person's mental health lay in the endocrine glands (such as the pituitary, thyroid, adrenal, and thymus), and that mental illness would be eliminated as soon as doctors understood the effects of hormones on the body. Endocrinology (the study of endocrine glands and hormones), however, was in its infancy. And as of yet, Bowman had uncovered little evidence to link a dysfunctional gland with an identifiable psychiatric illness. Was it possible his examinations of Nathan and Richard could provide that correlation? Bowman hoped so. He intended to focus particularly on the teenagers' thyroid, pituitary, and pineal glands, all of which manifested abnormalities through changes in urine, blood, pulse, and blood pressure. Such physical irregularities just *might* indicate a change in mental health, too.

Dr. Harold Hulbert, a Chicago-area psychiatrist in private practice, was pleasant, open, and in his midthirties. Despite his youth,
he had plenty of experience. He'd worked in the Tennessee prison
system, identifying those who had been put in jail rather than mental institutions, and was considered an expert at diagnosing psychiatric disorders.

A room away from the other prisoners at the county jail had
been set aside for the examinations. It contained a table with
chairs, a sink with hot and cold running water, a metal-framed bed,
and a window overlooking the jail's courtyard. Pleased with the
space, Drs. Hulbert and Bowman transformed it into their private
laboratory.

For the next fourteen days, they examined the teenagers. They
calculated their metabolic rates and measured variations in blood
pressure during emotional stimulation. An X-ray machine examined
cranial and facial bones, thoraxes, and the bones of the forearms,
wrists, and fingers.

The tests showed Richard to be in exceptionally good physical
health. Nathan's tests, however, were unusual. X-rays of his skull
showed that some of the suture lines (the fibrous bands of tissue
that connect the bones of the skull) were obliterated. This indicated
osteosclerosis, or hardening of the bones, a condition typically oc-
curring in middle age. Bowman also noted that the pineal gland, an
endocrine gland at the base of the skull, had prematurely hardened
and calcified. Again, this shouldn't have happened until Nathan was
in his midthirties. Could there be a link between these findings and
the teenager's mental condition? Bowman didn't know. Still, he reported them to Darrow.

The attorney didn't think these discoveries helped the case. How in the world could he convince a jury that this calcification had caused a glandular disorder that in turn had caused mental illness? Keep digging, he told the doctors.

They began probing into the teenagers' personalities. No question was too personal. No topic was too private.

At first, Nathan enjoyed these sessions. It gave him a chance to talk about himself. Some days he didn't want to stop, begging the doctors to stay past dinnertime so he could tell them more. And he told them *everything.* He chronicled his childhood sexual abuse, his distress at the loss of his mother, his king-slave fantasies, his Nietzschean beliefs. He talked about sex and his attraction to men. He confessed his obsession with Richard Loeb.

Did he feel sorry about what he'd done?

No, replied Nathan. He didn't feel he'd done anything morally wrong, because there was no such thing as morals. Instead, he believed that whatever gave him pleasure was right and anything he found unpleasant was wrong. Curiously, he admitted that crime gave him "no pleasure. With [me] it was purely an intellectual affair, devoid of any emotion."

But as the days of questioning continued, Nathan grew irritable and less cooperative. He paced the examination room, chain-smoking.

"Horseshit!" he erupted one morning. "I think this medical psychiatric stuff is all horseshit." He wasn't insane, he insisted. "[I] knew what [I] was doing at the time." He detested the idea of the world thinking he was crazy. His intellect was anything but defective. He knew he was extraordinary, and he refused to let the public think otherwise.

Richard, meanwhile, found the sessions with Bowman and

Hulbert boring. Sometimes he even fell asleep. Only when he was spinning stories about the crime did he come alive. At those times, "the patient looked decidedly interested," reported the doctors, "drew up his chair and talked almost in dramatic whispers with considerable tension, his eyes roaming the room."

Richard admitted that at the moment of the killing he experienced "great excitement, great heart-beating, faster, which was pleasant." He felt proud that he'd remained "cool and self-possessed" while Nathan had been upset. "I had quite a time quieting down [Leopold]. . . . I told him it was all right, and joked and laughed. . . ."

Richard was also animated when he talked about the public's reaction to the crime, reveling in all the press attention.

Would Richard do it again if he thought he wouldn't get caught?

"I would if I could get the money," he replied. Not that he needed the $10,000, but he was disappointed that he hadn't gotten to play out the most complicated part of the crime.

"I know I should feel sorry I killed that boy and all that, but I just don't feel it," said Richard. "I didn't have much feeling about this from the first. That's why I could do it. There was nothing inside me to stop me. Of course, I'm sorry about my family, but not as much as I ought to be."

He told the doctors all about his fantasies. He explained picturalization and shadowing and his feelings about being a master criminal. He talked about his obsession with detective novels, and opened up about the petty crimes he'd been committing since childhood. He told them about his life under the controlling Miss Struthers.

Like Nathan, Richard didn't believe in morals. He'd attempted going to temple twice in his life, the same number of times he'd been inside a Catholic church. He believed in his superiority but took Nathan's superman theories with "a big dose of salt." It felt phony to him, something cooked up by Nathan so he could go around acting disdainful and condescending.

Did he truly like Nathan?

Not really, replied Richard. He admitted to having considered shooting Nathan. He'd even concocted an elaborate scheme to murder Nathan that involved "hitting him over the head with [a] chisel, shooting him, robbing him, and breaking the crystal of his watch to give the impression that [Nathan] had been robbed and killed during the struggle." He'd decided against the plan because he figured he'd be the prime suspect. "If I could have snapped my fingers and made him pass away [from] a heart attack, I would have," he told Dr. Hulbert.

If he truly felt this way, why did he stay friends with Nathan?

Who else would have joined him in his crimes? Who would have admired him? Without Nathan, he'd be alone.

Sometimes Richard wondered about himself. Was he "all there"?

● ● ●

On an afternoon in mid-June, a dour woman, carefully dressed in a black skirt and blouse, arrived at the county jail. It was Emily Struthers, and without being asked, she'd traveled all the way from Boston, where she now lived, to help save Richard.

Drs. Bowman and Hulbert escorted her into the jail's makeshift examination room. Bowman noticed that the governess's eyes were red, as if she'd been crying. She also seemed tense and irritated. Why was she being asked to speak with psychiatrists? She wanted to see Richard.

Hulbert explained, "A complete understanding of this boy [is] essential for an accurate diagnosis."

Miss Struthers pursed her lips.

Could she tell them about any fears Richard had had as a child? Hulbert asked.

He had none, she replied.

What about sleep disorders?

He had none, she said again.

Any incidents of naughtiness?

There were none.

The doctors found this hard to believe. Richard had never once talked back or refused to do as he was told?

Miss Struthers insisted he hadn't.

Bowman studied the woman. Her answers were evasive, and her posture had become defensive. She'd clamped her jaws tightly together, and her arms were crossed over her chest. He tried a different tack. What about sex? Did the boy have any "sex impulses"?

The governess acted shocked. Absolutely not!

He'd never asked about sex matters?

Never.

Both doctors found this hard to believe, too. Richard was fifteen when she'd left the house. Had he really shown no curiosity about sex?

They asked about her time in the Loeb household.

Her account matched Richard's, except, of course, that she had no criticism of either him or herself. She had been the perfect governess. He had been the perfect boy . . . until she'd left and "others taught him to drink and go out with girls."

Dr. Bowman noted that she had an annoying habit of talking with her lips pursed.

Miss Struthers did not say she still loved Richard. She did not say she wanted him to love her, or that she was jealous of his relation-ships with others. But Bowman surmised that she *was* jealous. He believed she felt spurned by Richard and had hoped that "the boy whom she had loved would be a man who had learned to love her."

After more than an hour of questioning, Miss Struthers stood. As abruptly as she had come, she left. There is no record that she saw Richard that day. Soon afterward, she sailed for Europe.

But her visit had an enormous impact on Bowman and Hul-bert. They diagnosed her as "paranoid toward men in general" and claimed her incapable of "real insights into child psychology," as well as "devoid of the understanding necessary to deal properly with children." Neither man seemed to have considered the question of *who* had hired Miss Struthers. Richard's parents were paying the psychiatrists' bills, so they absolved the Loebs of any responsibility. Instead, the doctors blamed Miss Struthers for warping Richard's childhood, just as Sweetie Wantz had ruined Nathan's.

Darrow soon learned about the cruelty doled out by both gov-ernesses. But he never considered calling either Miss Struthers or Sweetie to testify as witnesses. Childhood abuse was not relevant in murder cases in 1924. Besides, the women were sure to deny the allegations.

*   *   *

Bowman and Hulbert wrote a report with two sections: one on Na-than, a second on Richard. Together, the reports came to fifty thou-sand words and laid out the most intimate facts of the teenagers' lives. Each included a detailed family and physical history. Richard, it was noted, suffered from hemorrhoids and still had three baby teeth. Nathan had food allergies and had been "rather effeminate" until age nine. There were sections on their upbringing, education, fantasy lives, sexual experiences, and thoughts about crime. Each report also included sections on the murder and the teens' subsequent behavior and reactions.

Finally, at the end, the doctors drew their medical conclusions. They noted that in Nathan's king-slave fantasies, he took the role of slave 90 percent of the time, while Loeb was the king. At the same time, Richard fantasized about being a master criminal who needed a worshipful follower to help him carry out the brilliant crimes he liked to plan. It seemed obvious to the doctors that Richard was the driving force in the relationship. "Loeb is the king," they summed up. "It is he who has been mastermind throughout. He is almost without emotions." Nathan had been his follower, not his Svengali. The doctors agreed that both were very troubled boys.

❦ ❦ ❦

Life in jail got easier. In mid-June, Richard was moved to the sixth floor and placed in a cell two away from Nathan's. Now they could converse by calling out to each other, something they hadn't been able to do since their arrest.

Nathan wanted to know why Richard refused to admit he'd killed Bobby Franks. After all, the law didn't care who'd struck the actual blows. Nathan was convinced they would both be hanged.

"But, Nate," Richard replied, "that's one of the reasons to stick to my story. As you say, it makes no difference anyhow. And I figure it will be easier for each of our families if they believe the other fellow is the actual murderer. I know Mompsie feels less terrible than she might, thinking you did it. I'm not going to take that shred of comfort away from her."

June turned to July. Richard played baseball with the other inmates during exercise hour, and Nathan tore through the prison library, reading as many as eight books a week, including *The Last Days of Pompeii* and *The Refutation of Darwinism*. Richard, too, did some reading. *White Fang* by Jack London and a detective novel by Mary Roberts Rinehart called *The Circular Staircase* sat on his cot atop a thick stack of newspapers. Richard also tried to teach Nathan to play chess during the hours inmates were allowed out of the cells, but he soon gave up, exasperated. "You're too stupid to learn, Babe!" he exclaimed. The teenagers still were sent all their meals by their parents from a restaurant. They chain-smoked and played cards. And every night they read the papers aloud to each other, hooting with laughter about the ridiculous and sensational ways the press portrayed them. Nathan even began plans for a book that would lay out his life's philosophy. With all the attention surrounding the case, he felt sure it would be a bestseller. He figured he had just enough time to get it done before the state hanged him.

Nathan didn't dread hanging. It was his preference, he later claimed. "I believed . . . a speedy execution of the death penalty would be much easier than a slow, day-by-day torture of spending the rest of [my life] in prison." He said he was only going along with Darrow's insanity defense because his father wanted him to.

Richard didn't seem to care either way. "Life in prison, or hanging," he told reporters. "What does it matter?"

❋ ❋ ❋

Dr. William Alanson White, president of the American Psychiatric Association, arrived in Chicago on July 1. Hired by Walter Bachrach, he'd traveled from Washington, DC, to examine the teenagers. He wasted no time. Medical bag in hand, he went straight from the train station to the county jail.

He spoke with Richard first. Would the teenager tell him about university life and his classes? What about his favorite food? Did he have any pet peeves?

This was the classic psychoanalytical approach—speak soothingly about comfortable topics. Don't pry, not right away. Let the patients arrive on their own at an intimate level of discussion.

It worked. Soon Richard was answering far more personal questions and revealing his thoughts and feelings.

He'd always longed for fame, he confessed. He thought of himself as a brave explorer, forging new paths in crime. He told White about his jail fantasies. He told him about his childhood lying and stealing. He told him about his governess, Miss Struthers. And he gave his definition of the perfect crime: "Any kind of crime in which police are baffled; where there are no clues; in which it is carried out according to the original scheme; and results in an unsolved murder. Its perfection is in proportion to the number of complexities and difficulties overcome, and to the opportunity it offers for cleverness and finesse, and the maximum of newspaper coverage. It is also desirable that it should be right in the community where I live so that it will be a topic of discussion for weeks and months in the papers, among my friends and in my family."

White nodded, listened, and took notes.

The next day he spoke with Nathan. Nathan volunteered that he was fluent in six languages and had a prodigious memory. He was top of his class in school. Yes, it *was* his superiority that put him above the law. Yes, he was a Nietzschean. Yes, he did enjoy having sex with Richard. No, he had no qualms about killing Bobby Franks.

White clearly saw how each boy affected the shape of their relationship. Both believed they could commit the perfect crime—Nathan because of his delusions about being a superman and not being bound by laws; Richard because of his vivid fantasies about being a master criminal. Their coming together had created a unique and unusual confluence of two disordered personalities that had led to a horrific crime. The murder of Bobby Franks, White told Darrow, was "practically inevitable."

⊛　⊛　⊛

Dr. William Healy, a specialist in adolescent crime, arrived from Boston three days later. An innovative doctor, he challenged the commonly held notion that all criminals were genetically flawed. Some faulty gene with which one was born did not cause criminal behavior, contended Healy. Rather, criminal behavior was caused by unconscious motives—those hidden, unknown desires that drove one's actions and satisfied a need. Additionally, he had a special interest in early-childhood influences and their effect on adult behavior.

Healy had worked with hundreds of mentally ill teenagers in the course of his career. But, as he soon discovered, he had never met *any* youth like Richard or Nathan. In individual interviews, both spoke coldly and matter-of-factly about the killing. Neither showed the slightest guilt or remorse. Richard even chuckled when asked if he felt sorry for the grieving Franks family.

That such brilliant minds could be so utterly without empathy puzzled Healy. Could the gap between their intellectual ability and their emotional capacity be a form of mental illness?

Healy put the pair through a series of intelligence tests. Nathan breezed through them. On one assessment where a score of 145 was considered highly gifted, he scored a whopping 220. Richard, however, struggled. Healy placed his IQ at just slightly above normal. Eventually, the doctor submitted his conclusions to Darrow.

In his report, he described Richard's mental condition as "decidedly abnormal. . . . Anything he wanted to do was right, even kidnapping and murder." The planning and carrying out of the crime were only possible "because of Loeb's diseased mental life. . . . He has a pathological personality that does not allow for sympathy or feelings."

Nathan's personality was also disordered, Healy wrote. But this abnormality would never have resulted in his committing crimes if not for Richard. The kidnapping and murder were "the direct result of [the] diseased motivation of Loeb's mental life."

Dr. Healy learned something else, too. He included it in his report but hoped he wouldn't be asked to repeat it, at least not in open court.

◉　◉　◉

Dr. Bernard Glueck arrived at the Cook County Jail on July 8. The director of the psychiatric clinic at Sing Sing Prison in New York, Glueck was also a "new-school" psychiatrist who looked to mental illness as the cause of criminal behavior. And like his colleagues, he was struck by the teenagers' "absolute lack of any signs of normal feelings."

After Richard relived for him his childhood memories and

fantasies, Glueck concluded that the youth suffered from a deep feeling of inferiority. To compensate, he'd created a fantasy world in which he was a deviously brilliant master criminal. Bobby's murder was obviously linked to Richard's "need to compensate through criminal prowess his feelings of inadequacy."

Nathan had also retreated into fantasies, summed up Glueck. But his withdrawal was a way of dealing with his homosexuality. He had cultivated his "cynical and aloof intellectualism as a way of reconciling himself to his sexuality." So what if he was attracted to men, Nathan told himself. He was a superior being, far above society's norms and mores. But deep down, despite all his bravado, Nathan still felt revolted by his sexuality. Only with Richard did he feel comfortable about it. For the first time in his life, he could accept his "inclinations without self-loathing." This bonded Nathan to Richard. Wrote Glueck, "Nathan's complete realization as a homo-sexual was made possible only in connection with his association to Richard Loeb." Because of this, Nathan went along with anything his friend suggested.

*   *   *

What conclusions would today's psychiatrists draw about the pair's mental health?

Nathan would probably be diagnosed with a psychotic disorder. He exhibited many of the symptoms: holding false beliefs with firm conviction, despite what everyone else believes; refusing to give up those beliefs even in the face of incontrovertible proof to the contrary; and an overinflated sense of self-worth, power, or knowledge.

Recent research suggests a correlation between psychotic disorder and abuse. Nathan experienced repeated sexual abuse at the hands of his governess, Mathilda Wantz. And while doctors back in 1924 made no attempt to link this with his mental condition (they didn't even bring it up in court), today's psychiatrists would certainly focus on it. They would search for signs of post-traumatic stress disorder, common in those abused during childhood. Could Nathan have had a psychotic disorder caused by his childhood sexual abuse?

Today's psychiatrists would also use a CT scan to look further at those calcifications found by the X-rays of Nathan's skull. Psychotic disorder can be caused by brain injuries. Were there calcifications anywhere else in Nathan's brain? Had an injury affected his behavior?

These days, some brain injuries can be treated. So can a psychotic disorder. With modern medications and therapies—depending on Nathan's responsiveness to them—he might have lived a healthier, more normal life.

The same cannot be said for Richard, whom psychiatrists would most certainly diagnose as a psychopath. His symptoms were classic. Psychopathy is characterized by superficial charm, poor judgment, and a failure to learn from experiences. Psychopaths are attention-seekers and thrill-seekers. They lack remorse or shame, have a grandiose sense of themselves, lie pathologically, and are cunning and manipulative. Other people are merely objects to be used for the psychopath's benefit. Psychopaths are coldhearted and calculating.

Scientists are still learning about the causes of psychopathy. There is a correlation between psychopathy and childhood separation from a parent or a lack of parental involvement, as well as between psychopathy and abuse and neglect. Richard, certainly, experienced this when Albert and Anna gave over their parental authority to his governess, Miss Struthers.

Discovery of Richard's disorder, however, wouldn't have led to a more normal life for him. Sadly, there is no effective treatment for adult psychopathy. There is no cure.

PART FIVE

COURTROOM BATTLE

CHAPTER EIGHTEEN

SURPRISE STRATEGY

Jacob Loeb strode into the elevator and pressed the button for the eleventh floor. It was past ten p.m. on Thursday, July 17, and the office building felt eerily empty. Everyone had gone home long ago—except for those in Clarence Darrow's office. The attorney had something urgent to discuss, and secrecy was essential. That was the reason he'd called a meeting at such a late hour.

The elevator doors glided open and Loeb made his way down the hall to Darrow's office. Walter and Benjamin Bachrach were already there. So was Nathan Sr., his face tight with worry.

Darrow put his hands in his pockets and leaned back on his heels. He'd been thinking and thinking. Even though the boys had entered a plea of not guilty, there was no way he could prove their innocence. The state's attorney had an airtight case. There was no hope for acquittal. Their only defense was to plead not guilty by reason of insanity.

But in Illinois, by law, an insanity defense meant an automatic jury trial. The case would have to be heard before twelve jurors. And so Darrow had come to a hard truth. Despite their psychiatrists' opinions, he didn't believe a jury would ever accept an insanity defense. After all, the boys had lived seemingly normal lives before the crime. They'd studied for exams, made summer travel plans, socialized with friends. In addition, they'd planned the crime meticulously. He believed a jury would not only find Nathan and Richard guilty but also recommend the death penalty.

Jacob Loeb couldn't disguise his shock. There had to be some way to save the boys' lives.

Darrow had been pondering that. And, he told them, he had a plan—a risky one. He wanted to change the teenagers' pleas to guilty, which meant there would be no jury. Nor would there be a trial. Instead, proceedings would go straight to the sentencing stage. And the sentencing hearing was solely the responsibility of the judge. It was, Darrow believed, their only chance.

Nathan Sr. pointed to the overwhelming evidence against the boys. Why wouldn't the judge just sentence them to death?

Darrow explained that in a case involving the death penalty, prosecutors were allowed to argue "aggravating circumstances"—that is, circumstances surrounding the crime that made it even worse, such as killing a police officer or, in this case, a child. The defense was allowed to argue "mitigating circumstances"—that is, circumstances that diminished the seriousness of the crime, such as the offender acting under duress or being elderly or a juvenile.

Darrow planned to use the teens' mental illness as a mitigating circumstance. He would rely on the expert testimony of their psychiatrists to build a case for life imprisonment rather than death.

It was, Walter Bachrach pointed out, easier to convince one judge than twelve people on a jury. It also helped that the sentencing judge would be John Caverly.

A liberal Democrat, sixty-three-year-old Caverly was "clean." In all his years on the bench, there had never been a whiff of scandal about him—despite his friendships with corrupt politicians and gangsters. (When Big Jim Colosimo had been gunned down in his speakeasy in 1920, Caverly had served as one of his pallbearers.) This in itself was noteworthy for a Cook County judge. But Caverly was also unique because of his sensitivity and perception. Born in London, he'd never forgotten his immigrant roots, or his childhood poverty. (He'd paid for his legal education by carrying water in the steel mills for eighty-seven cents a day.) He'd worked for social reform, including helping to create the Cook County Juvenile Court in 1899. The first court of its kind in the nation, it was established to divert children from the harsh and punitive adult system into a more understanding and restorative one. Doing so, Caverly and other reformers believed, would give troubled kids a better shot at maturing into upstanding citizens.

Darrow, who'd known Caverly for decades, hoped the judge's sympathies toward young people might lead him to spare Nathan and Richard.

As Darrow saw it, the first step, and the biggest hurdle, would be convincing Caverly to admit their psychiatric evidence. After all, the defense wasn't arguing that the boys were *legally* insane, but rather that mental illness was to a lesser degree a cause of their committing the crime.

Darrow looked squarely at the others in his office. He wanted to be clear. This was a novel defense. Never before had evidence of a defendant's mental condition been offered in court to lessen a sentence. Never.

In fact, Darrow's legal strategy was years ahead of its time.

What he proposed was an argument for the concept of diminished capacity—the idea that defendants should not be held fully and criminally liable for breaking the law because their mental functions were diminished, or impaired. But in 1924, this concept did not yet exist in Illinois law. Defendants were either incapable of telling the difference between right and wrong, and thus insane, or not. There was no partial responsibility. They would be paddling into uncharted legal water with two lives at stake.

And then there was State's Attorney Crowe to consider. "Fighting Bob" was sure to vehemently object. Always combative in court, he would blast away at their arguments. And he might very well succeed in convincing the judge not to admit the psychiatric testimony as evidence in mitigation. If that happened, their defense would be over before it even began. Still, Darrow saw no other choice.

Jacob Loeb and Nathan Sr. agreed.

Darrow swore them to secrecy. He wasn't legally obligated to tell the state's attorney about their new strategy. And he didn't want Crowe to hear about it until July 21, when Darrow would present a motion for a change of plea to the court. If given the time, Darrow knew, the crafty state's attorney would find a way around it. The element of surprise was crucial.

◉ ◉ ◉

On July 21, Clarence Darrow and Benjamin Bachrach visited their clients. There was less than an hour before court began, and Nathan and Richard were already dressed and smoking in the lockup room.

Darrow motioned for them to come close. Lowering his voice, he said, "Boys, we're going to ask you to do something that may strike you as very strange." He explained the change in strategy. "We are all convinced it's the best way. Hell, boys, it's the only way."

He paused for their reactions.

Nathan wasn't surprised. He later claimed he'd expected Darrow to ask them to change their pleas. What else could the attorney do? Ask them to act crazy?

Richard nodded. From the beginning, he'd willingly left all legal matters to the lawyers, making no suggestions or objections, asking no questions.

Darrow apologized for waiting until the last minute to tell them. "But so many things could have happened," he explained. "Maybe one of you talks in his sleep? Maybe you might have been tempted to discuss it together . . . and been overheard. What the newspapers wouldn't have paid for a scoop like this!"

He patted their shoulders. Then he and Bachrach headed into the courtroom.

◎　◎　◎

Flanked by guards, Richard and Nathan entered the courtroom. As they did, the spectators turned as one to stare at them. Nathan looked down at his feet, but Richard stared back. He liked having all eyes on him.

The teens took their seats directly behind the defense table. Darrow turned to give them a brief but reassuring smile before returning to the papers spread out in front of him.

Across the aisle at the prosecution table, State's Attorney Crowe looked buoyant, confident. He was sure he had an airtight case, and his name had been in the newspapers for weeks. His reelection prospects looked bright.

Judge Caverly rapped his gavel and asked for Darrow to offer any motions he had.

Darrow stood. He reached under his jacket and tucked his thumbs beneath his suspenders. "It is unnecessary to say that this case has given us many perplexities and sleepless nights," he began. "We want to state frankly here that no one believes these defendants should be released. We believe they should be permanently isolated from society."

The reporters leaned forward to catch every word.

The lawyer continued. "After long reflection and thorough discussion we have determined to make a motion in this court . . . to withdraw our plea of not guilty and enter a plea of guilty."

Guilty?

The word ricocheted around the packed courtroom.

Guilty?

It was a stunning reversal. And no one had seen it coming.

Reporters dashed for telephones as spectators buzzed and the bailiff shouted, "Quiet in the courtroom!"

Nathan and Richard looked indifferent.

Two rows behind them, Nathan Sr. sat stiffly, looking worried.

Across the aisle from him, Jacob Franks lowered his head and began to weep silently. His son Jack patted his arm.

Darrow went on. He reminded the court that it was its duty to listen to witnesses and evidence in regard to both aggravating and mitigating circumstances. "We shall ask [to be] . . . permitted to offer evidence as to the mental condition of these two boys, to show the degree of responsibility they had, and to offer evidence [of their] youth . . . as further mitigation. With that we throw ourselves upon the mercy of this court, and this court alone."

There was no longer any need for a trial. Instead, there would be a sentencing hearing, in which the state's attorney would argue—in both opening and closing statements—his belief that the aggravating factors in the case warranted the death penalty. He would also offer evidence and testimony to prove his argument. Darrow would then argue for the presence of mitigating factors in support of a more lenient sentence: life in prison. He, too, would offer testimony to bolster his argument.

There was also no need for the opposing sides to share information about their cases. Illinois law at the time did not require this type of "discovery." Neither side even had to provide a list of witnesses.

Judge Caverly would listen to both sides' arguments and evidence, and then he alone would decide whether Richard and Nathan lived or died.

Just as Darrow had expected, Caverly moved up the date of the sentencing hearing. Neither side had to prepare for a lengthy trial. The hearing, he declared, would begin in two days.

Crowe's good mood had evaporated. He'd looked forward to a lengthy and showy legal battle that would have impressed the public. To the reporters who crowded around him when court ended, he said, "These boys . . . will be hanged!"

CHAPTER NINETEEN

A HOT DAY IN COURT

July 23 dawned hot and humid. Quivering heat waves obscured Lake Michigan's horizon, and temperatures were expected to soar to ninety-five degrees. Despite the heat, crowds jammed the streets surrounding the Criminal Courts Building. They came out of curiosity, hoping to look at the "fiendish boys" and hear "some forbidden testimony." Well dressed and mostly middle class, they fought for seats in the sweltering sixth-floor courtroom. But only those with pink tickets—given on a first-come, first-served basis—were allowed inside. Members of the press, too, needed a ticket for admittance. Theirs were blue, one per newspaper. But this ticket system did little to bring about order. So insistent was the seething crowd that a column of police extended from the street, through the hallways, and up to the staircase. A half-dozen police officers guarded the courtroom doors, too.

Below the grillwork walkway that connected the Cook County Jail to the Criminal Courts Building, a group of giddy young women had gathered. Eyes shining and intent, they looked up at the bridge, waiting for a glimpse of "Angel Face Dicky," as one newspaper had nicknamed Richard. Some of them had sent love notes to his jail cell. Others, if they managed to get inside the courtroom, would make eyes at him, or blow kisses. And one admirer even found a way into Robert Crowe's office. Richard, she told him, had been with her the entire night of the murder. Crowe didn't buy her story.

As they waited for court to convene, Nathan and Richard smoked cigarettes and chatted with a group of reporters. On this day, and every day during the hearing, members of the press would be allowed to visit the teenagers in the jail. Reporters got ten minutes in the morning before court and ten minutes in the afternoon following court. This was Darrow's doing. He hoped the reporters—many of them young men themselves—would be more sympathetic to the teenage killers if they got to know them on a personal level.

That morning, the teens were carefree, laughing and joking.

"Chipper," one reporter described them.

"Debonair," wrote another.

One of the reporters asked if they were nervous.

"Do I look it?" replied Nathan. He brushed a cigarette ash from the sleeve of his gray tweed suit. As usual, he was dressed impeccably. So was Richard, in a black suit and powder-blue shirt.

"I hear you fellows had a hard time describing our clothes the other day," Nathan said playfully. "I don't want you to make any mistakes this time. . . . Now look at me. What am I wearing? If I walked away this moment not one of you could tell me—accurately. So I'm going to help you out. Dick's hat is a soft fedora, as you can see. It's dull gray. Mine is slate blue." He laughed. "Now, did you get that straight?"

"Oh, shut up, Babe," snapped Richard.

At a little before ten a.m., the boys said goodbye to the press and were escorted across the walkway and into court. Already the place felt like an oven. And the whirring of the room's three small fans did nothing to alleviate the heat. Within minutes, they were soaked in sweat.

Crowe's opening statement was fiery. "The cautious, crafty, cruel and vicious youths are guilty of the most cruel, cowardly, dastardly murder ever committed in the annals of American jurisprudence," he declared. He intended to prove this "by facts and circumstances, by witnesses, by exhibits, by documents."

Crowe shouted. Sweat dripped from his face. His white shirt grew sodden. But he would not stop. "Their story is identical in all essential detail except each of them—careful of their own skin, much more careful than they were of the body of little Franks—says the scheme originated with the other. Each one says the other is the one who struck and choked out the life of this poor little boy."

The temperature outside had risen to ninety degrees, but it seemed even hotter in the crammed courtroom. Men took off their jackets. Women fanned themselves.

The heat didn't seem to daunt Crowe. He looked toward the defendants, then back at the judge. He promised the court that when he had shown all the state's evidence "in the name of the people of the State of Illinois, in the name of the womanhood and the fatherhood, and in the name of the children of the State of Illinois, we are going to demand the death penalty for both these cold-blooded murderers."

His dramatic rhetoric was not meant to convince the judge of the boys' depravity. Crowe was playing a political game. He knew reporters in the room would repeat his incendiary comments in their newspapers. Those comments would inflame readers, who in turn would demand a death sentence, which would put pressure on the judge.

After an hour's ranting, Crowe returned to his table and sat down.

Darrow was as cool as Crowe had been hot. As he stepped around the defense table, wisps of unruly hair fell over his forehead. He pushed them back. "We shall insist in this case, Your Honor, that terrible as this is, terrible as any killing is, it would be without precedent if two boys of this age should be hanged by the neck until dead, and it would in no way bring back Robert Franks or add to the peace and security of this community." He expressed his trust in Judge Caverly, saying that he knew the judge would listen calmly and honestly to the defense's case. And despite the state's attorney's blatant attempt to rile up the public, he knew the judge would ignore the "cry of angry people [and do] what is just, merciful and fair." Smiling pleasantly, he sat back down. He'd spoken for only five minutes.

Judge Caverly looked at the state's attorney. He was ready to hear the prosecution's case.

Crowe called his first witness: Bobby's uncle Edwin Gresham.

Benjamin Bachrach stood. "If the court pleases, I suggest there is no [reason] for testimony." The teenagers had confessed. Crowe did not have to prove their guilt. So why bother with evidence and witnesses?

Crowe approached the judge's bench. "Your Honor is going to be asked to fix the punishment here and I want to show . . . the mountain of evidence we have piled up. I want to show their guilt clearly and conclusively, and all the details of it, and ask that they be hanged." He paused a moment before adding, "I don't think I ought to be limited."

"You are permitted to go into every detail," ruled Caverly.

Bachrach sat back down. It was a defeat. Not only would the judge hear the prosecution's spin on the murder, in all its brutality, but so would the reporters and, by extension, the public.

Edwin Gresham took the stand. He was asked to describe the emotional ordeal of identifying his nephew's body. "When the boy was a child he had rickets," answered Gresham, "and that had left marks, or pearls, on his teeth. I looked at the teeth to make sure the pearls were there." He paused. Tears welled in his eyes. "They were there."

Jacob Franks took the stand next. He grimly told the court about receiving the kidnap letter, putting together the ransom money, being telephoned first by the kidnappers and then by Gresham.

Spectators murmured sympathetically.

It was the appearance of Flora Franks, however, that caused the most buzzing. The grieving mother had not been seen in public since Bobby's funeral. Now, dressed in mourning clothes and leaning heavily on Sam Ettelson's arm, she took the witness stand.

May 21 was the last time she'd seen her son, she told the court. And it was "Friday—no, Saturday" that she next saw him—his body.

Crowe placed Bobby's clothes before her. Could she identify them?

Mrs. Franks touched her son's shoes and stocking, his belt and class pin. Yes, they belonged to her boy.

Richard observed her intently. He felt not a scrap of sympathy.

Nathan looked down at the floor.

Flora Franks testified for just seven minutes before Sam Ettelson helped her out the door. She never returned to the courtroom.

Crowe called thirteen more witnesses that day—cashiers, salesclerks, and bellhops. A bank teller identified Nathan as having opened an account at the Hyde Park State Bank. A clerk remembered Richard checking into the Morrison Hotel.

Darrow chose not to cross-examine any of them. Why keep them talking longer than was necessary? It wasn't his job to try to poke holes in the state's case. After all, he wasn't trying to prove his clients' innocence. His job was to show why his clients' lives should be spared.

The newspapers weren't helping his cause. When Darrow opened his newspaper the next morning, a banner headline greeted him.

MRS. FRANKS BARES TRAGEDY

BOY'S MOTHER
SPARTAN-LIKE
ON THE STAND

CURBS EMOTIONS AS SHE TELLS STORY

By Genevieve Forbes

Mrs. Jacob Franks, a figure of listless sorrow, reticent in her grief, terrible in her voice, hopelessly unmindful of the future, took the stand yesterday. . . . When they put the crumpled shoes and the one brown stocking into her lap, she fingered them and identified them. But from out of a mosaic of the most brilliant colors, perhaps that have been painted into a sensational murder trial, an obscure, subdued, and broken segment of the pattern was suddenly lifted to a key position. For with her testimony, Mrs. Franks became the real victim of the murder for which Nathan F. Leopold, Jr. and Richard Loeb . . . are now awaiting sentence.

(From the *Chicago Daily Tribune*, July 24, 1924, page 1)

❂ ❂ ❂

That same night at the Loeb mansion, Richard's oldest brother, Allan, picked up the telephone and called his parents in Charlevoix. This would become a nightly ritual over the course of the hearing—Allan on one end of the line, reporting on the day's events; Anna and Albert listening on the other end with tears in their eyes.

At the Leopold house, Nathan's father refused to answer the door or speak to reporters on the phone. He sat alone in the library, bewildered, scared for his son's life, and consumed by grief. He would need to muster all his strength to get through the hearing.

And at the Franks house, Flora shuffled into Bobby's room and sat on the edge of his bed. Nothing in the room had been touched. The set of books by Charles Dickens still lined his shelf. The baseball with Babe Ruth's autograph—Bobby's prized possession—still sat on his bureau. Bobby was dead. Flora knew that now. She laid her head on her son's pillow.

CHAPTER TWENTY

BATTLES IN AND OUT OF COURT

Reporters pressed closer to the bars of Richard's jail cell, pencils poised above notebooks. The teenager wanted to make a statement.

Richard's tone was solemn. "We are united in great and profound hope for today. Mr. Leopold and I have gone over the matter and have come to a mutual decision."

He paused.

"We have just one hope: That it will be a damned sight cooler than it was yesterday."

As the reporters threw up their hands in annoyance, Richard laughed heartily. Then the bailiff arrived to escort him to his second day in court.

◉ ◉ ◉

Once again, the courtroom sweltered. Thirty-three witnesses for the prosecution paraded across the stand that day, among them the night watchman who found the chisel, members of Nathan's study group, and a chauffeur from Kenwood who claimed to have seen Richard driving the rental car the afternoon of the murder.

Through it all, the teenagers grinned and snickered. They elbowed each other and passed whispered remarks back and forth.

The stream of witnesses continued into the third day, too.

And Darrow continued to sit quietly at the defense table. He was so still, some people in the courtroom wondered if he was napping.

Then Crowe called Detective James Gortland to the stand. Gortland claimed to have heard Nathan boasting about a "friendly judge"—meaning a bribed one.

Darrow whirled around in his chair and said loudly to Nathan, "Did you say that, Babe?"

"Hell, no," replied Nathan just as loudly.

On cross-examination, Darrow stood and stalked toward Gortland. He pressed him for witnesses, notes, or other supporting evidence.

Gortland admitted he had none.

And Darrow pounced. "Who was with you [during this conversation]?" he demanded.

"Nobody but he and I."

"Did you make any memoranda on it?"

"Not at the time . . ."

"Mr. Officer," growled Darrow, "don't you know that this story of yours is pure fabrication made for the purpose of intimidating the court?"

The detective insisted his story was true. But Darrow had won the point.

He returned to the defense table and lapsed back into silence.

◦ ◦ ◦

That night, Ty Krum, a reporter for the *Chicago Daily Tribune,* visited Nathan. He passed the teenager a flask of bourbon through the cell bars. It was part of their bargain: booze for a scoop. They'd been making this exchange since the boys' first night in the county jail.

As Nathan took a swig, Krum said, "Babe, I feel sorry for you. Do you know that?"

"Now, listen," replied Nathan, "I certainly don't like that. I don't want you to feel sorry for me and, if you do, I wish you would change your mind. I don't feel sorry for myself for what I did. I did it, and that's all. I got myself in this jam and it's up to myself to get out. . . . As far as being remorseful, I can't see it. Life is what we make it, and I appear to have made mine what it is today. That's my lookout and nobody's else."

Minutes later, Krum visited Richard. After passing a second flask of bourbon through the bars, he said, "Dickie, the people on the outside are thinking you're about the coldest-blooded mortal in the world. . . . You laugh and josh and appear to be having a good time."

"Well, what do they want me to do?" Richard tossed back the booze and ran his hand across his mouth.

"I suppose they want you to act normal," said Krum.

Richard frowned. "That's exactly what I am doing. I sit in the courtroom and watch the play as it progresses. When the crowd laughs, I laugh. When it is time to be serious, I'm serious. I'm a spectator, you know, and like to feel myself as one. You can tell the people on the outside that there is no faking or pretending. I have watched others in the courtroom and they laugh, smile, yawn, look bored, and all the other things. Why should I be any different?"

Krum stared at the teenager. He realized that Richard Loeb was incapable of honest emotion. All he could do was imitate the actions of those around him.

* * *

LOEB 'MASTER MIND' OF FRANKS SLAYING, ALIENISTS REPORT

LEOPOLD HIS MENTAL SLAVE IN BURGLARIES, ARSON AND MURDER, DEFENSE SPECIALISTS ASSERT.

LONG DREAMED OF CRIME

MURDER PLOT WAS FORMED WHILE RETURNING FROM ROBBERY OF LOEB'S FRATERNITY HOUSE.

LACK NORMAL EMOTIONS

BOTH MENTALLY IRRESPONSIBLE FROM EARLY YOUTH, PSYCHIATRISTS FIND— HAD NO SENTIMENT.

(From the *New York Times,* July 28, 1924, page 1)

* * *

On Monday, July 28, the public awoke to find this and other sensational headlines splashed across their morning newspapers. What followed was the medical report made by Drs. Hulbert and Bowman, summarized and excerpted. That day, along with their toast and coffee, readers devoured the most intimate details of Richard's life: his obsession with detective novels, his fantasies as the master criminal, his nightly picturalizations. They gobbled up Nathan's most personal secrets, too: his king-slave fantasies, his inferiority complex, his belief in Nietzsche.

Darrow claimed that the report had been stolen from his office, although rumor had it that he'd released it to the papers himself. For weeks now, Crowe had been painting the teenagers as monsters and whipping up the public's anger. Darrow wanted to change the narrative. He hoped that after reading the youths' life stories, the public would come to see them as ill children—mentally irresponsible and lacking in normal emotion—rather than killers. (To further the image of them as children, he directed all members of the defense team, including the psychiatrists, to call the boys "Babe" and "Dickie," in stark contrast to the prosecution's use of "Mr. Leopold" and "Mr. Loeb.")

For days after the story broke, people spoke of little else. "Barbers talk about it between swipes of the razor," reported the *Chicago Daily Tribune*. "Stenographers in Loop offices whisper about it with the girls who sit at the next desk. Bootblacks look up from their work and wonder aloud. The farmers in the field discuss it across the fence."

Intentional or not, Darrow's strategy worked. Reading about Babe's fragile, lonely childhood, scarred by feelings of physical inferiority and the death of his beloved mother, wrenched the public's heart. People were moved, too, by the picture of poor little Dickie telling his dreams and fantasies to his teddy bear while his strict governess denied him playmates and forced him to study. As days passed, the public's perception of the crime changed. The horror of the murder gave way to pathos. Suddenly the pages of the country's major newspapers were littered with editorials and opinion pieces about what parents could learn from the case. And Nathan and Richard went from being monsters to being vulnerable children.

* * *

FRANKS CASE WARNING TO PARENTS, SAYS LINDSAY

TREND OF DANGEROUS AGE IN YOUTH
SHOWN BY 'INFANT' SLAYERS,
ASSERTS DENVER JUDGE

By Ben B. Lindsay
Judge of the Juvenile Court of Denver

The Leopold-Franks murder case . . . through all its grue-some, sickening details, is a children's story, a story of youth, and it concerns us all. . . . Like a bolt out of the blue, with their confessions, the perpetrators turn out to be nothing but children themselves! This is a murder of a child done by children. Yes, Loeb and Leopold are children . . . infants . . . who unbridled and undisciplined were allowed the mental freedom, without adult direction, to roam at will amidst the pitfalls of an adult world. They drifted into adult dangers . . . [becoming] two poor, marooned children who might have been glorious if rightly directed. . . . The pity of it, the loss. . . . Think upon these two children, Leo-pold and Loeb, who have unwittingly, stumblingly come to tears because of this foul crime. Think upon their brilliant, unbridled, yet childish minds wasted, the poor children, the poor boys. . . .

(From the *Los Angeles Daily Times,* July 28, 1924, page 3)

This article and others like it struck a chord with readers. Before the Leopold and Loeb case, it was commonly believed that juvenile delinquency was caused by deprivation and neglect in families. It had not been associated with gifted individuals, or those from privi-leged, educated, well-to-do families. But that belief had been turned on its head. Many wondered if Nathan and Richard were not so different from their own children after all. How could anyone know if their child (or a neighbor's child) might be a killer? Was there anything parents could do to stop mental distortions from developing in their son or daughter? The horrible tragedy felt very close to home.

● ● ●

The state rested its case on the morning of Wednesday, July 30. Crowe had called eighty-one witnesses and submitted a mountain of physical evidence, including the recovered typewriter, the blood-stained rental car, Bobby's remaining clothes, the bloody chisel, and the ransom notes. Additionally, he'd had both confessions read into the court transcript.

Through it all, Judge Caverly had listened carefully, often with his chin in his hand. Now he called on the defense.

Walter Bachrach stood and summoned Dr. William Alanson White to the witness stand.

Crowe leaped to his feet. "Just a minute. I object to that, if Your Honor please!"

"Why?" asked Caverly.

"It is immaterial," said Crowe.

"Why?" Caverly asked again.

"The only purpose of it would be to lay a foundation for [the witness] to testify as an expert on the question of insanity . . . and Your Honor has no right to go into that question. As soon as [insanity] appears in the trial, it is Your Honor's duty to call a jury."

"Overruled," said Caverly. He looked at Bachrach. "You may proceed."

But Crowe dug in. "I want to be heard on that, Your Honor . . . I insist that the matter of sanity or insanity is a matter under the law, for a jury." He pulled out the Illinois Revised Statutes of 1923 and read a passage.

Caverly looked annoyed. He knew the legal definition of insanity. He asked Crowe what previous courts had said about introducing psychiatric testimony as a mitigating circumstance.

Crowe didn't answer. Instead, he sputtered angrily, "What is the defense trying to do here? Are they attempting to avoid a trial upon a plea of not guilty with the defendants before twelve men that would hang them, and trying to produce a situation where they can get a trial before one man that they think won't hang them?"

It was a rhetorical question. That was exactly what Darrow was trying to do. And everyone in the courtroom knew it.

"There are not degrees . . . in responsibility," Crowe argued.

Neither Darrow nor anyone else on the defense team said a word. Their defense hinged entirely on Caverly's ruling in favor of hearing the defense psychiatrists' testimony. And so Darrow, who believed that the outcome of hearings often rested on little things such as likeability, let Crowe shout. He figured the state's attorney would eventually antagonize the judge.

Crowe banged his fist on the document table in front of Caverly's bench. Darrow was trying to turn a sentencing hearing into an insanity trial, he howled.

But Caverly refused to be bullied. He wanted to hear arguments for and against allowing the psychiatric testimony.

The lawyers for the prosecution and the defense buzzed around the bench, presenting their side and arguing against the opposing one.

Crowe was red-faced. "You do not take a microscope and look into a murderer's head to see what state of mind he was in, because if he is insane he is not responsible, and if he is sane he is responsible. You look not to mental condition, but you look to the facts surrounding the case. Did [a defendant] kill the man because the man had debauched his wife? If that is so, then there is mitigation here. Did he kill the man because the man had spread slanderous stories about him? Then there is mitigation. Did he kill the man in the heat of passion during a drunken fight? That is mitigation. But here is a cold-blooded murder. . . . To attempt on a plea of guilty to introduce an insanity defense before Your Honor is unprecedented. That statute says that is a matter that must be tried by a jury."

Walter Bachrach responded. They weren't trying to prove their clients were insane, he said. They simply wanted to show that the boys had a "medical condition, a pathological condition." After all, if drunkenness could be considered a mitigating circumstance, why not a medical condition? Both affected behavior.

And according to Illinois law, Darrow added, "the court may listen to anything . . . in mitigation." In his opinion, the statute had given the court plenty of latitude. As long as the testimony did not present legal insanity, but rather a weakness of mind, the court *could* consider it. That was, of course, he added, if the judge thought it was "right, just, and humane."

During all this, Dr. White sat calmly in the witness stand, waiting for the chance to testify. To pass the time, he opened his briefcase and pulled out some papers. He began making notes on them with his fountain pen.

The debate raged on for the remainder of the day and all through the next. Law books piled up on both tables as each side brought before the court previous legal decisions about using psychiatric testimony.

But there were no precedents regarding psychiatric testimony as a mitigating circumstance. The United States Supreme Court had never made any such decision. Neither had any court in Illinois, nor any court in any other state. Caverly's decision would *establish* legal precedent.

"What is a mitigating circumstance?" Darrow suddenly asked. "Is it youth? If so, why?"

Darrow knew youth was not a mitigating circumstance in this case, according to Illinois law. But he wanted to remind Caverly that the defendants were young—just nineteen—and suggest that their youth be considered anyway.

"Is youth a mitigating circumstance?" Darrow asked again. Leaning against the bar in his wrinkled seersucker suit, he answered his own question. "Well, we have all been young, and we know that fantasies . . . haunt the daily life of a child. We know the dream world they live in. We know that nothing is real. We know the lack of appreciation. We know the condition of the mind of a child. Here are two boys who are minors. The law would forbid them making contracts, forbid them marrying without consent of their parents, would forbid them to vote. Why? Because they haven't the judgment which only comes with years, because they are not fully responsible."

Crowe interrupted. How dare Darrow try to make out that these "cold-blooded murderers had merely committed some boyish prank and they are sitting here sobbing for mercy, crying their hearts out," he shouted. Then his voice grew serious. "I insist, under the law, under the rules of logic and reason, that his evidence be excluded."

It was midmorning on Friday, August 1. Neither Crowe nor Darrow had anything more to say on the issue of whether the court should hear the defense's psychiatric testimony. Both men looked to the judge.

The courtroom fell silent as Caverly considered.

"The court is of the opinion," he finally said, "that it is his duty to hear any evidence that the defense may present and it is not for the court to determine in advance what it may be. The court will hear it and give it such weight as he thinks it is entitled to."

Jacob Loeb smiled at the decision. Nathan Sr. visibly relaxed. And Nathan and Richard laughed before whispering furiously to each other.

Crowe leaped to his feet.

"What is [it]?" asked Caverly testily.

"It is an objection," bellowed Crowe.

Caverly held up his hand. "The objection . . . is overruled." He looked over at White, who was still on the stand. "The witness may proceed."

CHAPTER TWENTY-ONE

NEW-SCHOOL PSYCHIATRY TAKES THE STAND

Clarence Darrow had made legal history, but he didn't revel in his victory. Instead, he shuffled his papers and leaned back in his chair as Walter Bachrach stood to examine the witness.

On the stand, White reached into his briefcase and took out his notes on the case. He spoke in a quiet voice, using plain terms and talking in general about new-school psychiatry.

"The inner life signifies the real fundamental needs and aspirations and hopes and wishes of the individual," White told the court. "They give us the real story of what that individual seeks in life."

Inner life. It was a term new to most in the courtroom.

White went on. "This inner life is the life that goes on inside and is not consciously or intentionally expressed by the individual. It is the thoughts and feelings that are privy to every man's inner consciousness, and [a physician] needs to inquire into those and watch during an examination for any indications that show what they may have been, because we know that the inner life fulfills a very definite function. It has as its function—"

Crowe couldn't stand it. "I object," he cried. When was the doctor going to start talking about his examination of the defendants?

"I am asking him," retorted Walter Bachrach.

"All his answers are lectures," Crowe shot back.

"If the court please—" said Bachrach.

"He is just cutting a swamp in a learned discussion that you and I don't know much about, Your Honor," interrupted Crowe.

"That is true," said Caverly. "That is why I want to listen to him."

With a dramatic sigh, Crowe dropped back into his chair.

But he kept objecting, over and over, almost every time Bachrach asked White a question.

Caverly kept overruling him.

At last, White came to his examinations of the teenagers. "I will begin with Dickie Loeb," he said.

Crowe shot to his feet. "You mean Richard Loeb, the defendant in this case, Doctor?"

White was tired of Crowe's antics. "Yes. No objection to my calling him Dickie, is there?" he asked coolly.

Crowe shrugged dramatically. "Well, just so we can identify him." He sat down again.

"Dickie lied about all sorts of things," continued White. "He lied to Babe Leopold, his comrade, about college . . . his [grades] . . . continually building up all sorts of artificial situations until he himself says that he found it hard to distinguish between what was true and what was not true."

Crowe saw a chance. He jumped up again. "Now, just wait a minute . . . that means [Loeb] could not distinguish between right and wrong. Truth is right, the other is wrong. I submit we are getting now clearly into an insanity hearing and I suggest a jury be impaneled."

"Motion denied," said Caverly. "You may proceed, Doctor."

White told the court about Richard's recurrent fantasies of being a master criminal. The teenager's motive for the crime, the doctor explained, had nothing to do with ransom and everything to do with his desire to actually become that master criminal.

During all this, Richard sat with his legs crossed and his face emotionless. Nathan leaned forward in his chair and put his hand on his chin as if listening intently.

Crowe stood again. "Doctor, may I interrupt you?"

"Let the doctor proceed without interruption, and you may cross-examine when he gets through," Caverly said.

Crowe sat.

Bachrach encouraged White to continue.

"Dickie cannot distinguish between the real world and the fantasy," the psychiatrist said. "He has lost the ability to differentiate and to draw clear lines, to tell where he is." This explained why Richard seemed to relish his celebrity role in court. Jail was more reward than punishment for him. He was finally living the life he'd long fantasized about. "He [feels] comfortable in jail . . . feels as if he sort of belongs there."

Regarding Nathan: "He developed in early life a feeling that he himself was more or less set apart from others . . . in the direction of superiority. Very early in life he developed an antagonism toward tender feelings . . . because they made him suffer." As he grew, White explained, his attitude turned into "a hedonistic philosophy." When he was deciding whether to do something, Nathan's only consideration was, Would the action give him pleasure?

Bachrach asked how all this might help the court to understand the murder.

One had to understand the relationship between Richard and Nathan, replied White. Richard needed an audience. In his fantasies, his imaginary gang was his audience. But in real life, Nathan played that role. "I cannot see how Babe would have entered into it all alone because he had no criminalistic tendencies . . . as Dickie did, and I don't think Dickie would have ever functioned to this extent [planning and carrying out the crime] all by himself. So these two boys, with their peculiar inter-digited personalities, came into this emotional compact with the Franks homicide as a result."

Bachrach nodded. "You may cross-examine," he said to the prosecutors.

Crowe stalked toward the witness stand. The defense had spent the entire day focused on the criminals and their warped childhoods, but Crowe intended to remind the court about the dead boy. What about the real victim?

"Now, Doctor," he began, "when you were talking to Nathan Leopold did you ask him who actually struck the blows that resulted in the death of Bobby Franks?"

"No, I don't think I did."

"Have you any opinion as to who actually committed the crime?"

"I think so."

"Which one in your judgment?"

"I think it was Dickie."

A low buzz of conversation came from the spectators, and Jacob and Allan Loeb glared at the witness. Richard remained emotionless. Nathan grinned.

Crowe continued. When White interviewed the teens, how had he known they were telling the truth? Wouldn't they try to mislead him? Certainly, Loeb was a liar. But what about Leopold? Wasn't he a liar, too?

"I think he was frank, as frank as could be," replied White.

"Don't you think it strange that he lies to Loeb, and he lies to everybody else except you? That . . . doesn't make any impression on your mind at all? Does it?"

White looked a bit rattled.

Crowe grew more aggressive. Had the teenagers admitted any other crimes during their examination? What were these crimes? When and where were they committed?

Richard had told him they lit three fires, recalled White. He wasn't told the details.

"You didn't ask them?"

"It was out in the middle of a lot somewhere," conceded White.

Could he provide any more information? A date, maybe, so Crowe could check police reports and determine if the teens had lied to the doctor?

"No, I can't give anything to satisfy you," said White.

"And your conclusions depend entirely on the fact that you believe what the boys told you?"

Crowe pretended to be incredulous.

"If they have fooled you and consistently lied to you, then your conclusion isn't worth anything, is it?"

White couldn't come up with an answer. He looked toward Darrow. But the lawyer didn't object to Crowe's question.

The state's attorney ended his cross-examination.

And Caverly adjourned court until Monday, August 4.

* * *

Dr. William Healy took the stand on Monday morning. His testimony centered on the boys' relationship, which he described as "most strange and pathological."

Darrow, who'd taken up the questioning, asked him to elaborate.

"Their association began at fifteen years of age," said Healy. "It is very clear . . . that both came with peculiarities in their mental life. . . . Each arrived at these peculiarities by different routes; each supplemented the other's . . . abnormal needs in a most unique way."

Healy paused. He admitted that in all his psychiatric experience, he'd never encountered "so little normal motivation" for committing a crime. "The matter was so long planned, so unfeelingly carried out . . ."

He shook his head and returned to the subject at hand. "In the matter of their association, I have the boys' story, told separately, about an incredibly absurd childhood compact that bound them. . . . For [Dickie], he says the association gave him the opportunity of getting someone to carry out his criminalistic imaginings . . . In the case of [Babe], the direct cause of entering into criminalistic acts was this particularly childish compact."

Crowe bolted out of his seat. A compact? About what? He objected to not hearing the details of the compact.

Caverly agreed. The court should hear more about it.

Here was the secret Healy had hoped not to reveal in open court. He turned to the judge. "I am perfectly willing to tell it in chambers," he said, "but it is not a matter that I think should be told here."

"I insist we know what the compact is," roared Crowe.

"I suggest it be in chambers," said Darrow.

"Tell it in court," demanded Crowe. He had an idea of what it was about—the teenagers' sexual relationship—and he wanted the public to hear it. He was, of course, playing to society's homophobia.

"The [hearing] must be public, Your Honor . . . it ought to be told in the same way that we put the other evidence in," he shouted.

Judge Caverly motioned for the lawyers to approach the bench. A handful of reporters approached, too.

"Oh, no," said the judge, "this is not for the papers at all."

The reporters backed off. Still, they strained to hear. So did others in the courtroom. Some even stood on their chairs.

Nathan and Richard shared a glance. They knew what Healy was about to disclose.

Healy lowered his voice. "The compact . . . consisted of an agreement between them that Leopold, who has very definite homosexual tendencies which have been a part of his makeup for many years, was to have the privilege of—do you want me to be very specific?"

"Absolutely," declared Crowe, "because this is important."

Babe was to have the privilege of having sex with Dickie at "special rates," said Healy. "At one time it was to be three times in two months, if they continued their criminalistic activities together . . . and then it was once for every criminalistic deed."

While Healy had been whispering, two reporters had snuck up behind the defense table and were frantically taking notes.

Caverly pounded his gavel. "Will you go and sit down, you newspapermen? Take your seats. This should not be published."

The reporters backed off.

Walter Bachrach asked when the boys had begun this compact.

Healy told them about that first trip they'd taken by train to Charlevoix in February 1921. "[Babe] . . . found it gave him more pleasure than anything else he had ever done. To go on further with this, even in jail here, a look at Loeb's body or his touch upon his shoulder thrills him so, he says, immeasurably."

The psychiatrist looked at Crowe. "It that enough?"

"I think that is all," said Crowe.

Caverly waved everyone but Darrow away from the bench.

Darrow now asked Healy to tell the court some of the things Nathan had said during their conversations.

Healy opened his notebook and began reading:

"I have reveled in the fact that I have no qualms of conscience."

"I have tried to kill affection for years."

"I have never had any disappointments [in life]. I was not allowed to."

Darrow asked the doctor to interpret Babe's comments. The teen wasn't merely bad, was he? Could those comments point to something else?

Healy nodded. "There seems to be profound disorder of judgment as shown in contradiction of ideas and impulses. With all [his] self-love there was no normal self-regard." After all, if Nathan really cared about himself, he wouldn't have tossed away his wealth, privilege, and future so casually.

Was this abnormal behavior?

Yes, Healy postulated. But Babe exhibited lots of abnormal behavior—mixing fantasy and reality, believing he was a superman. All this had brought him to where he was now. As a result, the doctor said, "in my opinion, Babe is thoroughly unbalanced in his mental life, or to use another term, mentally diseased."

And Richard?

He was decidedly abnormal, said Healy. Unfeeling and manipulative, Dickie was "charming, very friendly and well-mannered, but because of his [mental illness] he is an extensive liar, unscrupulous, unfair, ungrateful and disloyal in many social relationships."

At this, the teenagers looked at each other. Nathan smirked. Richard giggled.

◦ ◦ ◦

The next day, Crowe got his chance to cross-examine Healy. He immediately returned to the compact.

"Doctor, you talk about a childish prank. . . . Do you know any children who make these [sorts of] agreements and enter into these pacts that are not criminals and perverts?"

"Yes, I have known of them," Healy replied matter-of-factly.

"So you regard perversion not as a crime, but as a childish act," persisted Crowe.

"This is not a, you know," replied Healy, refusing to use the term *homosexual relationship*. "As I said, it is a childish form of perversion. There are different kinds of perversion. But as far as that goes, there are many children, very innocent children of fine people who get into many things of that sort. Many children who have been nice children and grown up in very nice ways have at one time done things like that."

Healy, like many modern psychiatrists of his day, was expressing what was then considered an advanced view of homosexuality. He believed that every little boy passed through homosexuality on his way to heterosexuality. This was "normal." Once in a while, however, boys missed the heterosexual boat. The result? They were stuck in the abyss of sexual perversity. This theory was part of the reason the defense psychiatrists kept emphasizing the teenagers' emotional ages and labeling them as infantile. The implication was that Nathan and Richard were not morally depraved homosexuals but rather had not developed normally. The defense was arguing that adult homosexuality was a mental illness—another manifestation of aberrant behavior. (Some historians even believe this legal case paved the way for the American Psychiatric Association's official, though erroneous, classification, made in the early 1950s, of homosexuality as a mental illness.)

It was also the reason Darrow now decided to allow Healy to disclose the boys' "compact" to the courtroom audience without objection.

Crowe refused to accept Healy's opinion on the subject. "You think that [the pair's sexual activity] is a childish pact?"

Walter Bachrach objected. What was the purpose of having Healy's earlier testimony given quietly in chambers when the prosecutor could cross-examine him publicly about the same subject?

"I have no desire to bring this out in public," countered Crowe, "but when the doctor says that boys who agree to practice forms of perversion are merely doing childish things, I disagree with him."

Crowe's words appeared to annoy the judge. "Cross-examination . . . along that line will be done quietly without any heralding to the world," said Caverly.

Once again, the attorneys huddled around the judge's bench and spoke in hushed voices. Crowe repeated his question about Nathan and Richard's sexual relationship. Surely it could not be considered normal.

"Hundreds of children, sir, have done it," insisted Healy.

"Aren't you ashamed of yourself, Doctor, to testify on that matter?" demanded Crowe.

"No, I should say not," retorted Healy. He repeated himself. "I have known of very nice children of very nice families who have gotten through with things of that sort."

Crowe tried a different tack. He turned to Caverly. Weren't the defense psychiatrists arguing that Nathan and Richard were insane? "There is only one thing to do under the law and that is to call a jury," he said.

"The motion is denied," said Caverly.

Court was adjourned.

Healy stepped down from the witness stand.

❁   ❁   ❁

Dr. Bernard Glueck took the stand on Wednesday morning, August 6.

Yes, he agreed with his colleagues that both teenagers were mentally diseased.

Yes, he was amazed at their absolute lack of normal feelings.

Yes, it was his opinion that the murder was "the inevitable outcome of this curious coming together of two pathologically disordered personalities."

In the overwarm courtroom, observers grew bored and sleepy. They'd heard all this before. Then Benjamin Bachrach asked a question that grabbed their attention.

"Did [Dickie] say anything about who it was that struck the blow on the head of Robert Franks with the chisel?"

"He told me all the details of the crime, including the fact that he struck the blow," said Glueck.

At the defense table, Nathan leaned forward and slowly smiled. He turned to talk with Darrow. Beside him, Richard remained impassive.

Two rows behind him, Allan Loeb covered his face with his hands.

❁   ❁   ❁

The next day, a procession of classmates and former girlfriends took the stand. Their testimony was part of Darrow's plan to show how abnormally the teenagers behaved around their peers.

Fellow law school student Arnold Maremont testified that Nathan hadn't had any qualms about murder. "In fact, he made the statement one afternoon that . . . it would be perfectly alright in his philosophy to go out and murder a person."

Fraternity brother Max Schrayer told the court that Richard had fainted frequently, and drank so much he'd been officially censured by Zeta Beta Tau. At one point in his testimony, the lawyers began arguing over a minor point. Schrayer looked over at Richard. Grinning back, Richard made a rude gesture toward the attorneys. Then, in case Max didn't understand what he was saying about the lawyers' endless arguments, he cupped his mouth and said in a stage whisper, "Horseshit!"

Lorraine Nathan, the girl Richard had taken to a jazz club days after the murder, also took the stand. She described the night he'd come to her home and been introduced to some of her parents' friends. He'd behaved oddly, she said. "He started dancing down the middle of the room. [Later] we were passing some chocolates around, [and] he put his thumb into each to find the hard center. . . . Then he went out in the reception hall and tried on all the hats of the guests." It seemed so infantile and irrational. "We had [a] quarrel. I told him I found such a change in him that our relationship could not be anything else but brother and sister." She swiped away a tear. She'd been fond of Dickie.

On her way back to her seat, she passed Richard's chair. "Thanks, Lorraine," he said, "but I'm sorry you said that about me."

"I'm sorry I had to," she replied.

* * *

Dr. Harold Hulbert took the stand on Friday, August 8. Because of the leaked medical report, observers were familiar with his name. He described in detail the teenagers' blood pressure readings, blood sugar levels, and the amount of carbon dioxide in their blood, droning on all that day and into the next. At one point, he held up the X-ray of Nathan's skull and lectured about the pineal gland. At another, he reported that Richard's urine was of "clear transparency and amber color."

For once, even the boys looked bored.

* * *

In homes across America, many parents now saw in Nathan and Richard an object lesson in how *not* to raise their children. That week, Dr. Carleton Simon, a criminologist and police detective, wrote an article for the *Chicago Herald and Examiner* instructing parents on how to watch for early warning signs of mental illness in their own kids. The newspaper headlined it "This Is an Article Which Every Parent Should Read."

Other newspapers printed the IQ tests and puzzles completed by the teenagers. Parents were encouraged to compare their child's score to "Leopold the genius."

And Winifred Black, a columnist for the *Chicago Herald and Examiner,* asked readers to identify with the killers' parents. In her article titled "If Your Sons Were the Slayer," she wrote: "You sit there at your breakfast table, so comfortable, so much at peace with the world. . . . Would you stand for justice and for right, no matter if by taking a stand you had to walk to the very foot of the gallows with your own son?"

Any mother, it seemed, could be the mother of a Richard Loeb or a Nathan Leopold. Claimed one Chicago minister, the hearing and all its psychoanalytical discussion "caused more heart searching on the part of parents than any crime within memory."

⊚ ⊚ ⊚

Crowe began his cross-examination of Dr. Hulbert on the afternoon of Monday, August 11. Hot and irritable, the state's attorney haggled over petty details.

"Do you know the name of the [X-ray] machine you used?" he asked.

"A Victor portable," replied Hulbert.

"What kind of current, direct or alternating?"

"I don't know."

"What kind of tube?"

"All I know is, it was a new tube suitable for the portable machine. A Victor tube," said Hulbert.

"What transformer was used?"

"I don't know."

"Where was the transformer located on the machine?"

"I don't know."

"Was the Bucky diaphragm used?"

"I am not a radiologist."

Hulbert was getting irritable himself. Just because he didn't know how the X-ray machine worked didn't mean he couldn't understand what it showed.

But Crowe kept picking at the doctor, all that afternoon and into the next morning, trying to call Hulbert's expertise into question. He didn't quit until midday on August 12.

Finally, Darrow rose and called his last witness for the day—

Katherine Fitzgerald, Albert Loeb's secretary—to the stand. She testified that she'd been signing checks for Richard since he was nine years old—sometimes for as much as $250 (about $3,700 nowadays)—whenever he asked. She also corroborated that his monthly allowance was $125 ($1,850 today).

"Maybe that is one of the things that helped spoil him?" sniped Crowe during his cross-examination.

Darrow was pleased that the state's attorney had stated the fact outright. Richard Loeb *had* been spoiled. Darrow had called the secretary as a witness to show precisely that. It was proof that the teenager had lived an extravagant lifestyle—a lifestyle that was, in Darrow's opinion, partly to blame for Richard's actions. It also showed that the teenagers' motive for kidnapping and murder was definitely *not* the ransom money.

Mike Leopold took the stand the next morning. Like Richard, Nathan also received an allowance of $125 a month, plus extra money whenever he wanted it, Mike testified. Additionally, their father had planned to give Nathan $3,000 for his trip to Europe (around $45,000 currently).

Around the courtroom, spectators shook their heads in astonishment. At a time when the average annual American income was about $2,200 ($33,100 today), it was a stunning amount.

Darrow rested his case that afternoon.

And Crowe stood, ready to fight back. He called the prosecution's psychiatrists to the stand. Dr. Hugh Patrick testified first. Were the teenagers mentally ill?

"I found no evidence of mental illness," said Patrick.

But on cross-examination, Benjamin Bachrach sought to discredit that. How many people had been present in the room when

Patrick made this assessment? Bachrach asked. Did he think it was as many as fifteen?

"No, I shouldn't think so," said Patrick.

"Let us count them," said Bachrach. "There were the state's attorney and three assistants. That makes four."

"Four, and two prisoners makes six," said Patrick helpfully.

Bachrach added in three psychiatrists, a physician who'd popped in out of curiosity, and several police officers.

"Well, it might go to fifteen . . . ," admitted Patrick unhappily.

"And two stenographers?" added Bachrach.

"Yes, two stenographers. I guess it would reach—"

"About seventeen?"

"Well, I don't think so, but I don't know."

Bachrach agreed to settle on the conservative original estimate of fifteen people, all listening as Patrick spoke with Nathan and Richard. "Did you ever in your life make an examination . . . under circumstances of that kind?"

Patrick shook his head. "I think not."

Crowe called Dr. Archibald Church to the stand next. He, too, had found no mental disease in either boy.

This time Darrow stood to cross-examine. He was perplexed, he admitted. How could either of the doctors have made a diagnosis? They'd had just one chance, together, to examine the boys. That hardly seemed like enough time. Even more perplexing was *how* they'd examined Richard and Nathan. "Now, there were some fifteen people in the room when you were talking with these boys," he said.

"Hardly that many," replied Church argumentatively. "But there were many, I think."

"Too many for a thorough consultation," insisted Darrow.

"Too many for an ideal consultation," admitted Church.

Darrow wanted to know if the doctor had ever before examined a patient in front of that many people.

"No," said Church.

"Did you ask any questions?"

"Yes."

"Who did most of the questioning?"

Church looked toward the prosecutor's table. "Really, there were very few questions asked. Dr. Patrick asked a few, and Dr. Krohn asked a few, and Mr. Crowe asked a few—"

Darrow made a shocked face, signaling to the court his surprise that the state's attorney was asking patients questions during a medical examination. "Did you ask any questions to find out evidence of mental disease?"

Church shook his head. "No."

Again, Darrow feigned shock. It was incredible how in just one visit, with fifteen people present, and without asking a single question, Dr. Church had been able to declare the defendants free of any mental illness.

The doctor flushed with anger.

Nathan and Richard grinned.

Dr. William Krohn testified last. He agreed with the other state psychiatrists. The defendants showed absolutely no signs of mental illness. Yes, he did concede the inadequacy of the examination. No, he did not concede the inaccuracy of his diagnosis. On the day he observed the teenagers, their "eyes, ears, all of the senses were working normally. . . . [Their] stream of thought flowed without any interruptions. . . . There was not a single remark made that was beside the point. The answer to every question was responsive. . . .

There was not a single piece of evidence of any defect, any disorder, any lack of development, or any disease."

No matter what Darrow asked, he could not shake Krohn from this position.

Crowe was delighted. The state's psychiatrists had gotten the last word on the subject, and they'd declared the teenagers sane.

CHAPTER TWENTY-TWO

"THE AGEING LION" VS. "FIGHTING BOB"

Closing arguments began on August 19. Assistant State's Attorney Thomas Marshall rose and spoke first. Why should Leopold and Loeb, these pampered, coddled killers, escape the death penalty when those far less advantaged hanged?

He reminded the court of Bernard Grant and Walter Krauser, the teenagers who'd killed a police officer during a store robbery. Both youths had appealed their sentences that summer, and while Krauser's case was still pending, Grant had just received bitter news: his sentence stood. His execution had been scheduled for October.

And yet, Marshall pointed out, "[Grant] had no original intention to commit the murder. Shall Grant go to the gallows under the law, when men of the same age, of greater education, of better opportunity can deliberately scheme a murder and kidnapping for months and months, carry it out and escape the penalty?"

Marshall went on to name seventeen men—some of them younger than Nathan and Richard—who'd been sentenced to death. Not one of them had been rich and privileged. Not one had been able to afford fancy lawyers. What about nineteen-year-old David

Anderson, hanged in 1908 for the murder of a plainclothes detective? Anderson—illiterate and destitute—hadn't done the actual shooting. His companion had. Still, the teenager had hanged. And then there was Nicholas Viana. He'd been executed in 1920 on the morning of his eighteenth birthday for shooting a man during a pool hall robbery. The vicious Cardinelli gang had initiated Viana, who'd come from a broken home, into a life of crime at a young age. Shouldn't his circumstance have warranted mitigation of punishment? Instead, his life had ended on the gallows.

And here sat Leopold and Loeb, guilty of the most depraved crime Marshall had ever encountered. "There is nothing like it in Illinois jurisprudence . . . the premeditation, the deliberate malice, the cunning plans, the months of preparation. . . . There is only one sentence that can be imposed upon these vile culprits . . . any lesser penalty than [death] would make a mockery of the law."

        © © ©

Assistant State's Attorney Joseph Savage spoke next. He recited the crime's details so graphically that Jacob Franks fled the courtroom. The brutal remarks even shattered Nathan's cool facade. During a break, he gripped his brother's arm and cried, "My God, Mike, do you think we'll swing after that?"

Walter Bachrach followed the assistant state's attorneys. He took the opportunity to further educate the court about the medical advances in understanding and treating mental illness. The air grew thick with terms like *diseased personality, unconscious influence,* and *inner life.*

In the 1920s, in significant cases, it was common for multiple lawyers from both sides to speak. They often took many hours—spread out over two or three days—to give their closing arguments. It was also not unusual for the prosecution and defense to go back and forth.

It wasn't until the afternoon of Friday, August 22, that Darrow rose to speak.

Word spread like wildfire:

"Darrow this afternoon."

"Darrow is on."

"It's Darrow!"

The lawyer's speeches were legendary. As one reporter noted, "the Ageing Lion" made them without notes, and in "marvelous displays of intellect and concentration." Like a weaver, he'd range back and forth across a case, laying down the facts from different viewpoints. His rhetoric both sprawled and soared. He could be by turns angry, humorous, and sorrowful. And all the while, he could reshape a case and invite the court to look far beyond the issue of guilt or innocence.

Mobs made a beeline for the Criminal Courts Building. After sweeping past a skirmish line of bailiffs stationed at the main entrance, they spilled along the corridors and up the stairs and elevators. Pushing and shoving, they ripped doors off their hinges and flattened police. It was, reported the *Chicago Herald and Examiner,* "a maelstrom of rioters who trampled upon each other, clawed at the police and deputies, tore each other's clothing, cursed, and for a critical half hour threatened wholesale bloodshed."

Caverly ordered the courtroom's doors barred. Shouting and pounding could be heard from outside as police continued to battle the crowds. Then those in the courtroom heard the sickening thud of wooden clubs on human flesh. There came howls of pain and protest. Finally, there was silence.

Darrow rose. Arms folded, he spoke directly to the judge. There was no need to go into the detailed testimony of the defense's psychiatric experts, he said. It was crystal clear from the bizarre nature of the crime that forces beyond their control gripped Dickie and Babe. "It was the senseless act of immature and diseased children . . . wandering around in the darkness and moved by some emotions that we still, perhaps, have not the knowledge or the insight to thoroughly understand."

As he often did in his closing arguments, Darrow tried to make a larger point to his fellow Americans—in this case, about the evils of capital punishment. He'd brought it up briefly in his opening statement. Now he returned to the topic with fervor. "This world has been one long slaughterhouse from the beginning until today, and the killing goes on and on and on and will forever. Why not read something, why not study something, why not think instead of blindly calling for death? Kill them! Will that prevent other senseless boys or other vicious men or vicious women? No." The death penalty did not deter crime.

Caverly leaned forward and rested his chin on his clasped hands, listening.

Darrow went on. "I know that any mother might be the mother of a little Bobby Franks, who left his home and went to school, and whose life was taken, and who never came back," he said. But "I know that any mother might be the mother of Richard Loeb and Nathan Leopold. . . . Any mother might be the mother of any of them."

Walking back and forth before the bench, wiping sweat from his neck with his handkerchief, he said, "I remember a little poem . . ." Then in a voice so low only those in the front of the courtroom could hear him, he recited a verse by A. E. Housman:

And so the game is ended,
That should not have begun.
My father and my mother
They had a likely son,
And I have none.

Darrow turned to face Caverly again. "No one knows what will be the fate of the child they get or the child they bear. I am sorry for these fathers and these mothers. The mother who looks into the blue eyes of her little babe cannot help wonder what will be the end of this child, whether it will be crowned with the greatest promises which her mind can imagine, or whether he may meet death from the gallows." He paused. "All she can do is raise him with care, to watch over him tenderly, to meet life with hope and with trust and confidence and to leave the rest to fate." Moving back to the defense table, he sat. He was finished for the day.

People in the courtroom were sobbing. Even Nathan seemed moved. Minutes later, as the teenagers were led from the courtroom, he stumbled and appeared dazed.

Richard, too, was seemingly affected. That night from his jail cell he wrote to Darrow: "Only the tears in my eyes as you talked, and the feeling in my heart could express the admiration . . . I have for you. I have gone through so much of my life as a play actor—but I am sure you know when it is the heart that is speaking. A heart, Mr. Darrow, with a thick coating of deceit, of selfishness, but a heart that way down deep must, because I am the son of my father and mother, have some good in it, and my message comes from there."

Darrow was unmoved by these words. Richard, he knew, took pleasure in duping people by acting sincere. The shrewd attorney felt sure the letter had been written strictly for effect. He filed it away, believing it was nothing but manipulation.

             ◉   ◉   ◉

Crowds appeared again the next morning. This time, double lines of armed police stood at the ready. Contained outside on the sidewalk, the crowd fell quiet in hopes of hearing Darrow through the open courtroom windows.

Because it was Saturday, the session was just two hours long. Darrow filled every minute with his melodious baritone voice. As always, he spoke without notes. His solemn words were not about the murderers, but about the case being society's chance to throw off the barbaric practice of execution. It was a chance, he suggested, for them all to become human.

"I can picture [Dickie and Babe] wakened in the gray light of morning, furnished a suit of clothes by the state, led to the scaffold, their feet tied, a black cap drawn over their heads, placed on a trapdoor . . . so that it falls under them and they are only stopped by the rope around their necks."

Darrow took a deep breath and exhaled slowly. "Do I need to argue to Your Honor that cruelty only makes cruelty? That hatred only causes hatred? That if there is any way to . . . soften the human heart, which is hard enough at its best, if there is any way to kill evil and hatred and all that goes with it, it is not through evil and hatred and cruelty; it is through charity and love and understanding."

He shrugged and dropped his arms in a gesture of futility. "I am asking Your Honor not to visit that grave and dire and terrible misfortune . . . upon these two boys. . . . [It] is brutality and cruelty. And what would it gain?" He shook his head. "Nothing."

He returned to the defense table, tears streaming down his face, as Caverly adjourned court.

◉ ◉ ◉

The following Monday, the sixty-seven-year-old Darrow again rose. And again he spoke all day. In the heat of the courtroom, his seersucker suit showed sweat stains. What had caused the teenagers to commit this terrible crime? Darrow could only speculate, he admitted. But he had a theory. "Over and over in the courts, [judges] have been asked to consider boys who have no chance; and they have been asked to consider the poor, whose homes have been the street, with no education and no opportunity in life." This was, of course, the right thing to do. "But, Your Honor, it is just as often a great misfortune to be the child of the rich as it is to be a child of the poor."

Robert Crowe snorted loudly.

Darrow ignored him and went on. "Wealth has its misfortunes. Too much, too great opportunity and advantage given to a child has its misfortunes, and I am asking Your Honor to consider the rich as well as the poor.

"Can I find the wrong? I think I can. Here was [Dickie Loeb] at a tender age, placed in the hands of a governess . . . pushed in his studies as plants are forced in hot houses. . . . He had no pleasures, such as a boy should have, except in what he gained from lying and cheating," Darrow said. And in Dickie's brain grew a "twisted" hunger for crime. Could the court truly hang such a child? "This boy needed more of home, more love, more directing. He needed to have his emotions awakened. He needed guiding hands along the serious road that youth must travel."

Darrow turned to Nathan. "He was just a half-boy, an intellect, an intellectual machine going without balance. . . . At seventeen, at sixteen, at eighteen, while healthy boys were playing baseball or working on the farm, or doing odd jobs, he was reading Nietzsche. . . . [Yet] here is this boy, in the adolescent age, harassed by everything that harasses children, who takes this philosophy and swallows it, who believes it literally, lives his life on it."

In the courtroom, people had stopped fanning themselves so they could hear better. Many nodded. Others murmured their assent. Darrow was delivering a captivating sermon, intellectually far above the usual legal wrangling. He was advocating mercy for reasons that were new and completely unconventional. He was saying that Nathan's and Richard's privileged upbringings had left them as emotionally and psychologically scarred as living in poverty and neglect might have.

"I am trying to trace causes," Darrow went on. "I am trying to trace them honestly. I am trying to trace them with the light I have. I am trying to say to this court that these boys aren't responsible for this. . . . [I'm] asking this court not to visit the judgment of wrath upon them for things for which they are not to blame. . . ."

Darrow laid his hands on the judge's bench. "Sometimes, Your Honor, a boy of great promise is cut off in his early youth. Sometimes he dies and is placed in a culvert. Sometimes a boy of great promise stands on a trapdoor and is hanged until dead."

Shouldn't the defendants' young age be reason enough for mercy? "I do not know how much salvage there is in these two boys. I hate to say it in their presence, but what is there to look forward to?" Maybe, he mused, it would be more merciful for them to be hanged. "Merciful to them, but not to civilization, and not merciful to those who would be left behind. I do not know; to spend the balance of their days in prison is mighty little to look forward to, if anything . . . There's nothing but the night."

He wiped tears from his face with the back of his hand. So did many others in the courtroom, including Nathan Sr.

Nathan and Richard looked down at the floor.

"I have stood here . . . as somebody might stand at the seacoast trying to sweep back the tide. I hope the seas are subsiding and the wind is falling and I believe they are. But I wish to make no false pretense to this court. The easy thing and the popular thing to do is to hang my clients. I know it."

He sighed. "Men and women who do not think will applaud. The cruel and thoughtless will approve. Your Honor stands now between the future and the past. . . . I am pleading for life, understanding, charity and kindness and the infinite mercy that forgives all. I am pleading that we overcome cruelty with kindness, and hatred with love. I know the future is on my side. You may hang these boys; you may hang them from the neck till they're dead. But in doing it, you will turn your face to the past. In doing it, you are making it harder for every other boy."

He was coming to the end now, his voice choking with emotion. "[Or] you may save them and make it easier for every child that some time may stand here where these boys stand. . . . I am pleading for the future; I am pleading for a time when hatred and cruelty will not control the hearts of men. When we can learn by reason and judgment and understanding and faith that all life is worth saving, and that mercy is the highest attribute of man."

Again, he wiped away tears. "I was reading last night of the aspiration of that . . . poet Omar Khayyam. It appealed to me as the highest I can envision. I wish it was in my heart, and I wish it was in the heart of all, and I can do no better than to quote what he said:

So I be written in the Book of Love,
I do not care about that Book above.
Erase my name or write it as you will,
So I be written in the Book of Love.

Darrow's voice had grown so soft that only Judge Caverly and a few others could hear him. The courtroom waited in silence. One minute. Two minutes.

Darrow patted the judge's bench, nodded, and sat down. Tears coursed down his face.

Tears coursed down Judge Caverly's face, too.

◦ ◦ ◦

Clarence Darrow was mythic, claimed the *Chicago Daily Tribune*. He had "wandered in a labyrinth of laws" and "slain a dragon—Man's inhumanity to man." Spectators had arrived in the courtroom convinced that Leopold and Loeb should be hanged. But after experiencing Darrow's "marvelous skill as a pleader," they had "wavered and changed their minds, and come to believe that, after all, [the boys] must not be sent to the gallows." The lawyer had "performed a miracle," the newspaper concluded.

◦ ◦ ◦

Crowe began his closing argument the next morning by deriding Clarence Darrow as "the distinguished gentleman whose profession it is to protect murder in Cook County." He ridiculed the new-school psychiatrists as "the three wise men from the East who came to tell Your Honor about these babes." And for the next three days he would rant, shout, stomp, and wave his hands in the air. "Now he thrust his face, purple with the strain of apoplectic speech, into the faces of Loeb and Leopold, now he strode before Judge Caverly, shaking his fist," reported the *Chicago Daily News*. "There were no valleys in the speech, just peaks . . . strident, impassioned, almost delirious."

"Treat [the defendants] with kindness and consideration?" Crowe shouted. "Call them babes, call them children? Why, from the evidence in this case they are as much entitled to sympathy and mercy of this court as a couple of rattlesnakes, flushed with venom, coiled and ready to strike. They are entitled to as much mercy at the hands of Your Honor as two mad dogs. . . . They are no good to themselves. . . . The only useful thing that remains for them in life is to go out of it as quickly as possible under the law."

His tone switched from angry to mocking. "But Mr. Darrow says, 'These poor little sons of multimillionaires. It is their wealth that is their misfortune. . . .'" He gave a sarcastic laugh. "Their wealth, in my judgment, has nothing to do with this, except it permits a defense here seldom given to men in criminal court.

"Take away the millions of the Loebs and Leopolds, and Clarence Darrow's tongue is as silent as [a] tomb. . . .

"Take away their millions, and the wise men from the East would not be here. . . .

"Take away their money, and what happens? The same thing that has happened to all other men who have been tried in this building, who had no money."

Crowe's voice changed again, his sarcasm turning steely. "Clarence Darrow once said that a poor man on trial here was disposed of in fifteen minutes, but if he was rich and committed the same crime and he got a good lawyer, his trial would last twenty-one days. Well, they got *three* lawyers, and it has lasted just a little bit longer.

"What are we trying here . . . a murder as a result of a drunken brawl. . . . A murder committed by some young [waif] of the streets whose father is a drunkard and his mother loose; who was denied every opportunity, brought up in the slums; never had a decent example set before him? No. [We are trying] a murder committed by two super-intellects coming from the homes of the most respected families in Chicago. Every advantage that love, money and wealth and position could give them was theirs. . . . They had the power of choice, and they deliberately chose to adopt the wrong philosophy."

He stalked toward the judge's bench. "Mitigation! Mitigation!" he cried before attacking Darrow's "illegal use" of mental illness as mitigating circumstance. He mocked all the "big and foreign-sounding words" used by the defense experts. And he insisted that there *was* a reason for the crime. It wasn't done merely for thrills, as the defense maintained, or because the defendants lacked emotions and morals. It was done, boomed Crowe, "to satisfy unnatural lusts."

Spectators murmured.

"What happened?" Crowe shouted. "Immediately upon killing [Bobby Franks] they took his trousers off . . . and they did not take the balance of the clothes off until they pushed the body into the culvert."

"Objection!" cried Benjamin Bachrach. "The coroner's report said there was no sign of [sexual abuse]." He insisted Judge Caverly examine that report.

But Caverly seemed more concerned about the women in the courtroom. He didn't believe women should be subjected to such a sordid discussion. He ordered them out into the hall.

Most stayed in their seats.

Crowe was screaming. "From the fact that the pants were taken off and the fact that they were perverts, I have a right to argue they committed an act of perversion."

Despite the lack of corroborating evidence, Crowe was trying to connect the teenagers' homosexuality with pedophilia.

Caverly demanded that the bailiff bring him a copy of the coroner's report. Then he handed it to Walter Bachrach and asked him to read the page-and-a-half report aloud so it would be in the court record.

Once more, those in the courtroom heard the list of wounds found on Bobby Franks's body. The report also stated that no evidence of sexual abuse had been found.

Benjamin Bachrach nodded. The facts spoke for themselves.

"It is a matter of argument," declared Crowe.

"I don't think that is a matter of argument," countered Darrow.

Crowe whirled around. "I don't think you and I are going to agree. You have your theory, and I have mine."

"The coroner's report says there is no evidence of it," insisted Darrow.

"You have your contention, and I have mine."

During this exchange, Benjamin Bachrach fumed. He knew that Crowe's accusation—which he had saved until his closing argument—was meant to prejudice and inflame the court. It was unfair, Bachrach argued, to make the charge now, when the defense could not reply to it. Besides, he repeated, there was no evidence.

"The evidence is these defendants are perverts," bellowed Crowe stubbornly.

The judge had had enough. The corner's evidence was conclusive, he ruled. "We will let it rest with what the coroner says." With that, he rapped his gavel and adjourned court until morning.

The state's attorney was no calmer the second day of his closing arguments. Crowe continued with his harangue by attacking the Bowman-Hulbert report point by point. He hinted that the teenagers had committed other crimes more gruesome than this one. And he speculated (without evidence) that Nathan wanted the ransom money so he could go to Europe or Hawaii and pursue his "perverted lusts."

And still Crowe kept talking—all that second day, and into the third. He was less fiery on the third day, and his voice had grown hoarse. His final arguments were against Darrow's "dangerous philosophy of life." He wanted to "soften the law," said Crowe. But leniency had no place in this case. Neither did mercy. If the judge said the boys "ought not to hang when the laws say you should, a greater blow has struck our institutions than by a hundred, yes, a thousand murders."

Caverly listened closely.

Then Crowe brought up the testimony given by Detective Gortland about Nathan's desire to appear before a "friendly judge." "I don't know if Your Honor believes the officer, or not, but . . . everybody connected with this case [on the defense side] have laughed and sneered and jeered, and if the defendant, Leopold, did not say that he would plead guilty before a friendly judge, his actions demonstrated that he thinks he has got one."

It was a huge miscalculation by the prosecutor. Judge Caverly suddenly leaned forward with an outraged expression. Was Crowe suggesting that Nathan had, indeed, found that "friendly judge"? That Caverly had taken a bribe? He glared at the state's attorney but said nothing.

Crowe was stunned. All his swaggering bluster disappeared. "You have listened with a great deal of patience and kindness and consideration to the State and the defense," he said in a stammering rush. "I am not going to unduly trespass upon Your Honor's time, and I am going to close for the State."

At this point, Crowe directed the court's attention to the charge of kidnapping against Nathan and Richard. It was no more than a formality; they had already presented testimony both in mitigation and aggravation for the charge of murder. Jacob Franks testified that his son had been kidnapped and murdered, and the ransom note was read into the record. The defense presented no arguments or objections.

Through this entire process Caverly remained stony. And as soon as the state rested, he let Crowe have it. "The court will order stricken from the record the closing remarks of the state's attorney as being a cowardly and dastardly assault upon the integrity of this court."

"It was not so intended, Your Honor," Crowe began.

Caverly cut him off. "And it could not be used for any other purpose except to incite [the public] and try to intimidate this court. It will be stricken from the record."

Crowe tried to smooth over the situation.

But the judge cut him off again. "The court will not be intimidated by anybody at any time or place. . . ." He waved his hands, refusing to let Crowe speak another word. Then he looked at his calendar, announced that he would rule on September 10, and left the room.

CHAPTER TWENTY-THREE

WAITING

Nathan and Richard found plenty of ways to fill their time as they waited for Caverly's verdict. The very afternoon their hearing ended, they headed over to the jail's indoor baseball diamond to blow off some steam.

Richard, who was the captain of his team, the Seventh Floors (despite his now being kept on the sixth floor), took his position on the pitcher's mound.

Nathan, who'd overcome his reluctance to interact with the other inmates, joined his team, the Alley Rats. He wasn't a good player, but he'd come to enjoy the game, perhaps because six members of the Chicago Cubs had turned up in the warden's office a few weeks earlier. They'd wanted to "tour the jail and see the young murderers," and the team's slugger, Gabby Hartnett, had ended up in the prison yard with Nathan. He'd corrected the teenager's batting stance and had given him some hitting tips.

As August turned to September, the number of visitors wanting to see Richard and Nathan grew. Reporters, former girlfriends, relatives, and classmates dropped in for a chat. Believing the teenagers would hang, the warden let them visit with whomever they chose.

One of those visitors was Patches Reinhardt, the flapper and sometimes girlfriend Richard had taken dancing two nights after the murder. When he learned she was down in the waiting area, he quickly changed out of his prison uniform. Minutes later, he greeted her looking more like a college student than a murderer, in a brand-new pea-green tweed suit and his gold University of Michigan class pin. Patches flung her arms around him. As Richard grinned and the jail guards watched, she peppered him with kisses.

On some Sundays, the prison held concerts. The teenagers enjoyed them, and occasionally Nathan even stepped forward to play a few songs on the piano. One of these tunes, "Hot Lips," reminded Richard of the first time he'd heard it. It was at a "dancing party on a yacht on Lake Michigan," he told reporters. "I was dancing with my partner along the deck, close to the rail . . . the boat pitching and tossing to that tune." And now he was hearing it again inside the county jail. Still, things could be worse, he added. Truly, he didn't feel unhappy. He now had "regular meals and regular sleep. . . . Instead of getting in at 3 a.m. and getting up at 7 to play tennis or golf, I now get at least eight hours regular sleep." His words, however, had a hollow ring.

Nathan told reporters he'd already drawn up his will. He had decided to donate his beloved bird collection to Chicago's Field Museum of Natural History. He also made a list of ten questions he would try to answer after his death if scientists managed to contact him. They included "Are the experiences in human life carried into the hereafter?" and "Is the intellectual or the spiritual the dominant note after death?"

Nathan had read in one of the newspapers that bookies were offering three-to-one odds against hanging. One day, he suggested to the reporters gathered around his cell that they make their own wager. In fact, he joked, he'd like to bet on the outcome himself. Too bad the county jail had a rule against prisoners gambling.

Another day, Nathan told reporters he planned to make a farewell speech from the gallows. "I will say something that will make the world listen," he declared. He also hoped a jazz band would play at the event, and that "plenty of hard cider" would be served.

Richard didn't care about wills or final words. He claimed not to care about Caverly's verdict, either. "I don't give a damn whether I am hanged or not," he told reporters. "The folks are to be considered, but for myself, it doesn't mean that much."

◉ ◉ ◉

On August 31, the *Chicago Daily Tribune* reported that the Frankses had sold their home. They took almost nothing with them, just personal keepsakes and photographs, including all of Bobby's games, his books, and his radio set, as well as the stained-glass window from the first-floor landing that depicted him with his siblings. The rest of their belongings were offered at auction.

A preview of those items in early September drew hundreds of curiosity-seekers. According to one reporter, people "fought to get into the rooms where Robert Franks had slept before he was made the victim of Loeb's and Leopold's experiments."

The family was spared seeing this. They'd already moved downtown to the Drake Hotel.

◉ ◉ ◉

Newspapers speculated about Anna and Albert Loeb. Would they return for Judge Caverly's decision? It seemed doubtful. Albert—who hadn't been seen in public since his son's confession—had suffered another heart attack on August 31. His doctor told reporters that it had been brought on by grief and worry. At least for now, Richard's parents would remain in Charlevoix.

◉ ◉ ◉

Meanwhile, Nathan Sr. took solace in his Kenwood home. The place was filled with memories, and the grief-stricken father found comfort in looking back on better times.

Was he happy there? reporters asked him.

He doubted he could be happy anywhere, he replied. But "no matter where I go, I can find no greater peace [than] here."

CHAPTER TWENTY-FOUR

"NOTHING BUT THE NIGHT"

On Wednesday, September 10, the day of the sentencing, Judge Caverly rose early. After finishing his breakfast, he was accompanied by two bodyguards on a walk along the shore of Lake Michigan. The sultry summer weather had at last broken, and a crisp breeze blew off the lake. The courtroom's temperature would be bearable. It was a small blessing.

For Caverly, the hot, tense days in court had been followed by two stressful weeks. Threats had flooded into both his office and his home. One letter writer promised to blow up the Criminal Courts Building if the judge didn't impose the death penalty. Another said he'd shoot Caverly if he *did* impose it. And one day, while the judge was attending a funeral, a cruel prankster telephoned Caverly's apartment pretending to be a police officer. "Your husband . . . has been shot to death [at] . . . the gate of Calvary Cemetery. Come quick!" he said. Caverly's terrified wife had leaped into a taxi—and arrived at the cemetery just as her husband came strolling, unharmed, through the gates. Sobbing hysterically, she fell into his arms.

The enraged judge had his phone disconnected. Police guards

were placed at his front door. "I am not afraid of these insane threats," he said, but it must have made deliberation on the case even more difficult.

After he returned from the lake, the judge changed into his black suit and went out to meet the three squad cars assigned to take him to the courthouse. He climbed into the backseat of the middle one. Two sharpshooters took their places on either side of him.

As they neared the courthouse, Caverly looked warily out at the crowds. Police refused to let anyone get within a block of the building. Still, five thousand people already clogged the streets. Suspense had reached a fever pitch. Would the teenagers live or die?

Inside the building, people were filing into the courtroom. As always, Nathan Sr. and his son Mike entered together. Both looked strained. They took seats next to Jacob and Allan Loeb. Allan placed a steadying hand on Nathan Sr.'s arm.

A reporter approached Darrow at the defense table. He asked how the lawyer felt.

"Well, I'm always a little nervous on these occasions," Darrow replied.

Next to him, Benjamin and Walter Bachrach nodded in agreement, while across the aisle, Crowe and his men leaned back in their chairs, looking confident. The state's attorney smiled for a photographer.

Jacob Franks had stayed home.

Meanwhile, Nathan and Richard chain-smoked cigarettes and waited to be led into the courtroom. Reporters asked if they were worried.

"Why worry?" said Richard. "Judge Caverly has made up his mind, and worrying isn't going to change it."

At exactly nine-thirty, an exhausted-looking Caverly took the bench. On either side of him stood an armed guard. He called for the defendants to be brought in.

Nathan kept his eyes pinned to the floor as he entered. But Richard looked around. He smiled at his uncle and brother.

The pair moved to the defense table, where they remained standing. Benjamin Bachrach rose to stand with them.

"Have the two defendants anything to say in either case?" asked Judge Caverly.

Benjamin Bachrach spoke for them. "No, Your Honor."

The teenagers sat, and Nathan Sr., who was seated directly behind them, gripped the arms of his chair.

Caverly looked down at the three sheets on which he'd written his sentence. He began reading. "In view of the profound and unusual interest [in] this case—"

Cameras flashed.

The judge paused. "Go ahead now," he told the photographers. "Take your pictures. I will wait until you are through."

And so, while the defendants waited to learn if they would live or die, the newspaper photographers snapped away.

At last, Caverly ended the picture-taking and started again. Nathan Leopold and Richard Loeb, he declared, were not insane, although they were certainly abnormal. "Had they been normal they would not have committed the crime," he said. Yes, the testimony of the defense's psychiatrists had been fascinating. It was, he believed, a valuable contribution to criminology. But none of it had affected his decision. "The court is satisfied that neither in the act itself, nor in its motives or lack of motives, or in the [childhood] of the offenders, can it find any mitigating circumstances."

No mitigating circumstances.

With that one sentence, the judge shattered Darrow's psychological defense.

Nathan Sr.'s eyes filled with tears.

"It's hanging," people in the courtroom whispered.

Reporters edged toward the door.

But Darrow had also argued in his closing statement against the death penalty as a societal remedy to crime. Had the judge been moved by his eloquent appeal?

Caverly continued. "It would have been the path of least resistance to impose the extreme penalty of the law."

Nathan's head jerked up.

The judge's next words shot through Nathan like an arrow. "In choosing imprisonment instead of death, the court is moved chiefly by the consideration of the age of the defendants. . . . The court believes it is within his [authority] to decline to impose the sentence of death on persons who are not full age."

The courtroom was buzzing again.

Caverly silenced it with a fierce look before continuing with his decision. No, the defendant's youth was not a mitigating circumstance in the legal sense. But taking their age into account was, he said, "in accordance with . . . the dictates of enlightened humanity. More than that, it seems to be in accordance with Illinois precedence. . . . The records of Illinois show only two cases of minors who were put to death by legal process . . . to which number the court does not feel inclined to make an addition."

Caverly paused a moment. Then he formally passed sentence:

"In No. 33,623, indictment for murder, the sentence of the court is that you, Nathan F. Leopold Jr., be confined in the penitentiary at Joliet for the term of your natural life."

"In No. 33,623, indictment for murder, the sentence of the court is that you, Richard Loeb, be confined in the penitentiary at Joliet for the term of your natural life."

"In No. 33,624, kidnapping for ransom, it is the sentence of the court that you, Nathan F. Leopold Jr., be confined in the penitentiary at Joliet for the term of 99 years."

"In No. 33,624, kidnapping for ransom, it is the sentence of the court that you, Richard Loeb, be confined in the penitentiary at Joliet for the term of 99 years."

Life plus ninety-nine years.

Nathan Sr. was crying freely now. He reached forward and laid his trembling hand on Nathan's shoulder. Nathan looked relieved. Not, he later claimed, because he'd escaped the gallows, but because "the tension of uncertainty" had been alleviated. He now knew his future. Richard turned and smiled at his brother. Reporters raced from the room to file their stories.

At the back of the room, a deputy sheriff poked his head into the corridor. "Rest o' natural life," he told the police officer standing guard. The officer passed the verdict on to a bailiff, who passed it along to another officer. Eventually, it spread to the guards stationed at the main entrance. One of them cupped his mouth and shouted to a motorcycle cop, "It's life!" He carried the news to the crowd, and in a twinkling five thousand people were repeating it over and over. "Yeah, it's life."

It was a tremendous victory for Clarence Darrow. He turned to shake his clients' hands. Their fingers barely touched before guards whisked Richard and Nathan away.

Reporters flocked around the attorney. "I have always hated capital punishment," he told them. "This decision caps my career as a criminal lawyer."

Would the boys ever get paroled?

Darrow nodded. Based on his understanding of the law, he thought the pair might be eligible for parole within thirty years or so.

Reporters swirled around Nathan's and Richard's relatives, too. Jacob Loeb spoke for both families: "There is little to say. We have been spared the death penalty, but what have [we] to look forward to? . . . What is there in the future but grief and sorrow, darkness and despair?"

Robert Crowe refused to talk with reporters. His face stormy, he crossed over to Darrow and shook his hand. Then he elbowed his way out the door. Back in his office, he wrote an official statement, which he distributed to the press. "The state's attorney's duty was performed," he reminded the public, who would be casting their votes in less than eight weeks. "He is in no measure responsible for the decision of the court."

Within minutes of the sentencing, reporters were pounding on the Frankses' door at the Drake Hotel. Jacob wasn't there, but Flora said a few words: "Bobby didn't believe in capital punishment. He wrote about it and read his article at school, and told me it was wrong and somehow—after that—how could I ask it? I didn't want to say or do anything that interfered with the prosecution, of course, but—I didn't want them to hang."

And in the Cook County Jail, Nathan and Richard celebrated. Tomorrow they'd be sent to the Illinois State Penitentiary in Joliet. But tonight they would feast.

"Go out and order us a big meal," Nathan told his jailers. "Get us two steaks this thick." With his thumb and finger, he measured off three inches.

"Yes," agreed Richard, "and be sure they are smothered in onions.

And bring every side dish that you can find. This may be our last good meal."

"And bring chocolate éclairs for dessert," added Nathan.

◎ ◎ ◎

"Faced with the facts of the gruesome case, the death sentence should have been an easy one," the *San Francisco Bulletin* declared. It found Caverly's argument about the defendants' youth nothing more than an excuse. The real reason Leopold and Loeb got off was that "there is one law for the obscure, and one law for the socially prominent."

The *Kansas City Post* agreed: "The theory that there is one set of laws for the rich and another for the friendless poor [is] gnawing at the very vitals of national confidence and pride."

So did the *New York Sun:* "The sentence shakes the faith of the people in the blind equality of justice. They will not believe any poor man who committed [such] a crime . . . would have escaped death."

But other newspapers applauded the decision. The *New York Times* homed in on the fact that Caverly had based his decision on the criminals' age, not their wealth. In fact, all the pricey lawyers and experts "went for nothing," editors wrote. "Judge Caverly simply ignored [them]. Had the youthful murderers been poor and friendless, they would have escaped capital punishment as Leopold and Loeb escaped it." This proved that there was not "one law for the poor and one for the rich."

In Chicago, many people were left scratching their heads. There wasn't any Illinois law that excused criminals younger than twenty-one from hanging. Indeed, as both Crowe and Assistant State's

Attorney Thomas Marshall had pointed out in their closing arguments, the state *had* twice executed youths. To some, it appeared
that Caverly had seized on the pair's ages as a convenient excuse for
helping out the rich families. Others wondered when the judge had
made his decision. He'd known the boys' ages from the day they'd
been arrested. Had he always believed their youth precluded them
from hanging?

And what about Bernard Grant, who was scheduled to hang
in six weeks? Wasn't he as deserving of life in prison as Leopold
and Loeb—perhaps even more so? Mary Grant, his mother, bitterly
compared her son's fate to theirs. "What can *we* do?" she asked reporters. "We were not able to hire [psychiatrists] at $250 a day to say
he is insane." In an editorial printed on September 14, just four days
after Caverly's decision, the *Chicago Sunday Tribune* urged clemency
for Grant. "If he hangs while Leopold and Loeb live, the inequality in
our process of justice will be gross." Six days later, Illinois governor
Len Small stayed Grant's execution, but his sentence was never commuted. He was stabbed to death in prison by his partner in crime,
Walter Krauser, before that could happen. Krauser went on to serve
two consecutive life sentences—one for the murder of the police officer and the other for the murder of Bernard Grant.

The public was especially worried that the killers would somehow get an early release. The wording of Judge Caverly's decision
fueled this concern. For some reason, it did not specifically state
that the sentences—life plus ninety-nine years—should be served
one after the other. This meant that the sentences would run con-
currently, with the prisoner serving the longer of the two. Had the
judge done this on purpose, or had it been an oversight?

Some people believed it was intentional.

But others claimed it didn't matter. Life was life. What could be longer than that?

Hinton G. Clabaugh, Illinois supervisor of pardons and paroles, weighed in. According to the law, men serving life sentences were eligible for parole after twenty years. Additionally, they could reduce their time through good behavior and the prison's merit system. Either teen, he said, could be out of prison in eleven years and three months. "They will still be young men scarcely over 30 years old," he said. "I don't mean to say [they] will necessarily be out in eleven years . . . but I do say it is hard to see how their legal privileges can be denied them any more than to other convicts."

Eleven years! Chicagoans were aghast. And even more convinced that the families had bought their sons' way out of trouble. The *Chicago Daily Tribune* summed up the sentiment best. "Life-imprisonment . . . [is] justified only if these two youthful murderers are placed in confinement so deep they will never be heard from again."

         ◉ ◉ ◉

Sometime in the hours before he was taken to the penitentiary in Joliet, Nathan Leopold scrawled a long letter of thanks to Clarence Darrow. He praised the lawyer, claiming he'd never met anyone as brave or intelligent. "This alone would cause me to bow down in abject hero-worship," he wrote. "It would be an inconsistent Superman indeed who did not reverence his superior." But it was Darrow's heart that surprised Nathan the most, "a heart in which there is room for all the world even including murderers and state's attorneys." Nathan marveled at the "spontaneous sympathy and understanding which instantly goes out of you to the most dastardly criminal. It [would be] sacrilege for me, who is so utterly lacking them, to attempt to measure them. But even lacking them, I can admire and wonder in awe."

Darrow would reply three weeks later, and give the teen this advice:

> *Most of life is within us and man is a wonderfully adaptable animal. I think you know this, too. Of course, you will be there for a long time & will naturally find out the best way to make things tolerable. . . . I am ambitious for you to write your bird book. I have had a good deal of pleasure, or rather forgetfulness in writing books which no one reads, & I want you to write one which will be read. Anyhow, I won't forget you and I'm sure I can help you in many ways.*
>
> *Always your friend,*
>
> *Clarence Darrow*

Darrow knew John Whitman, the warden at Joliet, well and planned to periodically check in with him on the teenagers' behalf. His continued presence, he knew, would provide them a bit of additional protection within the penitentiary's walls.

The following evening at dusk, the assistant jailer slapped handcuffs on the two young men. Then he marched them between double rows of rifle-toting guards to a row of cars parked in front of the jail's courtyard. This show of force was to safeguard their lives. Since the sentencing, the prison had received bomb threats, and a crowd was constantly gathered outside the jail.

The cars' engines were already running when Nathan and Richard, along with their jailer, climbed into the backseat of a black Packard. Two Cadillacs would escort them, one driving in front of their vehicle and the other behind. Each was packed with armed deputy sheriffs. As they pulled away, cars filled with reporters and photographers followed. Sirens screaming, the motorcade sped along at fifty-five miles an hour down Archer Avenue. Soon it left the city behind. The landscape became one of rolling farmland broken occasionally by a small town.

Night had already fallen when the motorcade arrived at the penitentiary thirty-three miles from Chicago. As it approached the prison gates, the cars' headlights swept over the stone fortress. It occurred to Nathan that until now he hadn't considered what the prison in Joliet might be like.

"Well, boys," said Richard with bravado. "Let it be written that we came through here on the eleventh of September, 1924."

Inside the prison grounds, an army of reporters waited. As Richard and Nathan climbed from the car, flashbulbs popped. The pair blinked, momentarily blinded. A second later, they got their first look at their new home.

Twenty-five-foot-high limestone walls, appearing as if they'd been dipped in a cauldron of bile, surrounded them. The administration building—a looming, castlelike fortress—was equally awful. The prison had been built to be intimidating, and it was.

Richard's bravado evaporated. As he moved toward an open doorway, the muscle in his cheek twitched. He stumbled on the uneven paving stones.

Nathan peered around and saw prison guards dressed in blue uniforms patrolling the thick walls. Each carried a rifle.

The pair was shoved through the doorway and into a waiting room. Nathan glanced back at the reporters. He spied Ty Krum, the newspaperman who had smuggled bourbon into their cells at the county jail each night. "It's 1924," he called back to Krum through the still-open doorway. "It will probably be 1957 when we get out, and I'll have a beard so long." He motioned from his chin to his waist.

"Shut up and face the wall," ordered a prison guard.

The steel door clanged shut.

CHAPTER TWENTY-FIVE

"LIFE IN PRISON IS JUST WHAT YOU MAKE"

On a November afternoon in 1963, carrying a paper cone of white lilies, his shoulders hunched against the cold, Nathan Leopold wove his way through the Jewish section of Chicago's Rosehill Cemetery. Almost four decades had passed since he'd been here, but he remembered the way. His mother's grave was just ahead.

Once he'd come weekly to stand at her headstone, the last time just days before murdering Bobby Franks. Back then he'd been a sophisticated Jazz Age teen. Now he was a pudgy fifty-nine-year-old ex-con with a heart condition.

Decades behind bars had taken their toll.

The cramped, slightly damp cells; the bedbugs; the weekly three-minute showers; even the slop buckets for toilets—by inches, fastidious Nathan had adjusted to it all. But he never got used to the "deadly, leaden, unrelieved monotony" of prison life. If only Richard had been there to liven things up. But the warden had separated them. Kept in opposite wings of the prison, they'd never seen each other.

The public rarely saw or heard about either of them. Only small bits of information about Leopold and Loeb escaped the prison in Joliet. Brief stories occasionally appeared in the back pages of newspapers. It was reported that Nathan had undergone surgery for appendicitis; Richard had caught the measles; Nathan worked in the prison's shoe shop doing clerical work; Richard cleaned the prison yard.

On the first anniversary of the pair's imprisonment, reporters flocked to the penitentiary for a follow-up story. The warden had granted permission for the pair to talk with them through the prison's heavy iron gate. Nathan refused to be interviewed. But Richard went out and stuck his hands through the bars and shook hands all around. James Mulroy of the *Chicago Daily News* thought he "presented a particularly pitiable figure, compared with the dapper Loeb of old."

"I can't talk to you boys," said Richard. "I'd like to say something, but I'm afraid I'd get in bad. I bear no grudges against any of you, and I'm trying to do my best down here to make good."

Mulroy learned from a prison guard that both teenagers' nerves were "scorched," and they went about with "drawn faces, twitching lips, brooding expressions." They were, the guard added, "suffering tremendously." Warden Whitman agreed. He predicted Loeb would be "lucky to last five years."

A few other brief reports made the papers over the years. But for the most part, Leopold and Loeb faded from public view, though Nathan years later wrote a book about his prison experiences. Richard did not. His daily life behind bars remains, for the most part, a mystery.

In 1925, Leopold and Loeb's separation grew wider. Prison officials transferred Nathan to Stateville, a new correctional facility three miles north of Joliet. "Life in prison is just what you make," the warden told him on the day he arrived. "Behave and you'll get along pretty well. Act badly, and you'll get into trouble. It's up to you."

Nathan chose trouble. He spent time in "the hole," or solitary confinement, for stealing sugar and getting into fights with other inmates and forging the chaplains' names to slips that permitted prisoners to go to the chapel. This last offense earned him seven days.

Seven days in solitary confinement was hard time. The small concrete cell had no furniture, just a blanket and the inevitable slop bucket. For most of each day, Nathan was handcuffed to the cell's inner barred door, with the solid steel outer door closed and locked. He was left to stand there for hours on end, and his feet swelled and his legs cramped. Twice a day, he was released. He fell to the concrete floor, exhausted and aching, and lay there until the guards called him back to the barred door.

Nathan was unruly for six years. Then one day, he recalled, "I sat down and considered carefully [this] question: Should I attempt to escape, should I commit suicide, or should I serve out my sentence?"

He decided to make what he could of his life in prison. He began a program of self-study, teaching himself calculus, logic, and Egyptian hieroglyphs. He stopped getting into fights. His improved behavior earned him better jobs. Because of his education, he was given the task of reorganizing the prison library, a job he relished. He also willingly used his education to do the various clerical jobs needed to run the prison, such as typing up the daily logs about inmate behavior and organizing prisoner files. He gained the warden's trust. By 1931, during those hours when prisoners were allowed out of their cells, Nathan could go anywhere in the prison.

But he still missed Richard.

And then, miraculously, his friend was transferred to Stateville. "The next four years from 1932–1936 were, in many ways, the best I have known in prison," Nathan later recalled. Both Richard and Nathan had an education far in advance of most of the other prisoners, so with the warden's blessing, they started a school. This activity allowed them to spend long hours together each day, even though they didn't share a cell. "Dick and I were as close as it is possible for two men to be," said Nathan.

At lunchtime on January 28, 1936, an inmate stopped by Nathan's cell. "[Loeb's] hurt," he said. Nathan rushed to the prison hospital to find Richard on the operating table. His throat had been slashed with a straight razor, and his body was covered in gashes—fifty-four in all. He'd been attacked in the shower by James Day, a convict with a long record of offenses, including armed robbery. Day claimed Richard had made sexual advances and that he'd acted in self-defense, but few people believed this. Why, if it was self-defense, was Richard's throat cut from *behind*? And why slash him all those additional times? Without any witnesses to the attack, these questions went unanswered. Day, however, was placed in solitary confinement until the following June.

There was little the doctors could do to save Richard. Nathan stood at the end of the operating table, watching his best friend's life slowly drain away. It was three o'clock in the afternoon when Richard Loeb died. He was thirty years old.

Nathan helped the surgical nurse wash the body. "We covered him at last with a sheet, but after a moment, I folded the sheet back

Clarence Darrow in court looking typically disheveled, 1924.

Judge John Caverly at the
bench, 1924.

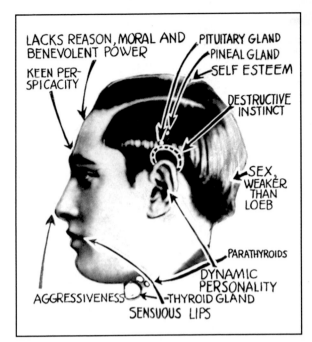

LACKS REASON, MORAL AND
BENEVOLENT POWER

KEEN PER-
SPICACITY

PITUITARY GLAND

PINEAL GLAND

SELF ESTEEM

DESTRUCTIVE
INSTINCT

SEX,
WEAKER
THAN
LOEB

PARATHYROIDS

DYNAMIC
PERSONALITY

AGGRESSIVENESS

THYROID GLAND

SENSUOUS LIPS

This pseudoscientific analysis of Nathan's face was featured in the *New York Daily News* in 1924, an attempt by the press to help readers understand a crime that seemed to have no rational motive. It also helped to vilify Nathan, painting him as the Svengali of the pair.

Cocky and unruffled, Nathan (front left) and Richard (center) head to Cook County Jail for cell assignments on June 2, 1924.

Crowds jam the sidewalks around the Criminal Courts Building in hopes of getting a glimpse of the teenage killers on their first day in court.

Photo montage showing "character studies of the two youthful slayers, 'Babe' Leopold (top left) and 'Dickie' Loeb (top right)." Below, Richard (center) and Nathan (left) plead not guilty at their arraignment. The courtroom was so packed that spectators pushed all the way up to the judge's bench, crowding the defendants. Defense attorney Benjamin Bachrach can be seen to the right, facing his clients but unable to reach them.

From left to right: Nathan, Richard, and Clarence Darrow look toward a newspaper photographer during a break in the court proceedings. Benjamin Bachrach is seated directly in front of them, July 1924.

Flora Franks testifies, July 23, 1924, while Judge Caverly listens sympathetically.

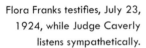

Nathan (left) and Richard (right) laugh in court.

Above, State's Attorney Robert Crowe and Clarence Darrow confer in court. In the background, a bank of white-shirted reporters sit in the jury box. Below, the new-school psychiatrists (from left to right) Drs. William Healy, Ralph Hamil (a medical observer who neither examined the teens nor testified), William Alanson White, and Bernard Glueck.

On the witness stand: upper left, Sven Englund, the Leopold family chauffeur who shattered the teenagers' alibi; upper right, Nathan's brother Mike; bottom, Lorraine Nathan, one of Richard's former sweethearts.

Dr. Harold Hulbert, one of the co-authors of the Hulbert-Bowman Report, holds up an X-ray of Nathan's skull while on the witness stand, August 8, 1924.

An exhausted and tearful Nathan Leopold Sr. just minutes after Judge Caverly gave his verdict, September 10, 1924.

Still full of bravado, Nathan (center left) and Richard (center right) are led down a flight of stairs upon their arrival at Joliet prison on September 11, 1924, to begin serving their life sentences.

Prisoner intake record for prisoner #9305, Richard Loeb, after having his head shaved and his expensive suit replaced by a prison uniform.

Prisoner #9306, Nathan Leopold. Wearing the penitentiary's standard-issue denim shirt and khaki trousers, the teenager had his Valentino-style hair shaved off by a convict barber.

Nathan's cell at Stateville prison. In addition to a small desk and library, he had three birdcages in which he raised canaries. At the time, inmates were allowed to raise animals to sell to pet stores.

Joliet prison, 1924.

Richard Loeb makes banner headlines for the last time following his murder in prison on January 28, 1936.

Fifty-three-year-old Nathan Leopold teaches Greek to fellow inmates at Stateville prison in 1957.

On March 13, 1958, a paroled Nathan Leopold stepped out of Stateville prison to face a crowd of reporters. "The only piece of news about me is that I have ceased to be news," he told them.

from his face and sat down on the stool by the table where he lay. I wanted a long last look at him."

• • •

Nathan was bereaved. "I missed [Richard] terribly," he later admitted. "We had shared everything and planned everything together. I was very lonely." He tried to keep busy. He studied twelve more languages. He took more college courses by mail and became a trained X-ray technician. During World War II, he offered himself for the malaria-treatment experiments being conducted in the prison hospital. He also kept up with ornithology, reading all the journals. He even raised a brood of canaries in his cell.

He also wrote his autobiography, *Life Plus 99 Years,* which begins *after* the boys had left Bobby Franks's body in the culvert. "I am not going to describe my childhood and youth," Nathan explains in the book's opening pages, "especially, I am not going to describe the crime. . . . I simply cannot bring myself to poke and probe again at the horrible . . . experiences. To pick the scab from the wound."

Published in 1957, while Nathan was still in prison, the book received a lukewarm reception. Wrote the *New York Times Book Review:* "[Readers] learn about Leopold's dramatic trial and the legal defense of Clarence Darrow; of how he had mastered twelve languages since his imprisonment in 1924, learned to be an x-ray technician and taught himself Braille . . . [but] are left to dimly imagine the forces that contributed to his committing the crime." *Kirkus Reviews* was more pointed: "Leopold, in spite of his intellectual gifts, doesn't write particularly well."

Just a year earlier, Meyer Levin—a fellow Chicagoan who'd covered the crime as a cub reporter for the *Chicago Daily News*—had released a fictional re-creation of Leopold and Loeb's crime titled *Compulsion.* The book involved invented scenes and dramatic characters. Levin focused on the psychological makeup of his characters, renaming them Judd Steiner (Nathan) and Artie Straus (Richard). But Levin also incorporated lots of true events in his work, as well as factual material from the trial transcripts, the confessions, and even Nathan's and Richard's psychiatric examinations. Selling 130,000 copies in its first year, *Compulsion* was the third-best-selling novel of 1956. It was later adapted into a feature film, as well as a Broadway play.

One would think its popularity would have created interest in Nathan's book. It didn't.

Life Plus 99 Years sold just 20,000 copies.

Nathan was both envious and angry. *Compulsion,* he said, was "insidious [and] devastating. . . . [Levin] has taken a large amount of fact, and to it he has added an even larger amount of fiction—or pure balderdash. And he has done it in such a [way] that the seams don't show. No reader can possibly know what is true and what is contrived. I confess that I, on several occasions, had to stop and think hard to be sure whether certain details were true or imaginary."

Probably most infuriating was the novel's last scene, in which Levin assigned a motive for the murder to the Nathan character. Levin wrote: "Judd was not merely Artie's accomplice. He wasn't there only because he was in love. He had to do the murder because of some compulsions in himself. Just the way Artie did."

This was *not* the image Nathan had been carefully reconstructing of himself. In his autobiography—written largely to demonstrate his rehabilitation to the parole board and drum up popular support for his cause—Nathan lays blame for the crime firmly at Richard's feet.

"It was he who had originated the idea of committing the crime," he declared. "He who had planned it out. He who had insisted on doing what we eventually did." He'd gone along, more or less, "for the thrill of it." The survivors, of course, write history.

But was Nathan really rehabilitated?

According to fellow inmate Gene Lovitz, Nathan still believed he was a Nietzschean superman. Dr. Bernard Glueck, one of the "new-school" psychiatrists who'd examined Nathan in 1924, verified this. He had a long (and sadly unrecorded) visit with the prisoner. When Glueck returned home, he told his son that Nathan hadn't changed. Despite all the good work he'd done, he was still manipulative, still a liar, and still a believer in Nietzsche.

Nathan, however, looked and acted like a model prisoner. It seemed parole might be possible.

Robert Crowe was dead set against it. "I thought at the time [Leopold] ought to hang," he told reporters before Nathan's first parole hearing. "I still think the same way." The now-retired lawyer *had* been reelected to the state's attorney's office after the Leopold and Loeb trial. But by 1928, he'd lost favor with voters for failing to rid the city of gangs and crime as he'd promised. Eventually, he was appointed a judge in the circuit court. He now added, "There are no extenuating circumstances; it was a brutal murder."

In February 1958, Nathan told the parole board that Clarence Darrow would have hoped for his release. The year after defending Leopold and Loeb, Darrow had taken on another high-profile court case: the so-called Monkey Trial, involving a Tennessee teacher named John Scopes who'd been arrested for teaching Darwin's theories of evolution to his high school students. This trial, plus the teenagers' hearing, had made Darrow America's most famous lawyer. He'd spent the last years of his life (he died in 1938) doing little trial work. Instead, he'd given lectures and had written. Nathan produced a letter Darrow had sent him in 1928. "I don't know how anybody else feels about it," Darrow had written, "but I shall always cling to the idea that sometime you will be out. . . ."

The attorney's words seemed to carry weight with the parole board.

Why had Nathan committed the murder? one board member asked.

Nathan struggled for an answer. Finally, he said, "I committed my crime because I admired Loeb extravagantly, because I didn't want to be a quitter, and because I wanted to show I had the nerve to do what he insisted on doing. They are, admittedly, not very reasonable motives. They don't, now, make very good sense to me. . . . But I was a boy of nineteen. . . . I had not then learned to control the fierce emotions of adolescence." He shook his head and added, "I have gotten over being nineteen."

It was the same explanation—the irrationality of youth—that Clarence Darrow had given in his closing argument.

The board granted Leopold parole.

On March 13, 1958, Nathan emerged from jail wearing an ill-fitting blue suit made for him by the prison tailor. He'd been behind bars for thirty-three years.

The day after his release, Nathan flew to Puerto Rico. As a condition of his parole, he had needed employment, as well as a sponsor. The Church of the Brethren, a Christian group, had stepped up. They'd offered him a job as an X-ray technician in a hospital in Castaner, a tiny village three hours' drive from San Juan. Here he would remain on parole—unable to travel without special permission, own or drive a car, drink alcohol, or socialize with other ex-cons—for another five years. He also had a ten-thirty curfew and was required to report to his parole officer regularly.

Nathan chafed at these rules. But he stayed out of trouble and filled his time with meaningful occupations. He did his work at the hospital conscientiously. He went to graduate school at the University of Puerto Rico and obtained a master's degree. He also published a book on ornithology titled *Checklist of Birds of Puerto Rico and the Virgin Islands.* Most surprising, perhaps, he married a widow named Gertrude Feldman Garcia de Quevedo. It seemed like a marriage of convenience—Nathan once described her as his "number one choice to push my wheelchair."

A framed picture of Richard was prominently on display in his apartment.

In the fall of 1963, Nathan's parole ended. He was now free to travel without restriction. He intended to see the world. Asia. South America. Europe. He would visit them all.

But first he went to Chicago to visit his family's graves.

● ● ●

On that chilly November afternoon, Nathan wound his way through Rosehill Cemetery. The plots of all three families involved in the events of 1924 were close to one another. Nathan's route took him past the Loebs' resting place first. Both of Richard's parents were here, buried beneath a sprawling oak tree. A bench carved simply with LOEB invited passersby to sit with the family awhile.

Richard wasn't there. A grief-stricken Anna Loeb had taken her son's body from the prison just hours after his death. The next day, after a private service at the Loebs' mansion on Ellis Avenue, the body had been cremated. The whereabouts of his ashes remain secret.

Nathan walked on. It was just eighty-five steps from the Loebs' plot to the Frankses' mausoleum. Over the years, Bobby had been joined by both Flora and Jacob, as well as his brother, Jack. Small tributes were tucked into the grillwork of the mausoleum's doors— notes, toys, pennies, ribbons. Chicagoans had not forgotten the murdered boy. Whether they had visited on purpose or had come across his resting place by accident, many felt compelled to leave something behind.

Nathan neither paused nor left a token. He gave no hint of what he might have been feeling. Instead, he moved on. Just a few feet farther, around a gentle curve, he came to the white obelisk with LEOPOLD inscribed on its base.

His mother no longer lay alone. In 1929, Nathan Sr. had joined her, just a week short of the murder's fifth anniversary. Nathan's brother Mike was gone now, too, but he rested beneath a stone in a nearby plot that read LEBOLD. Unable to live with the notorious name Leopold, he and his brother Samuel had changed their last name.

The fall wind rattled the bare tree branches. Nathan removed his hat and looked down at his parents' grave. He *did* have regrets. He regretted never having had a home and family. He regretted never having fulfilled his extraordinary promise. He regretted the grief he'd caused his father and the humiliation he'd brought his broth- ers. And yes, he regretted—so very much regretted—killing Bobby Franks and spending nearly a third of a century behind bars.

But he never regretted Richard Loeb.

Before Nathan's death from a heart attack on August 29, 1971, he tried to explain his devotion. "In many ways [Dick] was not only a charming person, but [he] had great character traits, in spite of everything. . . . I don't see how you could understand it, not having known the man, but Dick had a lot of good in him. Certainly he was the cause of my downfall. Certainly he was the worst enemy I ever had. He lost me my life. Still, he was the best pal I ever had. Is that understandable?"

AFTERWORD

It has been almost a century since Nathan Leopold and Richard Loeb committed what they hoped would be the perfect crime. Since then their story has been told and retold in books, movies, and plays. Just a year after the killing, F. Scott Fitzgerald—that preeminent chronicler of America's Jazz Age youth—told a reporter he was working on a novel about it. He claimed it would be "darker and more pessimistic" than anything he'd previously written. Fitzgerald's book never materialized, but four years later, in 1929, British writer Patrick Hamilton based his stage play on the murder. *Rope* was a smash hit.

In 1948, director Alfred Hitchcock made Hamilton's play into a movie. Also called *Rope,* it initially flopped at the box office but has since become a film classic. Other movies about the murder have also been made: *Swoon* (1992) and *Murder by Numbers* (2002). The event even spawned an Off-Broadway musical, *Thrill Me: The Leopold and Loeb Story* (2005). In one of its scenes, Nathan sings to Richard:

Tell me who can you have conversations with
Share your twisted observations with

Who else has a roughly similar view
If not me?

What is the cause of this story's odd magnetism? Why have writers and moviemakers returned to it again and again?

Certainly, part of the attraction is the senseless, gory murder. So, too, is the dramatic courtroom battle. But maybe it is Nathan Leopold and Richard Loeb themselves—their precociousness, their privilege, their warped sense of morality—that most fascinate. Something of the monster is in both boys, and something of the mastermind, too. It's an enthralling paradox. Nathan and Richard's narrative promises a peek into the minds of murderers. Their terrible deed has set them apart from the rest of us; it is what makes them special and compelling. We can't stop ourselves from looking. Why did they do it? But the gaps in the story still drive people crazy. Why did they do it . . . *really?*

And why are we so hungry for murder stories? Is it possible we *long* to know about these dark places; that only here will we discover things about ourselves we cannot learn anywhere else? Perhaps by looking closely at Leopold and Loeb, we see the scariest and most unacceptable parts of ourselves.

ACKNOWLEDGMENTS

I am deeply grateful for all the people who have helped me with this project, especially my editor, Anne Schwartz, who enthusiastically believed in it from the beginning. Without her hard work and stellar suggestions, this book would never have seen the light of day. Thank you, Anne.

Cathy Bobak, Anne-Marie Varga, Lili Feinberg, Adrienne Waintraub, and the rest of my Random House family were, as usual, a joy to work with.

The following institutions helped me in ways large and small, and each indispensable: McCormick Library of Special Collections and University Archives at Northwestern University; the Chicago History Museum; Special Collections and Preservation Division, Harold Washington Library Center, Chicago Public Library; University of Chicago Library; Cook County Clerk of the Circuit Court; University of New Mexico Ornithological Research Archive; and the Library of Congress Manuscript Reading Room.

Special thanks to Caroline Loeb for providing fresh insight into her great-uncle's psychological makeup; Hal Higdon for reaching back into his memory to answer my many questions; and fellow Leopold and Loeb obsessive Sharyn November for reading an early version of the manuscript and offering invaluable insights.

In the first stages of this project, John J. Binder, historian, author, and expert on organized crime in Chicago, took time out of his research to help me with mine.

Deep and special gratitude goes to the generous Nina Barrett, founder and owner of Bookends & Beginnings, an independent bookstore in Evanston, Illinois, who curated Northwestern University's 2009 exhibition *The Murder That Wouldn't Die* and wrote *The Leopold and Loeb Files: An Intimate Look at One of America's Most Infamous Crimes.* Thank you for your time, your expertise, and your eagle eyes.

Finally, thanks to Eric Rohmann, for his mapmaking skills and for accompanying me on my many "murder trips." As always, your eyes and insights were invaluable.

BIBLIOGRAPHY

My living in Chicago has been a boon to this book's creation. The city's libraries, universities, and historical museums are replete with primary source material about the Leopold and Loeb case. All four thousand–plus pages of the sentencing hearing, along with Nathan's and Richard's psychiatric evaluations and transcripts of Nathan's parole board hearings, can be found at Northwestern University's libraries. Nathan's voluminous prison correspondence is housed at the Chicago History Museum. So, too, is his will (he donated his body to science), the original manuscript of his published autobiography, news photographs related to the case, a film of Nathan on a birding expedition in 1923, and—amazingly— the eyeglasses that eventually led police to the teenagers' doors. But by far the museum's greatest trove is the Higdon interviews. Fifty years ago, author Hal Higdon conducted dozens of interviews with people who'd known Nathan and Richard—fraternity brothers, reporters, study group friends, neighbors, prison inmates. These rich, vivid, and personal accounts became important building blocks in my reconstruction of the teen killers and their world.

News coverage from the summer of 1924 also deeply informed this story. There are hundreds of articles, chronicling every dramatic twist in the case. From them I plucked telling details, snippets of conversation, little-known anecdotes. Luckily, these newspapers can still be found—even the defunct ones—at the Chicago Public

Library's archival and microfilm collections at the Harold Washington Library Center.

Of course, my research would not have been complete without a visit to the teens' Kenwood neighborhood. The Leopold home has long since been torn down. So has the Loeb mansion, although the original brick wall surrounding the property is still there. Just across the street, the abandoned Franks home sags behind a chain-link fence, while three and a half blocks away, the Harvard School for Boys (now an apartment building) remains standing. The stone lintel over the front door is still inscribed with the school's name. Even with just the ghosts of these places to measure by, I easily followed Nathan and Richard's route—the one they took as they searched for victims on that fateful afternoon of May 21, 1924. I stood on the spot where they enticed Bobby into their car. I stood on the spot where they killed him, too. Then I drove out to Wolf Lake, although the spot where the body was dumped is no longer recognizable. Later, I drove to the Illinois State Penitentiary in Joliet (closed in 2002) to get a sense of the change in their worlds. And finally, I walked through Rosehill Cemetery, past the Loeb gravesite to the Leopolds'.

At the grillwork door of the Franks mausoleum, I left flowers.

PRIMARY SOURCES

BOOKS

Darrow, Clarence. *The Story of My Life.* New York: Da Capo Press, 1996.

Darrow, Clarence, and Alfred J. Talley. *The Debate of the Century: Capital Punishment?* New York: League for Public Discussion, 1924.

Hecht, Ben. *Gaily, Gaily: The Memoirs of a Cub Reporter in Chicago.* New York: Doubleday, 1963.

Illinois Association for Criminal Justice. *The Illinois Crime Survey.* Chicago: Illinois Association for Criminal Justice, 1929.

Leopold, Nathan F., Jr. *Life Plus 99 Years.* New York: Popular Library, 1958.

McKernan, Maureen. *The Amazing Crime and Trial of Leopold and Loeb.* Birmingham, AL: Notable Trials Library, 1989.

Rascoe, Burton. *Before I Forget.* Garden City, NY: Doubleday, Doran, 1937.

Sellers, Alvin V. *The Loeb-Leopold Case: With Excerpts from the Evidence of the Alienists and Including the Arguments to the Court by Counsel for the People and the Defense.* Brunswick, GA: Classic Publishing, 1926.

Urstein, Maurice. *Leopold and Loeb: A Psychiatric-Psychological Study.* New York: Lecouver Press, 1924.

MAGAZINE ARTICLES

Carter, John. "'These Wild Young People' by One of Them." *Atlantic Monthly,* September 1920.

"Darrow, the Enigma." *Pattern Makers' Journal,* September 1912.

de Grazia, Edward. "Aftermath of a 'Thrill.'" *New York Times Book Review,* March 23, 1958.

Dix, H. N. "The Youths of America." *Ladies' Home Journal,* October 1920.

MacDonald, Betty. "Life Plus 99 Years." *Kirkus Reviews,* March 6, 1957. kirkusreviews.com/book-reviews/a/betty-macdonald-7/life-plus-99-years.

Train, Arthur, and Upton Sinclair. "Can a Rich Man Be Convicted?" *Forum,* May 1928.

NEWSPAPER ARTICLES

Chicago Daily Journal

"Body of Boy Found in Swamp." May 22, 1924.

"Question Woman in Franks Murder." May 26, 1924.

"Kin Aid Two in Franks Tangle." May 30, 1924.

"'Let Law Take Its Course,' Says Franks, Father of Slain Boy." May 31, 1924.

"Franks, as Debater, Won on Plea to Save Necks of Murderers." June 4, 1924.

Chicago Daily News

"Gin Party Leopold Alibi." May 30, 1924.

"Seek Girls' Story." May 30, 1924.

"Cub Reporters Win Franks Case Glory." May 31, 1924.

"Sad for Parents of Boys in Kidnapping." May 31, 1924.

"Loeb, Leopold Plead Guilty: Begin Trial Next Wednesday." July 21, 1924.

"Boys Primp for Big Day." July 23, 1924.

"Leopold Weeps Under State's Attack." August 21, 1924.

"Row Stops Crowe's Attack on Slayers." August 26, 1924.

Leopold, Nathan F. "Life Plus 99 Years." November 4, 1957.

Chicago Daily Tribune

"Did You See the Kidnapping of Bobby Franks?" May 23, 1924.

"Kidnap Rich Boy; Kill Him." May 23, 1924.

"Whose Spectacles Are These?" May 23, 1924.

"Franks Most Controlled at Inquest." May 24, 1924.

Doherty, James. "Kidnapped Boy Died Fighting." May 24, 1924.

"Expert Fixes on Kind of Machine Kidnapper Used." May 25, 1924.

Watkins, Maurine. "Simple Funeral Services Held for Franks Boy." May 26, 1924.

"Raid Dope Rings for Franks Slayers." May 28, 1924.

"Millionaire's Son on the Grill." May 30, 1924.

Watkins, Maurine. "Big Experience Either Way Is Nathan's View." May 31, 1924.

"Youth Retain Friends' Faith During Their Long Ordeal." May 31, 1924.

Doherty, James. "Darrow Leads Court Battle for Writ Today." June 2, 1924.

Forbes, Genevieve. "Old Fashioned Discipline Need of Leopold Jr." June 2, 1924.

Krum, Morrow. "'This'll Be the Making of Me,' Says Loeb Boy." June 2, 1924.

Krum, Tyrrell. "Elite of the Jail Think Leopold 'Ain't So Much.'" June 4, 1924.

McKernan, Maureen. "Weeping Girls Mourn Plight of Richard Loeb." June 4, 1924.

"Nathan Strikes Guard to Halt New Evidence." June 6, 1924.

"Hypnotism May Play Role in Loeb Defense." June 10, 1924.

Watkins, Maurine. "Leopold, Loeb Trial Set for Monday, Aug. 4." June 12, 1924.

"Crowe to Push Trial with All Possible Speed." July 22, 1924.

Forbes, Genevieve. "Mrs. Franks Bares Tragedy." July 24, 1924.

Krum, Tyrrell. "Feel No Regret Over Killing Franks Boy." July 26, 1924.

Lee, Robert M. "Crowe Smashes at Darrow; Calls Darrow Arch Lawyer of Murderers." August 27, 1924.

"Leopold Hopes, If Hanged, to Test Hereafter." September 3, 1924.

Krum, Tyrrell. "Big Guard of Police for Decision." September 10, 1924.

Lee, Robert M. "Life in Prison Decreed for Leopold, Loeb." September 11, 1924.

"Text of Judge Caverly's Decision." September 11, 1924.

"What Principals Said." September 11, 1924.

Krum, Tyrrell. "Imperiled by Crash in Motor Dash to Joliet." September 12, 1924.

"Disintegrating Society." September 19, 1924.

Chicago Evening American

"Pence Vouches for His 3 Instructors." May 23, 1924.

"Tony Minke, Finder of Boy's Body, Gives Details of Discover." May 23, 1924.

"Darrow's Plea!" August 22, 1924.

"Crank Phoned Wife Caverly Was Shot." September 2, 1924.

"Loeb Recalls Last Time He Danced to Tune." September 4, 1924.

"Loebs to Sell Home to Escape Having Memories Is Report." September 9, 1924.

Chicago Evening Post

"Loeb, Leopold Plead Not Guilty; Trial August 4." June 11, 1924.

"Leopold-Loeb Defense Now Seen as Insanity." June 13, 1924.

"Concludes Tests of Franks Killers." June 17, 1924.

Chicago Herald and Examiner

"Kidnappers Slay Millionaire's Son." May 23, 1924.

" 'Hang Leopold and Loeb,' Says Crowe." May 31, 1924.

"Confess." June 1, 1924.

"Expert Charles A. Bonniwell Analyzes Character of the Two Student Slayers and Reveals Their Innermost Thoughts." June 1, 1924.

" 'Hang the Slayers,' Billy Sunday Says." June 1, 1924.

Sullivan, Wallace. " 'I Wrote Note, Loeb Killed Him,' Says Leopold in First Interview." June 2, 1924.

"Leopold-Loeb Case Battle of Alienists." June 3, 1924.

"City Demands Franks Boy Slayers Be Brought to Trial Immediately." June 4, 1924.

"Faces of Youthful Slayers Are Contrasted by Experts." June 4, 1924.

"Fathers Will Let Bar Fix Fees in Slayers' Defense." June 7, 1924.

Black, Winifred. "If Your Sons Were the Slayer." June 9, 1924.

"Dejected? No, Just Thinking Out Next Move." August 3, 1924.

"Women Faint as Crowd Mobs Court." August 23, 1924.

Walker, Betty. "Girl, Society Matron, See Two Killers." August 30, 1924.

Chicago Sunday Tribune

"Police Delve into Past of Boys' Teachers." May 25, 1924.

"Clinches Youths' Confessions." June 1, 1924.

Watkins, Maureen. " 'Dick's Innocent,' Loebs Protest; Plan Defense." June 1, 1924.

"Jacob Franks Thinks Slayers of Son Insane." June 1, 1924.

McKernan, Maureen. "Leopold Family a Big Factor in City's Business." June 1, 1924.

Dwyer, Orville. "Take Loeb and Leopold on Franks Death Route." June 1, 1924.

Forbes, Genevieve. "They Slew for a Laboratory Test in Emotion." June 1, 1924.

"Gray Jail Days Make Murderers Model Prisoners." June 8, 1924.

Dwyer, Orville. "Darrow Calls Slaying Mad Act of Fools." August 24, 1924.

"Franks Sell Their Home of Cruel Memory." August 31, 1924.

"Grant's Sentence Should Be Commuted." September 14, 1924.

"Pleads to Save Son from Gallows." September 14, 1924.

OTHER NEWSPAPERS

"Jazz Ruining Girls, Declares Reformer—Degrading Music Even Common in 'Society Circles.'" *New York American.* June 22, 1922.

"Leopold as Boy Had Mania for Killing Young Birds." *Atlanta Constitution.* June 4, 1924.

Dennison, Lindsay. "Leopold and Loeb Families Scorned by Close Friends." *New York World.* June 5, 1924.

Lindsay, Ben B. "'Franks Case Warning to Parents,' Says Lindsay." *Los Angeles Daily Times.* July 28, 1924.

"Famous Alienist Paints Loeb as a Boy Without Remorse." *Olean (NY) Times Herald.* August 6, 1924.

"The Franks Case Decision." *Kansas City Post.* September 10, 1924.

"Judge Caverly's Sentence." *San Francisco Bulletin.* September 10, 1924.

"Franks Slayers Get Life Imprisonment, Youth Avert Noose." *New York Times.* September 11, 1924.

"The Mercy of the Court." *New York Times.* September 11, 1924.

"Says Leopold and Loeb Can Be Paroled in 1935." *New York Times.* September 11, 1924.

"Perfectly Comprehensible." *Detroit Free Press.* September 15, 1924.

"Petition for Life of Chicago Youth." *Indianapolis Times.* September 15, 1924.

"The Mind of the Judge." *New York Sun.* September 16, 1924.

Salpeter, Harry. "Fitzgerald, Spenglerian." *New York World.* April 3, 1927.

Kogan, Herman. "Profile of Robert Crowe." *Chicago Sun-Times.* August 20, 1942. Hal Higdon Research Papers on the Leopold and Loeb Case, Series 4, Box 3, Chicago History Museum.

OTHER DOCUMENTS

Asher, Robert. Interview. Hal Higdon Research Papers on the Leopold and Loeb Case, Series 4, Box 2, Chicago History Museum.

Attorney Presentation Before Parole Board, 1958. Leopold and Loeb Collection, Box 33, Charles Deering McCormick Library of Special Collections, Northwestern University.

Bachrach, Walter. "Closing Argument." Leopold and Loeb Sentencing Hearing Transcript, Vol. 6, Leopold and Loeb Collection, Box 3, Charles Deering McCormick Library of Special Collections, Northwestern University.

Brown, Abel. Interview. Hal Higdon Research Papers on the Leopold and Loeb Case, Series 4, Box 2, Chicago History Museum.

Church, Dr. Archibald. Testimony. Leopold and Loeb Sentencing Hearing Transcript, Vol. 5, Leopold and Loeb Collection, Box 3, Charles Deering McCormick Library of Special Collections, Northwestern University.

Cronson, Mrs. Bert (Ethel). Interview. Hal Higdon Research Papers on the Leopold and Loeb Case, Series 4, Box 2, Chicago History Museum.

Crot, William. Testimony. Leopold and Loeb Sentencing Hearing Transcript, Vol. 1, Leopold and Loeb Collection, Box 1, Charles Deering McCormick Library of Special Collections, Northwestern University.

Crowe, Robert. "Closing Argument." Leopold and Loeb Sentencing Hearing Transcript, Vol. 7, Leopold and Loeb Collection, Box 3, Charles Deering McCormick Library of Special Collections, Northwestern University.

Crowe, Robert. "Opening Statement." Leopold and Loeb Sentencing Hearing Transcript, Vol. 1, Leopold and Loeb Collection, Box 1, Charles Deering McCormick Library of Special Collections, Northwestern University.

Crowe, Robert. "Robert Crowe Argument—Mitigation." Leopold and Loeb Sentencing Hearing Transcript, Vol. 2, Leopold and Loeb Collection, Box 1, Charles Deering McCormick Library of Special Collections, Northwestern University.

Darrow, Clarence. "Clarence Darrow Reply—Mitigation." Leopold and Loeb Sentencing Hearing Transcript, Vol. 2, Leopold and Loeb Collection, Box 1, Charles Deering McCormick Library of Special Collections, Northwestern University.

Darrow, Clarence. "Opening Statement." Leopold and Loeb Sentencing Hearing Transcript, Vol. 1, Leopold and Loeb Collection, Box 1, Charles Deering McCormick Library of Special Collections, Northwestern University.

Englund, Sven. Testimony. Leopold and Loeb Sentencing Hearing Transcript, Vol. 1, Leopold and Loeb Collection, Box 1, Charles Deering McCormick Library of Special Collections, Northwestern University.

"First Ransom Note." Harold S. Hulbert Papers, Series 55/23, Box 2, University Archives, Northwestern University.

Fitzgerald, Katherine. Testimony. Leopold and Loeb Sentencing Hearing Transcript, Vol. 4, Leopold and Loeb Collection, Box 2, Charles Deering McCormick Library of Special Collections, Northwestern University.

Franks, Flora. Testimony. Leopold and Loeb Sentencing Hearing Transcript, Vol. 1, Leopold and Loeb Collection, Box 1, Charles Deering McCormick Library of Special Collections, Northwestern University.

Glueck, Dr. Bernard. Testimony. Leopold and Loeb Sentencing Hearing Transcript, Vol. 3, Leopold and Loeb Collection, Box 2, Charles Deering McCormick Library of Special Collections, Northwestern University.

Goldstein, Alvin H. Testimony. Leopold and Loeb Sentencing Hearing Transcript, Vol. 1, Leopold and Loeb Collection, Box 1, Charles Deering McCormick Library of Special Collections, Northwestern University.

Gortland, James. Testimony. Leopold and Loeb Sentencing Hearing Transcript, Vol. 1, Leopold and Loeb Collection, Box 1, Charles Deering McCormick Library of Special Collections, Northwestern University.

Gresham, Edwin. Testimony. Leopold and Loeb Sentencing Hearing Transcript, Vol. 1, Leopold and Loeb Collection, Box 1, Charles Deering McCormick Library of Special Collections, Northwestern University.

Healy, Dr. William. Testimony. Leopold and Loeb Sentencing Hearing Transcript, Vol. 3, Leopold and Loeb Collection, Box 2, Charles Deering McCormick Library of Special Collections, Northwestern University.

Hektoen, Ludwig. "The Coroner (in Cook County)." In *The Illinois Crime Survey.* Chicago: Illinois Association for Criminal Justice, 1929.

Herndon, William. Testimony. Leopold and Loeb Sentencing Hearing Transcript, Vol. 1, Leopold and Loeb Collection, Box 1, Charles Deering McCormick Library of Special Collections, Northwestern University.

Hulbert, Dr. Harold S. Testimony. Leopold and Loeb Sentencing Hearing Transcript, Vol. 4, Leopold and Loeb Collection, Box 2, Charles Deering McCormick Library of Special Collections, Northwestern University.

Hulbert, Dr. Harold S., and Dr. Karl Bowman. "Neuro-Psychiatric Evaluation of Nathan F. Leopold Jr." Harold S. Hulbert Papers, Series 55/23, Box 2, University Archives, Northwestern University.

Hulbert, Dr. Harold S., and Dr. Karl Bowman. "Neuro-Psychiatric Evaluation of Richard Loeb." Harold S. Hulbert Papers, Series 55/23, Box 2, University Archives, Northwestern University.

Johnson, Frank A. Testimony. Leopold and Loeb Sentencing Hearing Transcript, Vol. 1, Leopold and Loeb Collection, Box 1, Charles Deering McCormick Library of Special Collections, Northwestern University.

Kogan, Herman. "Profile of Robert Crowe." *Chicago Sun-Times,* August 20, 1945, in Hal Higdon Research Papers on the Leopold and Loeb Case, Series 4, Box 2, Chicago History Museum.

Krohn, Dr. William O. Testimony. Hal Higdon Research Papers on the Leopold and Loeb Case, Series 4, Box 2, Chicago History Museum.

Leopold, Nathan F., Jr. "Confessions and Other Statements of Leopold and Loeb (1924)." Harold S. Hulbert Papers, Series 55/23, Box 3, University Archives, Northwestern University.

Leopold, Nathan F., Jr. "Original Manuscript of *Life Plus 99 Years*." Nathan F. Leopold Papers, Series 4, Box 22, Chicago History Museum.

Leopold, Nathan F., Jr., to Richard Loeb, October 9, 1923. Leopold and Loeb Sentencing Hearing Transcript, Vol. 2, Leopold and Loeb Collection, Box 1, Charles Deering McCormick Library of Special Collections, Northwestern University.

Leopold, Nathan F., Jr., to Clarence Darrow, September 10 or 11, 1924. Clarence Darrow Papers, Box 3, Library of Congress.

Leopold, Nathan F., Jr., to Ralph G. Newman, October 12, 1962. Nathan F. Leopold Papers, Series 3, Box 16, Chicago History Museum.

Levinson, John. Interview. Hal Higdon Research Papers on the Leopold and Loeb Case, Series 4, Box 2, Chicago History Museum.

Loeb, Richard. "Confessions and Other Statements of Leopold and Loeb (1924)." Harold S. Hulbert Papers, Series 55/23, Box 3, University Archives, Northwestern University.

Loeb, Richard, to Clarence Darrow. "Friday Night," 1924. Clarence Darrow Papers, Box 3, Library of Congress.

Maremont, Arnold. Interview. Hal Higdon Research Papers on the Leopold and Loeb Case, Series 4, Box 2, Chicago History Museum.

Maremont, Arnold. Testimony. Leopold and Loeb Sentencing Hearing Transcript, Vol. 4, Leopold and Loeb Collection, Box 2, Charles Deering McCormick Library of Special Collections, Northwestern University.

Marshall, Thomas. "Argument—Mitigation." Leopold and Loeb Sentencing Hearing Transcript, Vol. 2, Leopold and Loeb Collection, Box 1, Charles Deering McCormick Library of Special Collections, Northwestern University.

Marshall, Thomas. "Closing Argument." Hal Higdon Research Papers on the Leopold and Loeb Case, Series 4, Box 2, Chicago History Museum.

Mayer, Howard. Interview. Hal Higdon Research Papers on the Leopold and Loeb Case, Series 4, Box 2, Chicago History Museum.

Mayer, Howard. Testimony. Leopold and Loeb Sentencing Hearing Transcript, Vol. 1, Leopold and Loeb Collection, Box 1, Charles Deering McCormick Library of Special Collections, Northwestern University.

Nathan, Lorraine. Testimony. Leopold and Loeb Sentencing Hearing Transcript, Vol. 4, Leopold and Loeb Collection, Box 2, Charles Deering McCormick Library of Special Collections, Northwestern University.

Patrick, Dr. Hugh T. Testimony. Leopold and Loeb Sentencing Hearing Transcript, Vol. 5,

Leopold and Loeb Collection, Box 3, Charles Deering McCormick Library of Special Collections, Northwestern University.

Robinson, Charles. Testimony. Leopold and Loeb Sentencing Hearing Transcript, Vol. 2, Leopold and Loeb Collection, Box 1, Charles Deering McCormick Library of Special Collections, Northwestern University.

Schrayer, Max. Interview. Hal Higdon Research Papers on the Leopold and Loeb Case, Series 4, Box 2, Chicago History Museum.

Stern, Gardner. Interview. Hal Higdon Research Papers on the Leopold and Loeb Case, Series 4, Box 2, Chicago History Museum.

Strauss, Lucille. Interview. Hal Higdon Research Papers on the Leopold and Loeb Case, Series 4, Box 2, Chicago History Museum.

Vollmer, August. "The Police (in Chicago)." In *The Illinois Crime Survey.* Chicago: Illinois Association for Criminal Justice, 1929.

Wallace, Sullivan. Testimony. Leopold and Loeb Sentencing Hearing Transcript, Vol. 2, Leopold and Loeb Collection, Box 1, Charles Deering McCormick Library of Special Collections, Northwestern University.

Ward, Charles E. Testimony. Leopold and Loeb Sentencing Hearing Transcript, Vol. 1, Leopold and Loeb Collection, Box 1, Charles Deering McCormick Library of Special Collections, Northwestern University.

White, Dr. William Alanson. Notes Relating to the Leopold-Loeb Case (1924). E37, Box 1, Records of Superintendent William Alanson White, Records of St. Elizabeth Hospital, National Archives.

White, Dr. William Alanson. Testimony. Leopold and Loeb Sentencing Hearing Transcript, Vol. 3, Leopold and Loeb Collection, Box 2, Charles Deering McCormick Library of Special Collections, Northwestern University.

Wolf, Thomas C. Testimony. Leopold and Loeb Sentencing Hearing Transcript, Vol. 1, Leopold and Loeb Collection, Box 1, Charles Deering McCormick Library of Special Collections, Northwestern University.

SECONDARY SOURCES

BOOKS

Barrett, Nina. *The Leopold and Loeb Files: An Intimate Look at One of America's Most Infamous Cases.* Chicago: Midway Press, 2018.

Bruccoli, Matthew J. *Some Sort of Epic Grandeur: The Life of F. Scott Fitzgerald.* Columbia: University of South Carolina Press, 2002.

Fass, Paula S. *The Damned and the Beautiful: American Youth in the 1920s.* New York: Oxford University Press, 1977.

Folsom, Robert G. *The Money Trail: How Elmer Irey and His T-Men Brought Down America's Criminal Elite.* Washington, DC: Potomac Books, 2010.

Franklin, Paul B. "Jew Boys, Queer Boys: Rhetorics of Antisemitism and Homophobia in the Trial of Nathan 'Babe' Leopold Jr. and Richard 'Dickie' Loeb." In *Queer Theory and the Jewish Question,* edited by Daniel Boyarin et al., 133–159. New York: Columbia University Press, 2003.

Higdon, Hal. *Leopold and Loeb: The Crime of the Century.* Urbana: University of Illinois Press, 1999.

Levin, Meyer. *Compulsion.* Bedford, NY: Fig Tree Books, 2014.

Levin, Meyer. *In Search.* New York: Horizon Press, 1950.

Levin, Meyer. *The Obsession.* New York: Simon & Schuster, 1973.

Murray, George. *The Madhouse on Madison Street.* Chicago: Follett, 1965.

Shapiro, David L., et al. *Retrying Leopold and Loeb: A Neuropsychological Perspective.* Cham, Switzerland: Springer International Publishing, 2018.

Stone, Irving. *Clarence Darrow for the Defense.* New York: Doubleday, 1941.

MAGAZINE AND JOURNAL ARTICLES

Baatz, Simon. "Leopold and Loeb's Criminal Minds." *Smithsonian,* August 2008. smithsonianmag.com/history/leopold-and-loebs-criminal-minds-996498.

Cheatwood, Derral. "Capital Punishment for the Crime of Homicide in Chicago." *Journal of Criminal Law and Criminology,* Spring 2002.

Fass, Paula S. "Making and Remaking an Event: The Leopold and Loeb Case in American Culture." *Journal of American History,* December 1993.

OTHER SOURCES

Dolginoff, Stephen. "Everyone Wants Richard," *Thrill Me: The Leopold & Loeb Story,* 2005, genius.com/Stephen-dolginoff-and-doug-kreeger-everybody-wants-richard-lyrics.

NOTES

PART ONE: WHERE IS BOBBY?

Chapter One: May 21, 1924

"What are you doing after school?": John Levinson, interview, Hal Higdon Research Papers on the Leopold and Loeb Case, Series 4, Box 2, Chicago History Museum.

"I'm going to play baseball": ibid.

"There are some children playing": Nathan F. Leopold Jr., "Confessions and Other Statements of Leopold and Loeb (1924)," Harold S. Hulbert Papers, Series 55/23, Box 3, University Archives, Northwestern University.

"I know him": Richard Loeb, "Confessions and Other Statements of Leopold and Loeb (1924)," Harold S. Hulbert Papers, Series 55/23, Box 3, University Archives, Northwestern University.

"Hey, Bob": ibid.

"Come on in": ibid.

"You know Leopold": ibid.

"You don't mind": ibid.

"Certainly not": ibid.

Chapter Two: The Longest Night

"Baby": "Jacob Franks Thinks Slayers of Son Insane," *Chicago Sunday Tribune*, June 1, 1924, 4.

"Don't you realize my age?": ibid.

"Most criminals have": "Franks, as Debater, Won on Plea to Save Necks of Murderers," *Chicago Daily Journal*, June 4, 1924, 3.

"Maybe he's playing tennis": Hal Higdon, *Leopold and Loeb: The Crime of the Century*, Urbana: University of Illinois Press, 1999, 34.

"There must be some explanation": ibid., 36.

"Mr. Franks isn't here": Flora Franks, testimony, Leopold and Loeb Sentencing Hearing

Transcript, Vol. 1, Leopold and Loeb Collection, Box 1, Charles Deering McCormick Library of Special Collections, Northwestern University.

"Your son has been kidnapped": ibid.

"Who is this?": ibid.

"Johnson": ibid.

"What do you want?": ibid.

PART TWO: BOYS WILL BE BOYS

Chapter Three: Nathan and Richard

"tough boys": "Neuro-Psychiatric Evaluation of Nathan F. Leopold Jr.," Harold S. Hulbert Papers, Series 55/23, Box 2, University Archives, Northwestern University.

"The idea of nailing anybody to anything": Higdon, *Leopold and Loeb,* 197.

"Nathan was a mean child": "Leopold as Boy Had Mania for Killing Young Birds," *Atlanta Constitution,* June 4, 1924, 1.

"I should give a damn": ibid.

"Nein, nein, Mama!": "Neuro-Psychiatric Evaluation of Nathan F. Leopold Jr.," Harold S. Hulbert Papers, Series 55/23, Box 2, University Archives, Northwestern University.

"Sweetie": ibid.

"Your mother wishes she had a figure": ibid.

"a slave": ibid.

"king-slave fantasies": ibid.

"I was devoted to her": ibid.

"mink coat ghetto": Higdon, *Leopold and Loeb,* 18.

"flea": "Neuro-Psychiatric Evaluation of Nathan F. Leopold Jr.," Harold S. Hulbert Papers, Series 55/23, Box 2, University Archives, Northwestern University.

"shadowing": "Neuro-Psychiatric Evaluation of Richard Loeb," Harold S. Hulbert Papers, Series 55/23, Box 2, University Archives, Northwestern University.

"the master criminal": ibid.

"built to be important": Abel Brown, interview, Hal Higdon Research Papers on the Leopold and Loeb Case, Series 4, Box 2, Chicago History Museum.

"mind her to the minute": "Neuro-Psychiatric Evaluation of Richard Loeb," Harold S. Hulbert Papers, Series 55/23, Box 2, University Archives, Northwestern University.

"I was kept under": ibid.

"To get by her": ibid.

"picturalizations": Dr. William Healy, testimony, Leopold and Loeb Sentencing Hearing Transcript, Vol. 3, Leopold and Loeb Collection, Box 2, Charles Deering McCormick Library of Special Collections, Northwestern University.

"As you know, Teddy": Maureen McKernan, *The Amazing Crime and Trial of Leopold and Loeb,* Birmingham, AL: Notable Trials Library, 1989, 157.

"I sort of broke loose": "Neuro-Psychiatric Evaluation of Richard Loeb," Harold S. Hulbert Papers, Series 55/23, Box 2, University Archives, Northwestern University.

Chapter Four: The Superman and the Master Criminal

"What is happening": H. N. Dix, "The Youths of America," *Ladies' Home Journal,* October 1920, 67.

"The older generation": John Carter, "'These Wild Young People' by One of Them," *Atlantic Monthly,* September 1920, 301.

"pathological, nerve-irritating, sex-exciting": "Jazz Ruining Girls, Declares Reformer— Degrading Music Even Common in 'Society Circles,'" *New York American,* June 22, 1922, 21.

"Defying the bluenose moralists": Matthew J. Bruccoli, *Some Sort of Epic Grandeur: The Life of F. Scott Fitzgerald,* Columbia: University of South Carolina Press, 2002, 13.

"Young America is enamored of life": Paula S. Fass, *The Damned and the Beautiful: American Youth in the 1920s,* New York: Oxford University Press, 1977, 19.

"more pleasure than anything": Dr. William Healy, testimony, Leopold and Loeb Sentencing Hearing Transcript, Vol. 3, Leopold and Loeb Collection, Box 2, Charles Deering McCormick Library of Special Collections, Northwestern University.

"despised by humanity": Lucille Strauss, interview, Hal Higdon Research Papers on the Leopold and Loeb Case, Series 4, Box 2, Chicago History Museum.

"Do you swim?": ibid.

"No": ibid.

"are not right": ibid.

"jealous of the food and drink": Dr. Bernard Glueck, testimony, Leopold and Loeb

Sentencing Hearing Transcript, Vol. 3, Leopold and Loeb Collection, Box 2, Charles Deering McCormick Library of Special Collections, Northwestern University.

"Nobody liked Leopold": Max Schrayer, interview, Hal Higdon Research Papers on the Leopold and Loeb Case, Series 4, Box 2, Chicago History Museum.

"I realized that if I could kid myself": Higdon, *Leopold and Loeb,* 201.

"The only wrong I can do": "Neuro-Psychiatric Examination of Nathan F. Leopold Jr.," Harold S. Hulbert Papers, Series 55/23, Box 2, University Archives, Northwestern University.

Chapter Five: Apart and Together

"I knew I should": "Neuro-Psychiatric Examination of Nathan F. Leopold Jr.," Harold S. Hulbert Papers, Series 55/23, Box 2, University Archives, Northwestern University.

"You don't know what you're talking about": Arnold Maremont, interview, Hal Higdon Research Papers on the Leopold and Loeb Case, Series 4, Box 2, Chicago History Museum.

"You don't understand him": ibid.

"totally gullible": ibid.

"What a miserable son of a bitch": Abel Brown, interview, Hal Higdon Research Papers on the Leopold and Loeb Case, Series 4, Box 2, Chicago History Museum.

"He lied like hell": Gardner Stern, interview, Hal Higdon Research Papers on the Leopold and Loeb Case, Series 4, Box 2, Chicago History Museum.

"We had the line on him": Arnold Maremont, interview, Hal Higdon Research Papers on the Leopold and Loeb Case, Series 4, Box 2, Chicago History Museum.

"fishy": Abel Brown, interview, Hal Higdon Research Papers on the Leopold and Loeb Case, Series 4, Box 2, Chicago History Museum.

"The actual sex": "Neuro-Psychiatric Evaluation of Richard Loeb," Harold S. Hulbert Papers, Series 55/23, Box 2, University Archives, Northwestern University.

"thrill of watching it": ibid.

"We took everything": ibid.

"When you came to my house": Nathan F. Leopold Jr. to Richard Loeb, October 9, 1923, Leopold and Loeb Sentencing Hearing Transcript, Vol. 2, Leopold and Loeb Collection, Box 1, Charles Deering McCormick Library of Special Collections, Northwestern University.

"for Robert's sake": Dr. William Healy, testimony, Leopold and Loeb Sentencing Hearing Transcript, Vol. 3, Leopold and Loeb Collection, Box 2, Charles Deering McCormick Library of Special Collections, Northwestern University.

Chapter Six: Planning the Perfect Crime

"Shared culpability": Richard Loeb, "Confessions and Other Statements of Leopold and Loeb (1924)," Harold S. Hulbert Papers, Series 55/23, Box 3, University Archives, Northwestern University.

"We had several dozen": Nathan Leopold, "Confessions and Other Statements of Leopold and Loeb (1924)," Harold S. Hulbert Papers, Series 55/23, Box 3, University Archives, Northwestern University.

"Do you know anyone": Charles E. Ward, testimony, Leopold and Loeb Sentencing Hearing Transcript, Vol. 1, Leopold and Loeb Collection, Box 1, Charles Deering McCormick Library of Special Collections, Northwestern University.

"I don't know anybody": ibid.

"Morton D. Ballard, traveling salesman": ibid.

a Mr. Louis Mason: William Herndon, testimony, Leopold and Loeb Sentencing Hearing Transcript, Vol. 1, Leopold and Loeb Collection, Box 1, Charles Deering McCormick Library of Special Collections, Northwestern University.

"Is this Mr. Louis Mason talking?": Richard Loeb, "Confessions and Other Statements of Leopold and Loeb (1924)," Harold S. Hulbert Papers, Series 55/23, Box 3, University Archives, Northwestern University.

"Yes": ibid.

"Do you know": ibid.

"I've known him for years": ibid.

"You ought to come out": Robert Asher, interview, Hal Higdon Research Papers on the Leopold and Loeb Case, Series 4, Box 2, Chicago History Museum.

"How would I get out there?": ibid.

"I'll give you a lift": ibid.

"When?": ibid.

"How about next Wednesday": ibid.

"I have to go to the dentist": ibid.

"Well, maybe we could make it": ibid.

"Give me a pint": Nathan Leopold, "Confessions and Other Statements of Leopold and Loeb (1924)," Harold S. Hulbert Papers, Series 55/23, Box 3, University Archives, Northwestern University.

"What do you need it for?": ibid.

"An experiment": ibid.

"Be sure and keep it upright": ibid.

"Can you do anything about it?": Higdon, *Leopold and Loeb,* 31.

"You better be careful": ibid.

"I'd rather run into somebody": ibid.

PART THREE: TRACKING THE KILLERS

Chapter Seven: Thursday, May 22, 1924

Dear Sir: "First Ransom Note," Harold S. Hulbert Papers, Series 55/23, Box 2, University Archives, Northwestern University.

"The money must be old": ibid.

"we can assure you": ibid.

"My God!": Higdon, *Leopold and Loeb,* 40.

"We thought he might still be alive": ibid.

"Did you see anything else?": ibid.

"I knew if we just put our heads together": Nathan F. Leopold Jr., "Life Plus 99 Years," *Chicago Daily News,* November 4, 1957, 12.

"We've been doing a bit of bootlegging": "Clinches Youths' Confessions," *Chicago Sunday Tribune,* June 1, 1924, 1.

"I am sending a Yellow Cab": Nathan Leopold, "Confessions and Other Statements of Leopold and Loeb (1924)," Harold S. Hulbert Papers, Box 3, University Archives, Northwestern University.

"Just a minute": ibid.

"Yes": Edwin Gresham, testimony, Leopold and Loeb Sentencing Hearing Transcript, Vol. 1, Leopold and Loeb Collection, Box 1, Charles Deering McCormick Library of Special Collections, Northwestern University.

"Jake, it looks to me as if the worst has happened.": "Kidnappers Slay Millionaire's Son as $10,000 Ransom Waits," *Chicago Herald and Examiner,* May 23, 1924, 1.

"What do you mean?": ibid.

"Your boy is dead": ibid.

"Who sent you?": Charles Robinson, testimony, Leopold and Loeb Sentencing Hearing Transcript, Vol. 2, Leopold and Loeb Collection, Box 1, Charles Deering McCormick Library of Special Collections, Northwestern University.

"A Mr. Franks called": ibid.

"Body of Boy Found in Swamp": *Chicago Daily Journal*, May 22, 1924, 1.

"When are those damn papers printed?": Nathan F. Leopold Jr., "Original Manuscript of *Life Plus 99 Years*," Nathan F. Leopold Papers, Series 4, Box 22, Chicago History Museum.

"Hell, I don't know": ibid.

"That was some swell place": ibid.

"The game [is] up": ibid.

"It [can] do no harm": ibid.

"Isn't it terrible": Higdon, *Leopold and Loeb*, 48.

"Whoever committed the crime": Alvin H. Goldstein, testimony, Leopold and Loeb Sentencing Hearing Transcript, Vol. 1, Leopold and Loeb Collection, Box 1, Charles Deering McCormick Library of Special Collections, Northwestern University.

Chapter Eight: Search for the Killers

"We must and will": "Kidnap Rich Boy, Kill Him," *Chicago Daily Tribune*, May 23, 1924, 1.

"dishonest, brutal, stupid men": August Vollmer, "The Police (in Chicago)," in *The Illinois Crime Survey*, Chicago: Illinois Association for Criminal Justice, 1929, 360.

"And they will hang!": Herman Kogan, "Profile of Robert Crowe," *Chicago Sun-Times*, August 20, 1942, in Hal Higdon Research Papers on the Leopold and Loeb Case, Series 4, Box 2, Chicago History Museum.

"load of nonsense": ibid.

"Society should have no hesitancy": ibid.

"If the police can catch": ibid.

"a general round-up of all persons": James Doherty, "Kidnapped Boy Died Fighting," *Chicago Daily Tribune*, May 24, 1924, 1.

"The man who wrote this letter": "Expert Fixes on Kind of Machine Kidnapper Used," *Chicago Daily Tribune,* May 25, 1924, 1.

"[Bobby Franks's] father has nothing but money": "Police Delve into Past of Boys' Teachers," *Chicago Sunday Tribune,* May 25, 1924, 2.

"There are things going on": "Pence Vouches for His 3 Instructors," *Chicago Evening American,* May 23, 1924, 1.

"Get the story!": George Murray, *The Madhouse on Madison Street,* Chicago: Follett, 1965, 85.

"Wave a little blood around": Burton Rascoe, *Before I Forget,* Garden City, NY: Doubleday, Doran, 1937, 120.

"The things we do": ibid., 206.

"One of the men": "Question Woman in Franks Murder," *Chicago Daily Journal,* May 26, 1924, 3.

Chapter Nine: A Murderer's Theory; A Coroner's Inquest

"I don't believe": Howard Mayer, interview, Hal Higdon Research Papers on the Leopold and Loeb Case, Series 4, Box 2, Chicago History Museum.

"Why don't we make the rounds": ibid.

"You see?": ibid.

"This is the place!": ibid.

"This is what comes from reading": ibid.

"If I were going to murder anybody": "Cub Reporters Win Franks Case Glory," *Chicago Daily News,* May 31, 1924, 1.

"an official as notorious": Robert G. Folsom, *The Money Trail: How Elmer Irey and His T-Men Brought Down America's Criminal Elite,* Washington, DC: Potomac Books, 2010, 57.

"inexperienced [and their] examinations incomplete": Ludwig Hektoen, "The Coroner (in Cook County)," in *The Illinois Crime Survey,* Chicago: Illinois Association for Criminal Justice, 1929, 381.

"from an injury to the head": Higdon, *Leopold and Loeb,* 54.

"no complete autopsy": Ludwig Hektoen, "The Coroner (in Cook County)," in *The Illinois Crime Survey,* Chicago: Illinois Association for Criminal Justice, 1929, 382.

"pervert": Higdon, *Leopold and Loeb,* 54.

"The kidnappers could have had everything": "Jacobs Most Controlled at Inquest," *Chicago Daily Tribune*, May 24, 1924, 2.

"the best clue": "Whose Spectacles Are These?," *Chicago Daily Tribune*, May 23, 1924, 1.

"Hey, Dick": Nathan F. Leopold Jr., *Life Plus 99 Years*, New York: Popular Library, 1958, 28.

"This had better be": Nathan F. Leopold Jr., "Original Manuscript of *Life Plus 99 Years*," Nathan F. Leopold Papers, Series 4, Box 22, Chicago History Museum.

"How in hell": ibid.

"There must be a jillion pairs": ibid.

"I have got all the alibi": ibid.

"Make 'em come to you": ibid.

"half in love": Maurice Urstein, *Leopold and Loeb: A Psychiatric-Psychological Study*, New York: Lecouver Press, 1924, 59.

Chapter Ten: Saturday, May 24–Sunday, May 25, 1924

"I already have experienced everything": Arnold Maremont, interview, Hal Higdon Research Papers on the Leopold and Loeb Case, Series 4, Box 2, Chicago History Museum.

"You've just enjoyed": Abel Brown, interview, Hal Higdon Research Papers on the Leopold and Loeb Case, Series 4, Box 2, Chicago History Museum.

"madcap sense of humor": Higdon, *Leopold and Loeb*, 63.

"It seems unlikely": Leopold, *Life Plus 99 Years*, 40.

"[If] Bobby knew them": Higdon, *Leopold and Loeb*, 75.

"Then I'd appreciate it": ibid., 64.

"I hear you're": Leopold, *Life Plus 99 Years*, 30.

"That's right": ibid.

"Well, that's just why I called you in": ibid., 30–31.

"On May 18": Thomas C. Wolf, testimony, Leopold and Loeb Sentencing Hearing Transcript, Vol. 1, Leopold and Loeb Collection, Box 1, Charles Deering McCormick Library of Special Collections, Northwestern University.

"so ready and his demeanor so innocent": Higdon, *Leopold and Loeb*, 65.

"I have an insurance policy": Leopold, *Life Plus 99 Years*, 31.

"the liquid verses": ibid., 32.

"I will lift up mine eyes": Maurine Watkins, "Simple Funeral Services Held for Franks Boy," *Chicago Daily Tribune,* May 26, 1924, 1.

"Mrs. Franks, assisted by her son and daughter": ibid., 2.

"Sympathy from Mr. Johnson": Howard Mayer, interview, Hal Higdon Research Papers on the Leopold and Loeb Case, Series 4, Box 2, Chicago History Museum.

Chapter Eleven: Interrogation

"dizzying merry-go-round": Nathan F. Leopold Jr., "Original Manuscript of *Life Plus 99 Years,*" Nathan F. Leopold Papers, Series 4, Box 22, Chicago History Museum.

"Come on, Nate": Nathan F. Leopold Jr., "Original Manuscript of *Life Plus 99 Years,*" Nathan F. Leopold Papers, Series 4, Box 22, Chicago History Museum.

"What can I do for you gentlemen?": Leopold, *Life Plus 99 Years,* 33.

"I do, but I don't have them": William Crot, testimony, Leopold and Loeb Sentencing Hearing Transcript, Vol. 1, Leopold and Loeb Collection, Box 1, Charles Deering McCormick Library of Special Collections, Northwestern University.

"Did you lose your glasses?": ibid.

"No": ibid.

"Have you got them?": Frank A. Johnson, testimony, Leopold and Loeb Sentencing Hearing Transcript, Vol. 1, Leopold and Loeb Collection, Box 1, Charles Deering McCormick Library of Special Collections, Northwestern University.

"No, but I'm sure they're around here": ibid.

"I'll have to ask you": ibid.

"This is mighty awkward": Leopold, *Life Plus 99 Years,* 34.

"They sure look like mine": ibid.

"Yours are at home?": ibid.

"Yes": ibid.

"This place where they found the body": Nathan F. Leopold Jr., "Original Manuscript of *Life Plus 99 Years,*" Nathan F. Leopold Papers, Series 4, Box 22, Chicago History Museum.

"Look, Samuel Ettelson is our next-door neighbor": ibid.

"There's been some mistake": Leopold, *Life Plus 99 Years,* 35.

"There, the whole business [will] be settled": Nathan F. Leopold Jr., "Original Manuscript of *Life Plus 99 Years*," Nathan F. Leopold Papers, Series 4, Box 22, Chicago History Museum.

"The thing is absurd": ibid.

"Do you know": Nathan F. Leopold Jr., "Confessions and Other Statements of Leopold and Loeb (1924)," Harold S. Hulbert Papers, Series 55/23, Box 3, University Archives, Northwestern University.

"Yes, sir": ibid.

"Are you familiar with that spot?": ibid.

"How do you think you lost the glasses?": ibid.

"I had a pair of rubber boots": ibid.

"If you put your glasses in your pocket": ibid.

"My breast pocket": ibid.

"I do want to warn you": Nina Barrett, *The Leopold and Loeb Files: An Intimate Look at One of America's Most Infamous Cases,* Chicago: Midway Press, 2018, 43.

"What did you do": Leopold, *Life Plus 99 Years,* 37.

"Gee, I don't know": ibid.

"How are things going?": ibid.

"Fine": ibid.

"We played hooky": Nathan F. Leopold Jr., "Original Manuscript of *Life Plus 99 Years,* Nathan F. Leopold Papers, Series 4, Box 22, Chicago History Museum.

"Edna and Mae": Higdon, *Leopold and Loeb,* 82.

"Yes": Nathan F. Leopold Jr., "Confessions and Other Statements of Leopold and Loeb (1924)," Harold S. Hulbert Papers, Series 55/23, Box 3, University Archives, Northwestern University.

"Yes": ibid.

"What is the color of your car?": ibid.

"Red": ibid.

"That was three years ago": Richard Loeb, "Confessions and Other Statements of Leopold and Loeb (1924)," Harold S. Hulbert Papers, Series 55/23, Box 3, University Archives, Northwestern University.

"Wasn't that an intolerable condition": ibid.

"No": ibid.

"That was more than a week ago": ibid.

"Did you read": Nathan F. Leopold Jr., "Confessions and Other Statements of Leopold and Loeb (1924)," Harold S. Hulbert Papers, Series 55/23, Box 3, University Archives, Northwestern University.

"Yes, *Treasure Island*": ibid.

"*Kidnapped*?": ibid.

"Yes": ibid.

"What languages do you know?": ibid.

"I've studied fifteen languages": ibid.

"What is your idea": ibid.

"I do not believe": ibid.

"If you die": ibid.

"Your ashes return to ashes": ibid.

"Is there any difference": ibid.

"No, sir": ibid.

"Have you read the ransom note": ibid.

"Yes": ibid.

"Could you compose": ibid.

"Without any trouble": ibid.

"Do you own a typewriter?": ibid.

"Yes, a Hammond": ibid.

"Can you type?": ibid.

"Fairly well": ibid.

"Drunks, they looked like": Nathan F. Leopold Jr., "Original Manuscript of *Life Plus 99 Years*," Nathan F. Leopold Papers, Series 4, Box 22, Chicago History Museum.

"I hadn't been taking criminal law": ibid.

Chapter Twelve: Another Day in Custody

"There's no question": "Gin Party Leopold Alibi," *Chicago Daily News,* May 30, 1924, 1.

"His conduct": ibid.

"contaminated with moral miasma": " 'Hang the Slayers,' Billy Sunday Says," *Chicago Herald and Examiner,* June 1, 1924, 1.

"too silly to discuss": "Youth Retain Friends' Faith During Their Long Ordeal," *Chicago Daily Tribune,* May 31, 1924, 2.

"The affair will": "Kin Aid Two in Franks Tangle," *Chicago Daily Journal,* May 30, 1924, 1.

"While this is a terrible ordeal": ibid.

"I probably could": ibid.

"Get over to the Loeb mansion": Howard Mayer, testimony, Leopold and Loeb Sentencing Hearing Transcript, Vol. 1, Leopold and Loeb Collection, Box 1, Charles Deering McCormick Library of Special Collections, Northwestern University.

"That's impossible!": Howard Mayer, interview, Hal Higdon Research Papers on the Leopold and Loeb Case, Series 4, Box 2, Chicago History Museum.

"No, it's not": ibid.

"I'm telling the truth": ibid.

"That's not [Richard's] story": ibid.

"Tell him to remember": ibid.

"Dick, if you want to clear yourself": ibid.

"I don't want to talk": ibid.

"What did he say, Howie?": ibid.

"He said to tell the truth": ibid.

"They've got wealthy parents": Mrs. Bert (Ethel) Cronson, interview, Hal Higdon Research Papers on the Leopold and Loeb Case, Series 4, Box 2, Chicago History Museum.

"Master Babe's": Nathan F. Leopold Jr., "Original Manuscript of *Life Plus 99 Years,*" Nathan F. Leopold Papers, Series 4, Box 22, Chicago History Museum.

"Then when you finished": Sven Englund, testimony, Leopold and Loeb Sentencing Hearing Transcript, Vol. 1, Leopold and Loeb Collection, Box 1, Charles Deering McCormick Library of Special Collections, Northwestern University.

"Oh, no": ibid.

"Very sure": ibid.

"I think we've got them": Mrs. Bert (Ethel) Cronson, interview, Hal Higdon
Research Papers on the Leopold and Loeb Case, Series 4, Box 2, Chicago History
Museum.

PART FOUR: CONFESSIONS

Chapter Thirteen: "I Will Tell You the Real Truth"

"Who told you that?": "Confess," *Chicago Herald and Examiner,* June 1, 1924, 1.

"Englund": ibid.

"My God!": ibid.

"Yes, he did": ibid.

"I will tell you all": ibid.

"Well, your pal has just confessed": Robert Crowe, "Opening Statement," Leopold and
Loeb Sentencing Hearing Transcript, Vol. 7, Leopold and Loeb Collection, Box 3,
Charles Deering McCormick Library of Special Collections, Northwestern
University.

"Do you think I'm stupid?": ibid.

"Oh, yeah, Mr. Wise Guy?": Nathan F. Leopold Jr., "Original Manuscript of *Life Plus 99
Years,*" Nathan F. Leopold Papers, Series 4, Box 22, Chicago History Museum.

"[Richard] says he was driving": ibid.

"I will tell you the *real* truth": McKernan, *The Amazing Crime and Trial of Leopold and
Loeb,* 23.

"Now, Nathan": Nathan F. Leopold Jr., "Confessions and Other Statements of Leopold
and Loeb (1924)," Harold S. Hulbert Papers, Series 55/23, Box 3, University Archives,
Northwestern University.

"by pure accident": ibid.

"I was sitting": ibid.

"[Bobby] did not succumb": ibid.

"On Calumet Road": ibid.

"Having arrived at [Wolf Lake]": ibid.

"What kind of acid": ibid.

"Hydrochloric": ibid.

"Then I stepped into the water": ibid.

"And then?": ibid.

"We gathered up all the clothes": ibid.

"Calling your attention": Richard Loeb, "Confessions and Other Statements of Leopold and Loeb (1924)," Harold S. Hulbert Papers, Series 55/23, Box 3, University Archives, Northwestern University.

"On the twenty-first of May": ibid.

"What is his full name?": ibid.

"Nathan Leopold Junior": ibid.

"And adventure, as you would say?": ibid.

"Yes": ibid.

"We did this in order": ibid.

"Leopold got out": ibid.

"Leopold carried the feet": ibid.

"Leopold put on his hip boots": ibid.

"And then what did you do?": ibid.

"I went to the opposite side": ibid.

"The head had bled": ibid.

"Yes . . . quite freely": ibid.

"Around 9 p.m.": ibid.

"From there I spoke to Mrs. Franks": Nathan F. Leopold Jr., "Confessions and Other Statements of Leopold and Loeb (1924)," Harold S. Hulbert Papers, Series 55/23, Box 3, University Archives, Northwestern University.

"[We] destroyed the clothes": Richard Loeb, "Confessions and Other Statements of Leopold and Loeb (1924)," Harold S. Hulbert Papers, Series 55/23, Box 3, University Archives, Northwestern University.

"We intended burning the robe": Nathan F. Leopold Jr., "Confessions and Other Statements of Leopold and Loeb (1924)," Harold S. Hulbert Papers, Series 55/23, Box 3, University Archives, Northwestern University.

"proceeded to get a pail": Richard Loeb, "Confessions and Other Statements of Leopold and Loeb (1924)," Harold S. Hulbert Papers, Series 55/23, Box 3, University Archives, Northwestern University.

"We washed the more obnoxious bloodstains": ibid.

"didn't want to be monkeying around": Nathan F. Leopold Jr., "Confessions and Other Statements of Leopold and Loeb (1924)," Harold S. Hulbert Papers, Series 55/23, Box 3, University Archives, Northwestern University.

"On the way home": Richard Loeb, "Confessions and Other Statements of Leopold and Loeb (1924)," Harold S. Hulbert Papers, Series 55/23, Box 3, University Archives, Northwestern University.

"He threw the chisel out": Nathan F. Leopold Jr., "Confessions and Other Statements of Leopold and Loeb (1924)," Harold S. Hulbert Papers, Series 55/23, Box 3, University Archives, Northwestern University.

"He took me home": Richard Loeb, "Confessions and Other Statements of Leopold and Loeb (1924)," Harold S. Hulbert Papers, Series 55/23, Box 3, University Archives, Northwestern University.

"I went to bed": Nathan F. Leopold Jr., "Confessions and Other Statements of Leopold and Loeb (1924)," Harold S. Hulbert Papers, Series 55/23, Box 3, University Archives, Northwestern University.

"I have some corrections": Nathan F. Leopold Jr. and Richard Loeb, "Confessions and Other Statements of Leopold and Loeb (1924)," Harold S. Hulbert Papers, Series 55/23, Box 3, University Archives, Northwestern University.

"No, I never said that": ibid.

"The entire kidnap and murder scheme": ibid.

"There are certain corrections": ibid.

"He did": ibid.

"You told the stories": ibid.

"I tried to help you out!": ibid.

"Those are all absurd dirty lies": ibid.

"I am sorry": ibid.

"All [he's said] are lies": ibid.

"Now listen, boys": ibid.

"Yes?": ibid.

"You have been treated decently": ibid.

"Absolutely": ibid.

"No brutality or roughness?": ibid.

"No sir": ibid.

"Not one of you have a complaint": ibid.

"No sir": ibid.

"Have you, Loeb?": ibid.

"No": ibid.

Chapter Fourteen: Murderers' Field Trip

"The Franks murder mystery": Charles V. Slattery, " 'Hang Leopold and Loeb,' Says Crowe," *Chicago Herald and Examiner,* May 31, 1924, 1.

"Young Leopold has said": " 'Let Law Take Its Course,' Says Franks, Father of Slain Boy," *Chicago Daily Journal,* May 31, 1924, 1.

"There is no truth": Maureen Watkins, " 'Dick's Innocent,' Loebs Protest; Plan Defense," *Chicago Sunday Tribune,* June 1, 1924, 1.

"Impossible, ridiculous": Maureen McKernan, "Leopold Family a Big Factor in City's Business," *Chicago Sunday Tribune,* June 1, 1924, 1.

"delighted us by his charming personality": Higdon, *Leopold and Loeb,* 119.

"That's a damn lie": ibid.

"Though the father": Lindsay Dennison, "Leopold and Loeb Families Scorned by Close Friends," *New York World,* June 5, 1924, 3.

"The fact that the murdered boy": Higdon, *Leopold and Loeb,* 116.

"there was one gruesome note": Meyer Levin, *In Search,* New York: Horizon Press, 1950, 27.

"it concerns a particular people": Paul B. Franklin, "Jew Boys, Queer Boys: Rhetorics of Antisemitism and Homophobia in the Trial of Nathan 'Babe' Leopold Jr. and Richard 'Dickie' Loeb," in *Queer Theory and the Jewish Question,* edited by Daniel Boyarin et al., New York: Columbia University Press, 2003, 141.

"efficient and vigorous work": "Sad for Parents of Boys in Kidnapping," *Chicago Daily News,* May 31, 1924, 3.

"Let's eat!": Orville Dwyer, "Take Loeb and Leopold on Franks Death Route," *Chicago Sunday Tribune,* June 1, 1924, 2.

"Shuffle them here, there": Herman Kogan, "Profile of Robert Crowe," *Chicago Sun-Times,* August 20, 1942, in Hal Higdon Research Papers on the Leopold and Loeb Case, Series 4, Box, 2, Chicago History Museum.

"Pull in here": Dwyer, "Take Loeb and Leopold on Franks Death Route," 2.

"I knew, I suppose": Leopold, *Life Plus 99 Years,* 48–49.

"egotism and precocity": Dwyer, "Take Loeb and Leopold on Franks Death Route," 2.

"Stop here!": ibid.

"The case is one of the most remarkable": Murray, *The Madhouse on Madison Street,* 112.

Chapter Fifteen: "Impaling a Beetle on a Pin"

"We've got to see Clarence Darrow": Irving Stone, *Clarence Darrow for the Defense,* New York: Doubleday, 1941, 242.

"You must save our two boys": ibid.

"very weary": Clarence Darrow, *The Story of My Life,* New York: Da Capo Press, 1996, 232.

"drawl before a jury box": Ben Hecht, *Gaily, Gaily: The Memoirs of a Cub Reporter in Chicago,* New York: Doubleday, 1963, 70.

"Not only could I": Darrow, *The Story of My Life,* 32.

"men in overalls": "Darrow, the Enigma," *Pattern Makers' Journal,* September 1912, 7.

"the State laying its bloody hand": Clarence Darrow and Alfred J. Talley, *The Debate of the Century: Capital Punishment?,* New York: League for Public Discussion, 1924, 38.

"No client of mine": Darrow, *The Story of My Life,* 232.

"to do what I could": ibid.

"It was all Loeb's idea": Wallace Sullivan, "'I Wrote Note, Loeb Killed Him,' Says Leopold in First Interview," *Chicago Herald and Examiner,* June 2, 1924, 1.

"Aren't golf players nuts?": Wallace Sullivan, testimony, Leopold and Loeb Sentencing Hearing Transcript, Vol. 2, Leopold and Loeb Collection, Box 1, Charles Deering McCormick Library of Special Collections, Northwestern University.

"It was concise": ibid.

"We even rehearsed": ibid.

"It was just an experiment": James Doherty, "Darrow Leads Court Battle for Writ Today," *Chicago Daily Tribune,* June 2, 1924, 2.

"Making up my mind": David L. Shapiro et al., *Retrying Leopold and Loeb: A Neuropsychological Perspective,* Cham, Switzerland: Springer International Publishing, 2018, 23.

"Nathan said you killed Bobby Franks": Higdon, *Leopold and Loeb,* 128.

"No": ibid.

"This thing will be the making of me": Krum, " 'This'll Be the Making of Me,' Says Loeb Boy," *Chicago Daily Tribune,* June 2, 1924, 2.

"I could have carried the secret": Higdon, *Leopold and Loeb,* 127.

"Well, I wouldn't say that": Krum, " 'This'll Be the Making of Me,' " 2.

"an 'experience' that seems to bring him no regret": Maurine Watkins, "Big Experience Either Way Is Nathan's View," *Chicago Daily Tribune,* May 31, 1924, 3.

"undoubtedly the brains": "Expert Charles A. Bonniwell Analyzes Character of the Two Student Slayers and Reveals Their Innermost Thoughts," *Chicago Herald and Examiner,* June 1, 1924, 1.

"detached, philosophical killer": Genevieve Forbes, "They Slew for a Laboratory Test in Emotion," *Chicago Sunday Tribune,* June 1, 1924, 3.

"A thirst for knowledge": Simon Baatz, "Leopold and Loeb's Criminal Minds," *Smithsonian,* August 2008, smithsonianmag.com/history/leopold-and-loebs-criminal -minds-996498.

"Well, I'll leave it to you gentlemen": Higdon, *Leopold and Loeb,* 129.

"When you made this plan": Shapiro et al., *Retrying Leopold and Loeb,* 12.

"Yes": ibid.

"And you knew about the legal consequences": ibid.

"Yes": ibid.

"What could a lawyer": Leopold, *Life Plus 99 Years,* 49.

"Was there a moment": ibid.

"No. [I] do not want to be called a quitter": ibid.

"I don't know": Nathan F. Leopold Jr. and Richard Loeb, "Confessions and Other Statements of Leopold and Loeb (1924)," Harold S. Hulbert Papers, Series 55/23, Box 3, University Archives, Northwestern University.

"The thing that prompted [us]": ibid.

"You wouldn't take ten thousand dollars": ibid.

"It depends on whether": ibid.

"have something [incriminating]": Richard Loeb, "Confessions and Other Statements of Leopold and Loeb (1924)," Harold S. Hulbert Papers, Series 55/23, Box 3, University Archives, Northwestern University.

"Yes, this is the car": Genevieve Forbes, "Old Fashioned Discipline Need of Leopold Jr.," *Chicago Daily Tribune,* June 2, 1924, 3.

"Not with him": ibid.

"Poor fellow, he's weak": ibid.

"I presume you've never eaten seaweed": ibid.

"I beg your pardon": Frank A. Johnson, testimony, Leopold and Loeb Sentencing Hearing Transcript, Vol. 1, Leopold and Loeb Collection, Box 1, Charles Deering McCormick Library of Special Collections, Northwestern University.

"How'd you like to be able to lie": ibid.

Chapter Sixteen: Darrow for the Defense

"Could this scarecrow know anything": Nathan F. Leopold Jr., "Original Manuscript of *Life Plus 99 Years,*" Nathan F. Leopold Papers, Series 4, Box 22, Chicago History Museum.

"Be polite": ibid.

"We cannot talk": McKernan, *The Amazing Crime and Trial of Leopold and Loeb,* 68.

"Waiting for . . . what?": Nathan F. Leopold Jr., "Original Manuscript of *Life Plus 99 Years,*" Nathan F. Leopold Papers, Series 4, Box 22, Chicago History Museum.

"It could be worse": "Neuro-Psychiatric Evaluation of Richard Loeb," Harold S. Hulbert Papers, Series 55/23, Box 2, University Archives, Northwestern University.

"get the rope": "Gray Jail Days Make Murderers Model Prisoners," *Chicago Sunday Tribune,* June 8, 1924, 3.

"He better lay off": Krum, "Elite of the Jail Think Leopold 'Ain't So Much,'" *Chicago Daily Tribune,* June 4, 1924, 2.

"What the hell's the use?": "Nathan Strikes Guard to Halt New Evidence," *Chicago Daily Tribune,* June 6, 1924, 3.

"Yes, Dickie, we have quarreled": ibid.

"a pure love of excitement": Nathan F. Leopold Jr. and Richard Loeb, "Confessions and Other Statements of Leopold and Loeb (1924)," Harold S. Hulbert Papers, Box 3, University Archives, Northwestern University.

"only cure for youthful crime": "City Demands Franks Boy Slayers Be Brought to Trial Immediately," *Chicago Herald and Examiner,* June 4, 1924, 3.

"Capital punishment is God's last act of love": ibid.

"If the parents of these two": Franklin, "Jew Boys, Queer Boys," 144.

"Jewish mercantile millionaires": ibid.

"two Jewish fortunes": ibid.

"related to every branch": Paula S. Fass, "Making and Remaking an Event: The Leopold and Loeb Case in American Culture," *Journal of American History,* December 1993, 922.

"Jewish Mafia": ibid.

"The fathers of these boys": James Doherty, "Darrow Leads Court Battle for Writ Today," *Chicago Daily Tribune,* June 2, 1924, 1.

"Can a rich man be convicted?": Arthur Train and Upton Sinclair, "Can a Rich Man Be Convicted?," *Forum,* May 1928, 645.

"outside [the] labor force": Derral Cheatwood, "Capital Punishment for the Crime of Homicide in Chicago," *Journal of Criminal Law and Criminology,* Spring 2002, 850–851.

"had no means to make": "Pleads to Save Son from Gallows," *Chicago Sunday Tribune,* September 14, 1924, 3.

"in no event": "Fathers Will Let Bar Fix Fees in Slayers' Defense," *Chicago Herald and Examiner,* June 7, 1924, 1–2.

"If [I] had not fastened the crime": Alvin V. Sellers, *The Loeb-Leopold Case: With Excerpts from the Evidence of the Alienists and Including the Arguments to the Court by Counsel for the People and the Defense,* Brunswick, GA: Classic Publishing, 1926, 303–304.

"there was the suspicion": "Leopold-Loeb Case Battle of Alienists," *Chicago Herald and Examiner,* June 3, 1924, 3.

"It is an easy thing": Maureen McKernan, "Weeping Girls Mourn Plight of Richard Loeb," *Chicago Daily Tribune,* June 4, 1924, 2.

"Girls? Sure, I like girls": Krum, "'This'll Be the Making of Me,'" 2.

"Nathan with his brooding Semitic looks": "Faces of Youthful Slayers Are Contrasted by Experts," *Chicago Herald and Examiner,* June 4, 1924, 2.

"But I'm sure Bobby will be coming back": Barrett, *The Leopold and Loeb Files,* 139.

Chapter Seventeen: Searching for Insanity

"I've been pictured in the public mind": "Concludes Tests of Franks Killers," *Chicago Evening Post,* June 17, 1924, 3.

"Why come to me?": Meyer Levin, *The Obsession,* New York: Simon & Schuster, 1973, 106.

"Not guilty, sir": "Loeb, Leopold Plead Not Guilty; Trial August 4," *Chicago Evening Post,* June 11, 1924, 1.

"Not guilty": ibid.

"All motions will be heard": ibid.

"no pleasure": "Neuro-Psychiatric Evaluation of Nathan F. Leopold Jr.," Harold S. Hulbert Papers, Series 55/23, Box 2, University Archives, Northwestern University.

"Horseshit! I think": ibid.

"the patient looked decidedly interested": "Neuro-Psychiatric Evaluation of Richard Loeb," Harold S. Hulbert Papers, Series 55/23, Box 2, University Archives, Northwestern University.

"great excitement": ibid.

"I would if I could get the money": ibid.

"I know I should feel sorry": ibid.

"a big dose of salt": ibid.

"hitting him over the head": ibid.

"A complete understanding of this boy": ibid.

"sex impulses": ibid.

"others taught him to drink": ibid.

"the boy whom she had loved": ibid.

"paranoid toward men": ibid.

"rather effeminate": McKernan, *The Amazing Crime and Trial of Leopold and Loeb,* 109.

"Loeb is the king": ibid., 135.

"But Nate, that's one of the reasons": Nathan F. Leopold Jr., "Original Manuscript of *Life Plus 99 Years*," Nathan F. Leopold Papers, Series 4, Box 22, Chicago History Museum.

"You're too stupid to learn": ibid.

"I believed . . . a speedy execution": Leopold, *Life Plus 99 Years*, 84.

"Life in prison, or hanging": "Leopold-Loeb Defense Now Seen as Insanity," *Chicago Evening Post*, June 13, 1924, 6.

"Any kind of crime": Notes Relating to the Leopold-Loeb Case (1924), E37, Box 1, Records of Superintendent William Alanson White, Records of St. Elizabeth Hospital, National Archives.

"practically inevitable": ibid.

"decidedly abnormal": Dr. William Healy, testimony, Leopold and Loeb Sentencing Hearing Transcript, Vol. 3, Leopold and Loeb Collection, Box 2, Charles Deering McCormick Library of Special Collections, Northwestern University.

"the direct result": ibid.

"absolute lack": Dr. Bernard Glueck, testimony, Leopold and Loeb Sentencing Hearing Transcript, Vol. 3, Leopold and Loeb Collection, Box 2, Charles Deering McCormick Library of Special Collections, Northwestern University.

"need to compensate": ibid.

"cynical and aloof intellectualism": ibid.

PART FIVE: COURTROOM BATTLE

Chapter Eighteen: Surprise Strategy

"Boys, we're going to ask you": Leopold, *Life Plus 99 Years*, 61.

"But so many things could have happened": ibid., 62–63.

"It is unnecessary to say": "Loeb, Leopold Plead Guilty: Begin Trial Next Wednesday," *Chicago Daily News*, July 21, 1924, 1.

"After long reflection": ibid.

"Quiet in the courtroom!": ibid.

"We shall ask [to be] . . . permitted": ibid.

"These boys . . . will be hanged!": "Crowe to Push Trial with All Possible Speed," *Chicago Daily Tribune*, July 22, 1924, 1.

Chapter Nineteen: A Hot Day in Court

"fiendish boys": "Dejected? No, Just Thinking Out Next Move," *Chicago Herald and Examiner,* August 3, 1924, 3.

"Angel Face Dicky": "Famous Alienist Paints Loeb as a Boy Without Remorse," *Olean (NY) Times Herald,* August 6, 1924, 13.

"Chipper": "Boys Primp for Big Day," *Chicago Daily News,* July 23, 1924, 7.

"Debonair": ibid.

"Do I look it?": ibid.

"I hear you fellows had a hard time": ibid.

"Oh, shut up, Babe": ibid.

"The cautious, crafty, cruel and vicious youths": Robert Crowe, "Opening Statement," Leopold and Loeb Sentencing Hearing Transcript, Vol. 1, Leopold and Loeb Collection, Box 1, Charles Deering McCormick Library of Special Collections, Northwestern University.

"Their story is identical": ibid.

"in the name of the people of the State of Illinois": ibid.

"We shall insist in this case": Clarence Darrow, "Opening Statement," Leopold and Loeb Sentencing Hearing Transcript, Vol. 1, Leopold and Loeb Collection, Box 1, Charles Deering McCormick Library of Special Collections, Northwestern University.

"If the court pleases": Edwin Gresham, testimony, Leopold and Loeb Sentencing Hearing Transcript, Vol. 1, Leopold and Loeb Collection, Box 1, Charles Deering McCormick Library of Special Collections, Northwestern University.

"Your Honor is going to be asked": ibid.

"You are permitted": ibid.

"When the boy was a child": ibid.

"Friday—no, Saturday": Flora Franks, testimony, Leopold and Loeb Sentencing Hearing Transcript, Vol. 1, Leopold and Loeb Collection, Box 1, Charles Deering McCormick Library of Special Collections, Northwestern University.

Chapter Twenty: Battles in and out of Court

"We are united": Higdon, *Leopold and Loeb,* 181.

"We have just one hope": ibid.

"friendly judge": James Gortland, testimony, Leopold and Loeb Sentencing Hearing Transcript, Vol. 1, Leopold and Loeb Collection, Box 1, Charles Deering McCormick Library of Special Collections, Northwestern University.

"Did you say that, Babe?": Higdon, *Leopold and Loeb,* 184.

"Hell, no": ibid.

"Who was with you": James Gortland, testimony, Leopold and Loeb Sentencing Hearing Transcript, Vol. 1, Leopold and Loeb Collection, Box 1, Charles Deering McCormick Library of Special Collections, Northwestern University.

"Nobody but he and I": ibid.

"Did you make any memoranda": ibid.

"Not at the time": ibid.

"Mr. Officer, don't you know": ibid.

"Babe, I feel sorry for you": Krum, "Feel No Regret Over Killing Franks Boy," *Chicago Daily Tribune,* July 26, 1924, 1.

"Now, listen, I certainly don't like that": ibid.

"Dickie, the people on the outside": ibid.

"Well, what do they want me to do?": ibid.

"I suppose they want": ibid.

"That's exactly what I am doing": ibid.

"Barbers talk about it": ibid.

"Just a minute. I object": Thomas Marshall, "Argument—Mitigation," Leopold and Loeb Sentencing Hearing Transcript, Vol. 2, Leopold and Loeb Collection, Box 1, Charles Deering McCormick Library of Special Collections, Northwestern University.

"Why?": ibid.

"It is immaterial": ibid.

"Why?": ibid.

"The only purpose": ibid.

"Overruled": ibid.

"I want to be heard on that": ibid.

"What is the defense trying to do": ibid.

"There are not degrees": ibid.

"You do not take a microscope": ibid.

"medical condition, a pathological condition": ibid.

"the court may listen to anything": ibid.

"What is a mitigating circumstance?": Clarence Darrow, "Clarence Darrow Reply—
    Mitigation," Leopold and Loeb Sentencing Hearing Transcript, Vol. 2, Leopold and
    Loeb Collection, Box 1, Charles Deering McCormick Library of Special Collections,
    Northwestern University.

"Is youth a mitigating circumstance?": ibid.

"cold-blooded murderers": Robert Crowe, "Robert Crowe Argument—Mitigation,"
    Leopold and Loeb Sentencing Hearing Transcript, Vol. 2, Leopold and Loeb
    Collection, Box 1, Charles Deering McCormick Library of Special Collections,
    Northwestern University.

"The court is of the opinion": ibid.

"What is [it]?": ibid.

"It is an objection": ibid.

"The objection . . . is overruled": ibid.

Chapter Twenty-One: New-School Psychiatry Takes the Stand

"The inner life": Dr. William Alanson White, testimony, Leopold and Loeb Sentencing
    Hearing Transcript, Vol. 2, Leopold and Loeb Collection, Box 1, Charles Deering
    McCormick Library of Special Collections, Northwestern University.

"This inner life is the life": ibid.

"I object": ibid.

"I am asking him": ibid.

"All his answers are lectures": ibid.

"If the court please": ibid.

"He is just cutting a swamp": ibid.

"That is true": ibid.

"I will begin with Dickie Loeb": ibid.

"You mean Richard Loeb": ibid.

"Yes. No objection to my calling him Dickie": ibid.

"Well, just so we can identify him": ibid.

"Dickie lied about all sorts of things": ibid.

"Now, just wait a minute": ibid.

"Motion denied": ibid.

"Doctor, may I interrupt you?": ibid.

"Let the doctor proceed": ibid.

"Dickie cannot distinguish": ibid.

"He developed in early life": ibid.

"I cannot see how Babe": ibid.

"You may cross-examine": ibid.

"Now, Doctor, when you were talking": ibid.

"No, I don't think I did": ibid.

"Have you any opinion": ibid.

"I think so": ibid.

"Which one in your judgment?": ibid.

"I think it was Dickie": ibid.

"I think he was frank": ibid.

"Don't you think it strange": ibid.

"You didn't ask them?": ibid.

"It was out in the middle of a lot": ibid.

"No, I can't give anything": ibid.

"And your conclusions": ibid.

"If they have fooled you": ibid.

"most strange and pathological": Dr. William Healy, testimony, Leopold and Loeb Sentencing Hearing Transcript, Vol. 3, Leopold and Loeb Collection, Box 2, Charles Deering McCormick Library of Special Collections, Northwestern University.

"Their association began": ibid.

"so little normal motivation": ibid.

"In the matter of their association": ibid.

"I am perfectly willing to tell": ibid.

"I insist we know": ibid.

"I suggest it be in chambers": ibid.

"Tell it in court": ibid.

"The [hearing] must be public": ibid.

"Oh, no": ibid.

"The compact . . . consisted of an agreement": ibid.

"Absolutely, because this is important": ibid.

"special rates": ibid.

"Will you go and sit down": ibid.

"[Babe] . . . found it gave him more pleasure": ibid.

"Is that enough?": ibid.

"I think that is all": ibid.

"I have reveled": ibid.

"I have tried to kill affection": ibid.

"I have never had any disappointments": ibid.

"There seems to be profound disorder": ibid.

"in my opinion, Babe is thoroughly unbalanced": ibid.

"charming, very friendly": ibid.

"Doctor, you talk about a childish prank": ibid.

"Yes, I have known of them": ibid.

"So you regard perversion not as a crime": ibid.

"This is not a, you know": ibid.

"You think that": ibid.

"I have no desire": ibid.

"Cross-examination . . . along that line": ibid.

"Hundreds of children": ibid.

"Aren't you ashamed of yourself": ibid.

"No, I should say not": ibid.

"There is only one thing to do": ibid.

"The motion is denied": ibid.

"the inevitable outcome": Dr. Bernard Glueck, testimony, Leopold and Loeb Sentencing Hearing Transcript, Vol. 3, Leopold and Loeb Collection, Box 2, Charles Deering McCormick Library of Special Collections, Northwestern University.

"Did [Dickie] say anything": ibid.

"He told me all the details": ibid.

"In fact, he made the statement": Arnold Maremont, testimony, Leopold and Loeb Sentencing Hearing Transcript, Vol. 4, Leopold and Loeb Collection, Box 2, Charles Deering McCormick Library of Special Collections, Northwestern University.

"Horseshit!": Max Schrayer, interview, Hal Higdon Research Papers on the Leopold and Loeb Case, Series 4, Box 2, Chicago History Museum.

"He started dancing": Lorraine Nathan, testimony, Leopold and Loeb Sentencing Hearing Transcript, Vol. 4, Leopold and Loeb Collection, Box 2, Charles Deering McCormick Library of Special Collections, Northwestern University.

"Thanks, Lorraine": Higdon, *Leopold and Loeb,* 221.

"I'm sorry I had to": ibid.

"clear transparency": Dr. Harold S. Hulbert, testimony, Leopold and Loeb Sentencing Hearing Transcript, Vol. 4, Leopold and Loeb Collection, Box 2, Charles Deering McCormick Library of Special Collections, Northwestern University.

"This Is an Article": Fass, "Making and Remaking an Event," 936.

"Leopold the genius": ibid.

"You sit there at your breakfast table": Winifred Black, "If Your Sons Were the Slayer," *Chicago Herald and Examiner,* June 9, 1924, 3.

"caused more heart searching": Fass, "Making and Remaking an Event," 936.

"Do you know the name": Dr. Harold S. Hulbert, testimony, Leopold and Loeb Sentencing Hearing Transcript, Vol. 4, Leopold and Loeb Collection, Box 2, Charles Deering McCormick Library of Special Collections, Northwestern University.

"A Victor portable": ibid.

"What kind of current": ibid.

"I don't know": ibid.

"What kind of tube?": ibid.

"All I know is": ibid.

"What transformer was used?": ibid.

"I don't know": ibid.

"Where was the transformer": ibid.

"I don't know": ibid.

"Was the Bucky diaphragm used?": ibid.

"I am not a radiologist": ibid.

"Maybe that is one of the things": Katherine Fitzgerald, testimony, Leopold and Loeb Sentencing Hearing Transcript, Vol. 4, Leopold and Loeb Collection, Box 2, Charles Deering McCormick Library of Special Collections, Northwestern University.

"I found no evidence of mental illness": Dr. Hugh T. Patrick, testimony, Leopold and Loeb Sentencing Hearing Transcript, Vol. 5, Leopold and Loeb Collection, Box 2, Charles Deering McCormick Library of Special Collections, Northwestern University.

"No, I shouldn't think so": ibid.

"Let us count them": ibid.

"Four, and two prisoners makes six": ibid.

"Well, it might go to fifteen": ibid.

"And two stenographers": ibid.

"Yes, two": ibid.

"About seventeen?": ibid.

"Well, I don't think so": ibid.

"Did you ever in your life": ibid.

"I think not": ibid.

"Now, there were some fifteen people": Dr. Archibald Church, testimony, Leopold and Loeb Sentencing Hearing Transcript, Vol. 5, Leopold and Loeb Collection, Box 3, Charles Deering McCormick Library of Special Collections, Northwestern University.

"Hardly that many": ibid.

"Too many for a thorough consultation": ibid.

"Too many for an ideal consultation": ibid.

"No": ibid.

"Did you ask any questions?": ibid.

"Yes": ibid.

"Who did most of the questioning?": ibid.

"Really, there were very few questions": ibid.

"Did you ask any questions": ibid.

"No": ibid.

"eye, ears, all of the senses": Dr. William O. Krohn, testimony, Leopold and Loeb Sentencing Hearing Transcript, Vol. 5, Leopold and Loeb Collection, Box 3, Charles Deering McCormick Library of Special Collections, Northwestern University.

Chapter Twenty-Two: "The Ageing Lion" vs. "Fighting Bob"

"[Grant] had no original intention": Thomas Marshall, "Closing Argument," Leopold and Loeb Sentencing Hearing Transcript Vol. 6, Leopold and Loeb Collection, Box 3, Charles Deering McCormick Library of Special Collections, Northwestern University.

"There is nothing like it": ibid.

"My God, Mike": "Leopold Weeps Under State's Attack," *Chicago Daily News,* August 21, 1924, 2.

diseased personality, unconscious influence: Walter Bachrach, "Closing Argument," Leopold and Loeb Sentencing Hearing Transcript, Vol. 6, Leopold and Loeb Collection, Box 3, Charles Deering McCormick Library of Special Collections, Northwestern University.

"Darrow this afternoon": "Darrow's Plea!" *Chicago American,* August 22, 1924, 1.

"Darrow is on": ibid.

"It's Darrow!": ibid.

"the Ageing Lion": Robert M. Lee, "Crowe Smashes at Darrow; Calls Darrow Arch Lawyer of Murderers," *Chicago Daily Tribune,* August 27, 1924, 2.

"a maelstrom of rioters": "Women Faint as Crowd Mobs Court," *Chicago Herald and Examiner,* August 23, 1924, 1.

"It was the senseless act": McKernan, *The Amazing Crime and Trial of Leopold and Loeb,* 226.

"This world has been": ibid., 232.

"I know that any mother might be": ibid., 233.

"I remember a little poem": ibid.

"And so the game": ibid.

"No one knows what will be the fate": ibid., 234.

"Only the tears in my eyes": Richard Loeb to Clarence Darrow, "Friday Night," 1924, Clarence Darrow Papers, Box 3, Library of Congress.

"I can picture": Barrett, *The Leopold and Loeb Files,* 223.

"Do I need to argue": McKernan, *The Amazing Crime and Trial of Leopold and Loeb,* 250.

"I am asking Your Honor": ibid., 255.

"Over and over in the courts": ibid., 260.

"Wealth has its misfortunes": ibid.

"Can I find the wrong?": ibid.

"He was just a half-boy": ibid., 270–271.

"I am trying to trace causes": ibid., 300.

"Sometimes, Your Honor": ibid.

"I do not know how much salvage there is": ibid., 302.

"I have stood here": ibid., 303.

"Men and women who do not think": ibid., 304.

"[Or] you may save them": ibid.

"I was reading last night": ibid., 305.

"wandered in a labyrinth of laws": Orville Dwyer, "Darrow Calls Slaying Mad Act of Fools," *Chicago Sunday Tribune,* August 24, 1924, 1.

"the distinguished gentleman": Robert Crowe, "Closing Argument," Leopold and Loeb Sentencing Hearing Transcript, Vol. 7, Leopold and Loeb Collection, Box 3, Charles Deering McCormick Library of Special Collections, Northwestern University.

"Now he thrust his face": "Row Stops Crowe's Attack on Slayers," *Chicago Daily News,* August 26, 1924, 1.

"Treat [the defendants] with kindness": Robert Crowe, "Closing Argument," Leopold and Loeb Sentencing Hearing Transcript, Vol. 7, Leopold and Loeb Collection, Box 3, Charles Deering McCormick Library of Special Collections, Northwestern University.

"Oh, but Mr. Darrow says": ibid.

"Take away the millions": ibid.

"Take away their millions": ibid.

"Take away their money": ibid.

"The same thing that has happened": ibid.

"Clarence Darrow once said": ibid.

"What are we trying here": ibid.

"Mitigation! Mitigation!": ibid.

"What happened?": ibid.

"Objection! The coroner's report": ibid.

"From the fact": ibid.

"It is a matter of argument": ibid.

"I don't think that is a matter of argument": ibid.

"I don't think you and I are going to agree": ibid.

"The coroner's report says": ibid.

"You have your contention": ibid.

"The evidence is": ibid.

"We will let it rest": ibid.

"perverted lusts": ibid.

"dangerous philosophy of life": ibid.

"I don't know if Your Honor believes": ibid.

"You have listened with a great deal of patience": ibid.

"The court will order stricken from the record": ibid.

"It was not so intended": ibid.

"And it could not be used": ibid.

"The court will not": ibid.

Chapter Twenty-Three: Waiting

"tour the jail": Betty Walker, "Girl, Society Matron, See Two Killers," *Chicago Herald and Examiner,* August 30, 1924, 3.

"dancing party on a yacht": "Loeb Recalls Last Time He Danced to Tune," *Chicago Evening American,* September 4, 1924, 3.

"Are the experiences in human life": "Leopold Hopes, If Hanged, to Test Hereafter," *Chicago Daily Tribune,* September 3, 1924, 3.

"I will say something": ibid.

"I don't give a damn": "Loeb Recalls Last Time He Danced to Tune," *Chicago Evening American,* September 4, 1924, 3.

"fought to get into the rooms": "Franks Sell Their Home of Cruel Memory," *Chicago Sunday Tribune,* August 31, 1924, 8.

"no matter where I go": "Loebs to Sell Home to Escape Having Memories Is Report," *Chicago Evening American,* September 9, 1924, 4.

Chapter Twenty-Four: "Nothing but the Night"

"Your husband . . . has been shot": "Crank Phoned Wife Caverly Was Shot," *Chicago Evening American,* September 2, 1924, 1.

"I am not afraid": Krum, "Big Guard of Police for Decision," *Chicago Daily Tribune,* September 10, 1924, 1.

"Well, I'm always a little nervous": Robert M. Lee, "Life in Prison Decreed for Leopold, Loeb," *Chicago Daily Tribune,* September 11, 1924, 2.

"Why worry?": Nathan F. Leopold Jr., "Original Manuscript of *Life Plus 99 Years,*" Nathan F. Leopold Papers, Series 4, Box 22, Chicago History Museum.

"Have the two defendants anything to say": "Text of Judge Caverly's Decision," *Chicago Daily Tribune,* September 11, 1924, 2.

"No, Your Honor": ibid.

"In view of the profound and unusual interest": Lee, "Life in Prison Decreed for Leopold, Loeb," 2.

"Go ahead now": ibid.

"Had they been normal": McKernan, *The Amazing Crime and Trial of Leopold and Loeb,* 378.

"The court is satisfied": ibid., 378–379.

"It's hanging": Higdon, *Leopold and Loeb,* 266.

"It would have been the path": McKernan, *The Amazing Crime and Trial of Leopold and Loeb,* 379.

"In choosing imprisonment": ibid.

"in accordance with": ibid., 379.

"In No. 33,623": ibid., 380.

"In No. 33,623": ibid.

"In No. 33,624": ibid.

"In No. 33,624": ibid.

"the tension of uncertainty": Leopold, *Life Plus 99 Years,* 86.

"Rest o' natural life": "Franks Slayers Get Life Imprisonment, Youth Avert Noose," *New York Times,* September 11, 1924, 1.

"I have always hated capital punishment": "What Principals Said," *Chicago Daily Tribune,* September 11, 1924, 2.

"There is little to say": ibid.

"The state's attorney's duty": ibid.

"Bobby didn't believe in capital punishment": Barrett, *The Leopold and Loeb Files,* 253.

"Go out and order us a big meal": Lee, "Life in Prison Decreed for Leopold, Loeb," 2.

"Yes, and be sure": ibid.

"And bring chocolate éclairs": ibid.

"Faced with the facts": "Judge Caverly's Sentence," *San Francisco Bulletin,* September 10, 1924, 18.

"The theory that there is one set of laws": "The Franks Case Decision," *Kansas City Post,* September 10, 1924, 26.

"The sentence shakes the faith": "The Mind of the Judge," *New York Sun,* September 16, 1924, 14.

"went for nothing": "The Mercy of the Court," *New York Times,* September 11, 1924, 22.

"What can *we* do?": "Pleads to Save Son from Gallows," *Chicago Sunday Tribune,* September 14, 1924, 4.

"If he hangs": "Grant's Sentence Should Be Commuted," *Chicago Sunday Tribune,* September 14, 1924, 8.

"They will still be young men": "Says Leopold and Loeb Can Be Paroled in 1935," *New York Times,* September 11, 1924, 5.

"Life-imprisonment . . . [is] justified": "Disintegrating Society," *Chicago Daily Tribune,*
September 19, 1924, 21.

"This alone would cause me to bow down": Nathan F. Leopold to Clarence Darrow,
September 10 or 11, 1924, Clarence Darrow Papers, Box 3, Library of Congress.

Most of life is within us: Leopold, *Life Plus 99 Years,* 126–127.

"Well, boys. Let it be written": Higdon, *Leopold and Loeb,* 279.

"It's 1924": Tyrrell Krum, "Imperiled by Crash in Motor Dash to Joliet," *Chicago Daily
Tribune,* September 12, 1924, 1.

"Shut up and face the wall": Leopold, *Life Plus 99 Years,* 88.

Chapter Twenty-Five: "Life in Prison Is Just What You Make"

"deadly, leaden, unrelieved monotony": Leopold, *Life Plus 99 Years,* 117.

"presented a particularly pitiable": Higdon, *Leopold and Loeb,* 283.

"I can't talk to you boys": ibid.

"scorched": ibid.

"Life in prison is just what you make": Nathan F. Leopold Jr., "Original Manuscript
of *Life Plus 99 Years,*" Nathan F. Leopard Papers, Series 4, Box 22, Chicago History
Museum.

"I sat down and considered": ibid.

"The next four years": ibid.

"Dick and I were as close as it is possible": ibid.

"[Loeb's] hurt": ibid.

"We covered him at last": ibid.

"I missed [Richard] terribly": ibid.

"I am not going to describe my childhood": Leopold, *Life Plus 99 Years,* 21.

"[Readers] learn about": Edward de Grazia, "Aftermath of a 'Thrill,'" *New York Times
Book Review,* March 23, 1958, BR12.

"Leopold, in spite of his intellectual gifts": Betty MacDonald, "Life Plus 99 Years,"
Kirkus Reviews, March 6, 1957, kirkusreviews.com/book-reviews/a/betty-macdonald
-7/life-plus-99-years.

"insidious [and] devastating": Leopold, *Life Plus 99 Years,* 403.

"Judd was not merely Artie's accomplice": Meyer Levin, *Compulsion,* Bedford, NY: Fig Tree Books, 2014, 452.

"It was he who had originated the idea": Leopold, *Life Plus 99 Years,* 295.

"I thought at the time": Higdon, *Leopold and Loeb,* 212.

"I don't know how anybody else feels": Leopold, *Life Plus 99 Years,* 131.

"I committed my crime": Attorney Presentation Before Parole Board 1958, Leopold and Loeb Collection, Box 33, Charles Deering McCormick Library of Special Collections, Northwestern University.

"number one choice": Nathan F. Leopold to Ralph G. Newman October 12, 1962, Nathan F. Leopold Papers, Series 3, Box 16, Chicago History Museum.

"In many ways [Dick]": Barrett, *The Leopold and Loeb Files,* 278–279.

Afterword

"darker and more pessimistic": Harry Salpeter, "Fitzgerald, Spenglerian," *New York World,* April 3, 1927, 12.

Tell me who can you: Stephen Dolginoff, "Everyone Wants Richard," *Thrill Me: The Leopold & Loeb Story,* 2005, genius.com/Stephen-dolginoff-and-doug-kreeger -everybody-wants-richard-lyrics.

IMAGE CREDITS

FIRST INSERT

page 1, top: DN-0077990, *Chicago Daily News* Collection, Chicago History Museum

page 1, bottom: DN-0077991, *Chicago Daily News* Collection, Chicago History Museum

page 2, top: Library of Congress

page 2, bottom: *The Auk* (January 1924)

page 3, top and bottom: illustration for Maureen McKernan, *The Amazing Crime and Trial of Leopold and Loeb*

page 4, top: collection of the author

page 4, bottom left: DN-0077041, *Chicago Daily News* Collection, Chicago History Museum

page 4, bottom right: Eric Rohmann

page 5, top: DN-0077049, *Chicago Daily News* Collection, Chicago History Museum

page 5, bottom left and right: courtesy of Northwestern University, McCormick Library of Special Collections and University Archives

page 6, top: DN-0077999, *Chicago Daily News* Collection, Chicago History Museum

page 6, bottom: DN-0077995, *Chicago Daily News* Collection, Chicago History Museum

page 7, top: DN-0077495, *Chicago Daily News* Collection, Chicago History Museum

page 7, bottom: illustration for Maureen McKernan, *The Amazing Crime and Trial of Leopold and Loeb*

page 8, top: DN-0077058, *Chicago Daily News* Collection, Chicago History Museum

page 8, bottom: DN-0077053, *Chicago Daily News* Collection, Chicago History Museum

SECOND INSERT

page 1, top: DN-0077491, *Chicago Daily News* Collection, Chicago History Museum

page 1, bottom: DN-0077924, *Chicago Daily News* Collection, Chicago History Museum

page 2, top: *New York Daily News* via Getty Images

page 2, bottom: *New York Daily News* via Getty Images

page 3, top: DN-0078011, *Chicago Daily News* Collection, Chicago History Museum

page 3, bottom: illustration for Maureen McKernan, *The Amazing Crime and Trial of Leopold and Loeb*

page 4, top: DN-0078021, *Chicago Daily News* Collection, Chicago History Museum

page 4, center: DN-0077520, *Chicago Daily News* Collection, Chicago History Museum

page 4, bottom: Rolls Press/Popperfoto via Getty Images

page 5, top left: illustration for Maureen McKernan, *The Amazing Crime and Trial of Leopold and Loeb*

page 5, top right: illustration for Maureen McKernan, *The Amazing Crime and Trial of Leopold and Loeb*

page 5, bottom: DN-0077481, *Chicago Daily News* Collection, Chicago History Museum

page 6, top: DN-0078049, *Chicago Daily News* Collection, Chicago History Museum

page 6, bottom: DN-0078044, *Chicago Daily News* Collection, Chicago History Museum

page 7, top left: DN-0078243, *Chicago Daily News* Collection, Chicago History Museum

page 7, top right: DN-0078242, *Chicago Daily News* Collection, Chicago History Museum

page 7, center: Everett Collection Historical/Alamy Stock Photos

page 7, bottom: Library of Congress

page 8, top: American Newspaper Repository, Special Collections Library, Duke University, Courtesy Tribune Media Services

page 8, center: Francis Miller/The LIFE Picture Collection via Getty Images

page 8, bottom: Popperfoto via Getty Images/Getty Images

INDEX

Allen, E. M., 139

American Psychiatric Association, 186, 197, 239

Anderson, David, 248–249

antisemitism, 152, 176–177; *see also* Judaism

Asher, Bobby, 63

Atlantic Monthly, 32

Auk (ornithological journal), 46

Bachrach, Benjamin, 165, 184, 185, 205, 208–209, 215–216, 240, 244–245, 259–260, 268–269

Bachrach, Walter, 184, 186–187, 197, 205, 206, 225, 227, 230–233, 236, 239, 249, 260, 268
   closing argument of, 249

baseball, 4, 9, 24, 63, 65, 88, 155, 174, 196, 218, 255, 263

Black, Winifred, 242

Blair, Sam, 91

bootlegging, 33, 34, 35–36, 66, 76, 87; *see also* Prohibition

Boston Psychiatric Hospital, 188

Bowman, Carl, 187, 188–195, 222, 261

Brown, Abel, 46, 106

Buchman, Hamlin, 39–41, 57
   attempted murder of, 39–40

Calvary Cemetery, 267

capital punishment, *see* death penalty

Capone, Al, 35

Carson, Frank, 91

Catholicism, 17, 41, 151, 179, 191–192

Caverly, John R., 152–153, 171, 184–186, 206–207, 209, 211, 214–216, 225–229, 231–232, 234–240, 250–252, 254, 257–262, 263, 265, 266, 267–275
   reputation of, 207
   threats against, 267–268
   verdict of, 267–271, 273–275

Champion Manufacturing Company, 58, 59

Charlevoix, Michigan, 36, 38, 39, 132, 184, 218, 236, 266

Charlevoix Inn, 39

Checklist of Birds of Puerto Rico and the Virgin Islands, 287

Chicago Cubs, 263

Chicago Daily Journal, 80, 90

Chicago Daily News, 83, 90, 96, 128, 131, 132–133, 164, 258, 280, 283

Chicago Daily Tribune, 90, 93, 95, 99, 102, 111–112, 114, 127, 128, 152, 155, 162, 177, 180–181, 187–188, 217, 220, 223, 257, 265, 275

Chicago Evening American, 90, 95, 96, 129

Chicago Evening Post, 90

Chicago Herald and Examiner, 90, 91, 95, 128, 149–150, 162, 164, 165, 180, 242, 250

Chicago Police Department, ineptitude of, 84–85

Chicago Sunday Tribune, 150, 176, 178, 274

Church, Archibald, 166–167
testimony of, 245–246

Circular Staircase, The, 196

Clabaugh, Hinton G., 275

Coconut Grove, 107, 122

Collins, Morgan A., 84, 85, 87–88, 95, 105, 114

Colosimo, James "Big Jim," 35, 207

Colosimo's Cafe, 35

Compulsion, 283–284

Cook County Criminal Courts Building, 92, 130, 133, 149, 165, 166, 169, 171, 212, 250, 267
riot in, 250

Cook County Jail, 171, 172–174, 184, 188, 189, 192, 197, 199, 212, 221, 264–265, 272, 278

Coolidge, Calvin, 65, 91

Cronson, Bert, 133–134

Crot, William, 105, 115–116, 125, 129

Crowe, Robert, 85–87, 92–93, 105, 114, 116, 118–119, 121–126, 127, 132–134, 137–139, 145–148, 149, 153–154, 161, 165–169, 171–172, 179, 184, 185, 187, 208–211, 213–217, 220, 223, 225–229, 231–240, 243–247, 254, 257–262, 268, 272, 273–274, 285
closing argument of, 257–261, 262
death penalty and, 86, 211, 285
opening statement of, 214–215
opposition to Nathan's parole of, 285
political views of, 86–87
seeking motive for the murder, 168–169

Daily Jewish Courier, 176

Daley's Restaurant, 161–162

Darrow, Clarence, 158–161, 165–166, 171–172, 177, 179, 184–187, 189–190, 194, 196, 198, 199, 205–211, 213, 215, 217, 220, 223, 226–228, 230, 234, 235, 237, 239, 240–241, 243–247, 250–261, 268, 271–272, 275–276, 283, 285–286
appearance of, 158, 160, 171–172, 184, 215, 228, 254
closing argument of, 250–257, 270, 286
compassion of, 160
credentials of, 159–160
death of, 286
death penalty and, 159–161, 251–256, 271
"diminished capacity" argument of, 207–208
fee of, 179
hiring of, 158–161
letters to Nathan by, 276, 286
mistrust of Richard of, 252–253
Monkey Trial and, 285–286
opening statement of, 215, 251

Darrow, Ruby, 158

Day, James, 282

death penalty, 8, 86–87, 153, 159–161,
175–179, 206, 211, 214–215,
248–249, 251–257, 261, 265, 267–274
Bobby Franks's essay about, 8, 272
as crime deterrent, 87, 161, 251, 271
demographics of, 177–179, 248–249,
273–274
Nathan's and Richard's feelings about,
155, 195–196, 265
religious views on, 175–176
DeMille, Cecil B., 66
Detective Story Magazine, 65
Deutsch, Armand, 57–58
Dever, William, 152
Dew Drop Inn, 165
Doherty, James, 162
Doherty, Thomas, 173
Donker, Edward, 173
Douglas Public School, 16
Drake Hotel, 56, 265, 272
Dwyer, Orville, 155

Edgewater Beach Hotel, 104
Egan, Charles, 105
endocrinology, 188–189
Englund, Sven, 34, 49, 66–67, 76–77,
133–134, 137–138, 146–147
Ettelson, Samuel, 10–11, 72, 78–80, 98,
99, 117–118, 216

Farrell, John, 105
Field Museum of Natural History, 264
Fifth Church of Christ, Scientist, 111
Fitzgerald, F. Scott, 290
Fitzgerald, Katherine, 244
Forbes, Genevieve, 217
Forum magazine, 177

Four Deuces, 35
Franks, Bobby, 6–7, 8–11, 63, 78–82, 85,
87–90, 97–101, 108, 110–112, 127,
218, 265
autopsy of, 98–100
discovery of body of, 73–75, 81
essay on capital punishment by, 8,
272
funeral of, 110–112, 216
grave of, 288
Franks, Flora, 8–11, 72–73, 78, 89,
111–112, 144, 150, 181–182, 216,
217, 218, 272, 288
grave of, 288
testimony of, 216, 217
Franks, Jack, 9–10, 111, 210, 288
grave of, 288
Franks, Jacob, 9–11, 72, 77–80, 81, 87,
96–99, 101, 103, 105, 108, 112, 113,
117, 144, 150, 179, 184, 210, 216,
249, 262, 268, 272, 288
grave of, 288
testimony of, 216, 262
Franks, Josephine, 10, 111
Freud, Sigmund, 186
Friar's Inn, 35
Furth's Funeral Home, 98

Glueck, Bernard, 199–200, 240, 285
testimony of, 240
Golden Diner, 169
Goldstein, Alvin, 83, 96–98, 131
Gortland, James, 220, 261
Grant, Bernard, 178, 248, 274
clemency for, 274
Grant, Mary, 274
Gresham, Edwin, 78–79
testimony of, 215–216

Hamilton, Patrick, 290
Hartnett, Gabby, 263
Harvard Law School, 47, 61, 101
Harvard School for Boys, 4, 20–21, 58, 82, 84, 88, 89–90, 114, 141
Hawaii, 169, 170, 261
Healy, William, 198–199
  testimony of, 235–240
Hecht, Ben, 160
Hegewisch neighborhood, 73, 74
Higdon, Hal, 151
Hitchcock, Alfred, 290
homosexuality, 20, 36–42, 47, 89–90, 179–180, 238–240, 259–260
Hotel Windermere, 154, 156
"Hot Lips" (song), 264
Housman, A. E., 251–252
Hughes, Michael, 138, 139–140, 154, 155
Hulbert, Harold, 19, 187, 188–195, 222, 261
  testimony of, 242, 243
Hyde Lake, 109
Hyde Park State Bank, 61, 138, 217
hypnotism, 180–181

Illinois Association for Criminal Justice, 84, 85; see also Illinois Crime Survey
Illinois Central Railroad, 58, 59
Illinois Crime Survey, 99, 100
Illinois Revised Statutes of 1923, 226
Illinois State Penitentiary, 270–271, 272, 275–278, 279–280

Jackson Park, 24, 31, 45, 48, 67, 106, 107, 155
jazz, 33, 34, 36, 75, 106

Johnson, Frank, 105, 115–116, 125, 129–130
Joliet prison, see Illinois State Penitentiary
Judaism, 17, 20–21, 27, 30, 38, 41, 111, 151–152, 176–177, 180–181, 279
  Jewish community's reaction to killers' identity, 151–152, 176

Kansas City Post, 273
Kenwood neighborhood, 3–4, 20, 22–23, 30, 50, 59, 66, 82, 84, 98, 105, 107, 108, 113, 219, 266
Khayyam, Omar, 256–257
King, Alva Vest, 175
Kirkus Reviews, 283
Korff, Paul, 73–75, 119
Krauser, Walter, 178, 248, 274
Krohn, William, 166–167, 246–247
  testimony of, 246–247
Krum, Ty, 220–221, 277–278

Ladies' Home Journal, 32
LaSalle Hotel, 116, 118
Last Days of Pompeii, The, 196
Lebold, Mike, see Leopold, Foreman "Mike"
Leopold, Florence, 17, 18, 20
  death of, 42, 190
  grave of, 279, 288
Leopold, Foreman "Mike," 17, 116–118, 121, 156, 249, 268
  grave of, 288
  testimony of, 244
Leopold, Nathan
  alibi concocted by, 107–108, 122–123, 129–133, 146, 175

allowance received by, 244

arraignment of, 183–186, 187–188

arrest of, 125, 127–129, 133

atheism of, 42, 150, 164, 175

birding by, 15–16, 17–18, 19, 21, 22, 38,
45–46, 48, 56, 63–64, 65, 71, 102,
103, 109–110, 113–114, 115, 117,
118, 119, 125, 146, 180–181, 264,
283, 287

books written by, 280, 283–285, 287

bullying of, 16–17, 19, 21

commonalities with Richard, 30

confession of, 138–141, 144–148,
149, 153, 155, 156–157, 161, 167,
168–169, 175, 225

criminal responsibility of, 152–153

death of, 289

education of, 16, 20–22, 38, 42–43,
44–46, 47, 56, 61, 66, 71, 124, 128,
164, 175, 198, 281–282, 287

eyeglasses of, 74–75, 85, 90,
102–103, 106, 114–119, 128,
132–133, 141

field glasses of, 5, 15, 63

fires set by, 50, 234

food sent to in jail, 173

as George Johnson, 11, 79, 112, 144

grief for Richard of, 283

gullibility regarding Richard of, 45

gun owned by, 120

Hammond Multiplex typewriter owned
by, 124–125

hip boots owned by, 3, 143, 144, 145,
146, 155

homosexuality of, 20, 36–42, 47,
120–121, 179–181, 190, 198, 200,
235–236, 238–240, 260

hypnotism and, 180–181

indictment of, 174

intelligence of, 16, 18, 21–22, 128, 164,
190, 198, 199, 283

Judaism and, 17, 176–177, 180–181

kidnapping and ransom plans of,
56–65

king-slave fantasies of, 19–20, 190, 195,
222

lack of emotion of, 164

law school and, 47, 61, 101

letter to Clarence Darrow by, 275–276

life in jail of, 172–174, 195–196,
263–265, 272–273, 279–283

loyalty to Loeb of, 3

marriage of, 287

as Morton D. Ballard, 61, 62, 66, 138,
154

osteosclerosis of, 189–190, 201

parole of, 285–287

personality of, 30–31, 41

psychological evaluations of, 188–192,
194–195, 197–200, 232–237,
244–247

psychotic disorders and, 200–201, 237

questioning of by police, 115–123, 127

ransom notes written by, 65, 72, 77, 82,
88, 162, 225

relationship with Richard of, 31,
33–42, 47–54, 56–57, 120, 123, 175,
192, 282–283, 288–289

robberies committed by, 49–50, 51–53

sentencing hearing of, 212–262

sentencing of, 267–271

sexual abuse of, 19–20, 190, 200–201

sexual awakening of, 20

solitary confinement of, 281

"superman" theory and, 37–38, 45, 48,
164, 192, 198, 237, 275, 285

talent for languages of, 44

transfer to Joliet prison of, 275–278

Leopold, Nathan (*continued*)
  transfer to Stateville prison of, 280–281
  Underwood typewriter stolen by, 52–53, 56, 65, 84, 88, 106–107, 131–132, 133, 155, 225
  Willys-Knight sports car owned by, 34, 49, 50, 54, 66–67, 77, 82, 123, 133–134, 137–138, 144–145
  Willys-Knight sports car rented by, 66–67, 76–77, 80, 138, 144–145, 169, 219, 225
Leopold, Nathan, Sr., 16–17, 18, 116, 120, 125, 128–129, 145, 150, 151, 184, 205–206, 208, 210, 218, 229, 256, 266, 268–271
  grave of, 288
Leopold, Samuel, 17, 19, 288
  sexual abuse of, 19
Levee District, 35
Levin, Meyer, 151–152, 283–284
Levinson, Johnny, 4–5, 150
Levinson, Salmon, 150–151
Lewis, George, 64, 71, 82, 109
Life Plus 99 Years, 283–285
Lincoln Park, 107, 122
Lindsay, Ben B., 224
Loeb, Albert, 23–24, 27–28, 95–96, 121, 150, 152, 181, 202, 218, 244, 266
  health of, 95–96, 266
Loeb, Allan, 24, 25, 40, 150, 218, 233, 240, 268, 271
Loeb, Anna, 24, 27–29, 49, 95–96, 128, 150, 151, 181–182, 202, 218, 266, 287
  grave of, 287
Loeb, Ernest, 24
Loeb, Jacob, 158–159, 161, 165, 184, 205–206, 208, 229, 233, 268, 272
  grave of, 287

Loeb, Richard
  abandonment of Nathan by, 41–42
  alibi concocted by, 107–108, 122–123, 129–133, 146, 175
  allowance received by, 47, 244
  arraignment of, 183–186, 187–188
  arrest of, 126, 127, 129–131, 133
  attendance at Bobby's inquest, 98–101
  at Bobby's funeral, 111
  commonalities with Nathan, 30
  confession of, 137–139, 141–148, 149, 153, 156–157, 161, 167, 168–169, 175, 225, 266
  contempt for morality of, 48
  crime stories and detective novels read by, 25–26, 47, 97, 191, 196, 222
  criminal responsibility of, 152–153
  death of, 282–283, 287–288
  delusions of, 23, 191
  education of, 27–28, 38, 47, 56, 282
  fires set by, 50, 234
  food sent to in jail, 173
  girlfriends and female admirers of, 103–104, 180, 212–213, 241, 263–264
  indictment of, 174
  kidnapping and ransom plans of, 56–65
  letter expressing admiration for Clarence Darrow by, 252–253
  letter Nathan wrote to, 120–121
  life in jail of, 173–174, 195–196, 232, 263–265, 272–273, 280, 282
  as Louis Mason, 62
  lying by, 24, 231, 234
  "master criminal" fantasies of, 22–23, 26–27, 37, 48, 50, 55, 183, 191, 195, 198, 200, 222, 232

as Morton D. Ballard, 62, 138

personality of, 30–31

"picturalizations" of, 26–27, 191, 222

psychological evaluations of, 188–192, 194–195, 197–200, 231–237, 244–247

psychopathy and, 201–202, 237

ransom notes written by, 65, 72, 77, 82, 88, 162, 225

relationship with Nathan of, 31, 33–42, 47–54, 56–57, 120, 123, 175, 192, 282

robberies committed by, 49–50, 51–53

selection of murder victim by, 4–7, 139

sentencing hearing of, 212–262

sentencing of, 267–271

sexual exploits of, 29

"shadowing" by, 22–23, 39

shoplifting and petty crimes committed by, 27, 37, 191

transfer to Joliet prison of, 275–278

transfer to Stateville prison of, 282

Loeb, Tommy, 4, 24, 29, 95

London, Jack, 196

Long, Simon, 175

Los Angeles Daily Times, 224

Lovitz, Gene, 285

Lurie, Susan, 56, 106, 110

Maremont, Arnold, 45, 106, 131

testimony of, 241

Marshall, Thomas, 184, 273–274

closing argument of, 248–249

Marshall Fields, 107

Martyn, Wyndham, 26

Mayer, Howard, 96–98, 101, 129–131

Melamed, S. M., 176

Michigan City, Indiana, 59, 77

Minke, Tony, 73–74, 95

Mitchell, Mott Kirk, 82, 89–90

Moll, Philip, 105

Morrison Hotel, 61–62, 138, 217

Mulroy, James, 78, 96–98, 131, 280

Murder by Numbers (film), 290

Nathan, Lorraine, 106

testimony of, 241

newspapers; *see also individual papers*

competition among, 90–92

importance of, 91

relationship with police of, 92, 161

special editions of, 165

New York American, 33

New York Sun, 273

New York Times, 157, 222, 273

New York Times Book Review, 283

Nietzsche, Friedrich, 37, 45, 164, 190, 198, 222, 255, 285

"superman" theory of, 37–38, 45, 48, 164, 192, 198, 237, 275, 285

Northwestern University, 166

O'Grady, Michael, 105

Packard, Frank L., 25–26

Patrick, Hugh, 166–168, 246

testimony of, 244–245

Pere Marquette train, 36

Phi Beta Kappa, 21, 46

physiognomy, 180

Prohibition, 32–33; *see also* bootlegging

psychoanalysis, 186, 197, 243

psychopathy, 201–202

Puerto Rico, 286–287

Quantico, 51
Quevedo, Gertrude Feldman Garcia de, 287

Refutation of Darwinism, The, 196
Reinhardt, Patches, 103–104, 264
Rent-A-Car Company, 62, 66, 154
Rinehart, Mary Roberts, 196
Roaring Twenties; *see also* bootlegging
  hedonism of, 32–35
Rockford Watch Company, 11
Rope (film), 290
Rope (play), 290
Rosehill Cemetery, 111, 279, 287
Roseland Presbyterian Church, 175
Rosenwald, Julius, 57–58, 157
Rubel, Dick, 56, 57, 113, 151
Ruth, Babe, 65, 218

San Francisco Bulletin, 273
Savage, Joseph, 118–119, 121–122, 138,
  139–141, 184
  closing argument of, 249
Sbarbaro, John, 118, 121–122, 137–138,
  141–143, 184
scarlet fever, 40
Schrayer, Max, 52
  testimony of, 241
Scopes, John, 285
Sears, Roebuck & Company, 23, 57–58
Shapino, Tony, 74–75
Sheeder, F. A., 141
Sheridan Plaza Hotel, 93
Shoemaker, William, 141, 143, 163
Simon, Carleton, 242
Simpson, Emma, 159
Sinai Congregation, 151

Sing Sing Prison, 199
Small, Len, 274
Smith, Milton, 184
Souders, Ralph, 178
South Shore Country Club, 162
Springer, Joseph, 99–101
Stateville prison, 280–282
Stein, Sidney, 64, 109
Struthers, Emily, 24–29, 37, 191, 192–194,
  197, 202
  resignation of, 29
Sullivan, Wallace, 162, 163
Sutton, H. P., 84, 88, 131
Swoon (film), 290

Ten Commandments, The (film), 66
Thompson, William "Big Bill," 35
Thrill Me: The Leopold and Loeb Story
  (musical), 290–291
Torrio, Johnny, 35

Underwood typewriter, 52–53, 56, 65,
  84, 88, 106–107, 131–132, 133, 155,
  225
  destruction of, 107
University High School, 27
University of Chicago, 21–22, 27, 38, 39,
  43, 44, 47, 53, 56, 132, 151
  Campus Club of, 22, 29, 30
University of Michigan, 38, 40, 42, 47,
  51, 264
University of Puerto Rico, 287

Van de Bogert & Ross drugstore, 97, 103
Van den Bosch, Paula, 17–18
Viana, Nicholas, 249

Wantz, Mathilda "Sweetie," 18–20, 194, 201
  firing of, 20
  Nathan's devotion to, 20
  sexual abuse of Nathan by, 19–20, 190
Washington Post, 157
Watkins, Maurine, 187–188
Weinstein, Jacob, 114–115
Weiss Restaurant, 169–170
White, William Alanson, 197–198
  testimony of, 225, 227, 229, 230–234
White Fang, 196
Whitman, John, 276, 280
Wicker Park Lutheran Church, 175

Williams, R. P., 88–89
Wolfe, Thomas C., 109–110, 116
Wolff, Oscar, 98–101
Wolf Lake, 45, 64, 73, 78, 84, 102, 109–110, 133, 140, 143
World War I, 32
World War II, 283

Yellow Cab Company, 77, 79

Zeta Beta Tau fraternity, 41–42, 51, 56, 83, 96, 114, 241

ABOUT THE AUTHOR

CANDACE FLEMING is the prolific and versatile author of many award-winning books for children and young adults, including *The Rise and Fall of Charles Lindbergh*, which was a *Kirkus Reviews, Publishers Weekly, Booklist,* and *School Library Journal* Best Book of the Year, received the 2021 YALSA Award for Excellence in Nonfiction for Young Adults, and was hailed by the *Wall Street Journal* as a "fascinating chronicle." *The Family Romanov: Murder, Rebellion, and the Fall of Imperial Russia* won the *Boston Globe–Horn Book* Award for Nonfiction and the *Los Angeles Times* Book Prize, as well as a Robert F. Sibert Honor. *Amelia Lost: The Life and Disappearance of Amelia Earhart* was selected as a *New York Times* Notable Children's Book of the Year and was featured in the National Geographic documentary *Expedition Amelia. The Lincolns: A Scrapbook Look at Abraham and Mary* also won the *Boston Globe–Horn Book* Award for Nonfiction, and her picture book *Honeybee,* illustrated by Eric Rohmann, won the Robert F. Sibert Medal.

Candace lives in Oak Park, Illinois, just a fifteen-minute car ride from where Nathan Leopold and Richard Loeb kidnapped Bobby Franks. Visit her at candacefleming.com.